Guildcraft

Table of Contents

Contents

Designers

Peter Leitch, Chris Maxfield, Mark Somers,
and "Uncle" Wes Nicholson

Additional Design

Greg Dent

Lead Editor

Janice Sellers

Creative Director

Jim Butler

Art Director

Todd Morasch

Cover Artist

Michael Orwick

Artwork

Andrew Baker, Andy Blase, Ginger Kubic,
Mark Jones, and Michael Orwick

Cartography

Jeremy Simmons

Typesetters

Jim Butler and Todd Morasch

Playtesters

Allan Libby, Andree Ricker, Andy Terrill, Brendon Hayes,
Christian Pliete, Crystal McMichael, Dave McMicheal, Heiner de Wendt, Jeff Terrill, Kevin Ruesch, Nicole Kitzmann,
Ralf Gehling, and Tyson Moyer.

Distributed worldwide to the hobby, toy, comic, and book trade by Osseum Entertainment (www.osseum.com) and regional distributors.

Introduction to Guildcraft

Welcome to the world of *Guildcraft*. This book is a tool to enhance the roleplaying experience of your campaign and to allow you to explore new avenues of adventure using your character's skills and class traits in new and exciting ways. In these pages you will find all you need to make use of those skills your characters have and complain they can never use. Each of the core character classes from the d20 fantasy worlds has at least one guild to join. Many of the common and less common skills and trades have guilds also, and player characters are welcome members in these. Political intrigue, secret missions, rival organizations—all of these and more can be found in these pages. Our aim is to give you an added dimension to your campaign, so that instead of beating up bad guys and monsters, your characters can be agents of a larger collective, and the potential exists for different characters to have different secret goals on the same adventure. The roleplaying possibilities are endless.

Historical Guilds

Guilds were the forerunner to the trade union, the Chamber of Commerce, and the cooperative society. They were the civilian counterpart to the armed forces—a group of people bound together by a common interest who worked for the good of the organization as well as that of the individual member.

All cooperative associations charge some kind of dues from members in order to make them viable. These dues may be in the form of monetary payment for the benefits of membership, or they be a certain amount of the member's time spent working for the cause. Some groups require both. For example, the parent/teacher association at just about every school in the free world has a small annual fee and expects each member to donate some time and effort in helping run various fundraisers throughout the year. Community clean-up campaigns (like Adopt a Highway) require only the donation of time on a regular basis. Hobby-based clubs generally require only the payment of annual dues, although they encourage the donation of time as well.

Historically, traders formed guilds to reduce overhead and to increase profits. These guilds were usually in the form of a cooperative. Fishermen still work in co-ops in many places around the world because none of them can afford the cost of setting up their own fish market. Silver- and goldsmiths formed guilds to keep secret the tricks of their craft and also to ensure the survival of the secrets by way of carefully selected apprentices or by handing them down from generation to generation. Mercenary companies form together because it is a better negotiating base to have 100 soldiers for hire rather than one. Merchants formed guilds to keep down the costs of hiring caravan guards, or even the wagons and horses needed to haul their wares from place to place. Eight wagons don't need twice the guards that four do, and few merchants require a whole number of wagons for their products.

Using the Guilds

The guilds presented in this book can serve many purposes. Some are there to give your players bonuses (or balance penalties in some cases) to skills or in combat. Some are there primarily to act as nemeses to your player characters, and others to encourage roleplaying within your group. Each of the organizations presented has some of each of these factors. It is up to the GM to determine how many of them fit into the campaign and how they fit in.

World Neutrality

All of the entries in this book are designed to be "world neutral" while not appearing generic. The term "world neutral" means that the information presented has been crafted so that it can be dropped into nearly any campaign world without excess changes or development work and without breaking the principles of the world in question. The term generic implies a lack of color or personality, which has been avoided here. The guilds and NPC's in this book have unique names, goals, and functions, although their locations have been left as open as possible. Guilds are typically centered around towns and can either be dropped into an existing town in the campaign or added to a new town created for the purpose of giving the guild a home. GMs are more than welcome to change the names, terms, and details presented in this book in order to suit the individual campaign, and the entries have been written to allow this to be done as painlessly as possible.

How to Read the Entries

The first four chapters in this book contain a variety of fully detailed guilds for use in any number of campaigns. Chapter 1 contains guilds centered around specific classes, Chapter 2 contains guilds centered around particular skills or occupations, and Chapter 3 contains guilds created because of particular social situations. Chapter 4 details a guild designed specifically for adventurers. This guild is the easiest to introduce into most campaigns and provides services invaluable to most PCs.

Within the chapters, each guild is presented with its own name, type, background, and a variety of details on membership and function. The game details of each guild are summed up in the guild's advancement table, which explains the benefits and costs of joining the guild as well as the guild's structure. At the end of the entries are ideas on how to incorporate the guild into your campaign, as well as adventure hooks to get things going quickly. The last section of the entries suggest variations on the guild that the GM can use to better suit his world. Chapter 5 walks you through the process needed to create your own guilds and also explains the full details of the terms used in defining the guilds.

Terminology

In this book, the word "level" refers to a character's total level, derived from his total XP. Rank refers to the number of skill points put into a particular skill. Grade refers to a character's status within a specific guild. This is a little muddy in the mercenary company, where rank is also used in the military sense of the word. We've tried to keep the three concepts separate to avoid any confusion.

Guild Membership & Advancement

Some of the guilds in this book cost nothing to join. Others have a monetary cost, and still others have an XP cost to join. Some have both monetary and XP costs. All but one of the guilds require XP investments in order to progress through the grades, along with other requirements. The XP used to gain a grade are spent just as a wizard spends XP to craft a magical item.

Guild grades do not stack with character levels, nor do they confer any hit points, "to hit" bonuses, or other level-based benefits unless these are explicitly stated in the text.

Cross-Membership

Some guilds have exclusive membership requirements. For example, mercenary companies do not allow their members to have any other associations. Other groups not only tolerate cross-membership, they encourage it. An adventurer's guild has links to every other guild imaginable, unless that group is either mercenary or secretive. As you read through the guilds in this book and tie them into your campaign, it will become apparent which ones make sense to allow cross-membership and which do not.

Chapter 1 - Class Guilds

This chapter presents a variety of guilds, each based around the particular strengths of a single character class. Each of the core classes has been given its own guild, and some characters may even be able to join more than one. Adventuring PCs are likely to wish to join class-based guilds, and the guilds themselves can serve as impetus for expeditions.

Barbarian Horde

Since the dawn of recorded history, small tribes of nomadic warriors have occasionally banded together for short periods to accomplish goals which were beyond the reach of any one tribe. Most often the goal has been to sack a city or civilization that has encroached on the lands of the nomads and threatened their very existence. To people outside the horde, these nomads are known as barbarians.

Membership

Belief/Code: All members of a barbarian horde share the same belief in bringing down whatever threatens their existence. While this is likely a civilization seeking to expand its borders, it may be a terrible monster such as an ancient dragon that has taken up residence and either eaten or scared away the herds which the barbarians rely on for food and clothing.

Location: All members of a horde come from the same general area, although each tribe has its own roughly defined hunting grounds within that area.

Joining the Horde

Edict: When the lands of the nomads are threatened, the tribal chiefs meet and decide whether the threat is great enough to warrant a horde. If they decide it is, all members of all tribes are automatically members of the horde.

Application: Often, local rangers and druids share the concerns of the nomads and may elect to join the cause.

Size and Scope

The size of a horde can vary enormously, from a single extended family of around 50 to several complete tribes numbering in the low thousands. The perceived level of threat to the tribes will dictate how many join the horde, but even a threat which moves every tribe to action will be limited to at most a couple of thousand. The harsh reality of tribal nomadic life limits the number of people who can survive, let alone thrive.

Hordes seldom venture outside the region they consider to be their hunting grounds. A horde from the northern wastes is not going to sweep through an entire continent just to get to a major city in the subtropical south. On the other hand, nomadic tribes are often warlike as a necessary adjunct to hunting for sometimes scarce resources, and it is not unknown for two tribes to invoke the horde and battle each other for the right to hunt in an area.

The range of a horde is normally defined by the terrain. It may be hundreds of square miles of savannah or prairie, or it may be limited to the immediate surrounds of a lake or part of a river. It may be a hidden valley deep in the mountains or the frozen tundra of the polar regions. Whatever the range, it will be clearly defined by some natural geographical feature.

Guild Structure & Advancement

Barbarians are chaotic by nature and abhor any kind of organized structure. The make-up of the horde reflects this in that there are few defined grades and advancement is informal.

The majority of barbarians are considered fodder. They charge into battle, careless of their own lives and those who stand before them.

Fodder who show prowess and courage may gain recognition as Chosen Ones. Others of their clan or

tribe will follow them into battle when next the horde is on the move.

Chosen Ones who cleave their way through the enemy ranks may rise to the height of War Leader and gain the respect of all the clans or tribes in the region.

War Leaders who survive a few battles end up as Chieftains in their own right, attracting numbers of followers to start their own tribes (or, rarely, their own clans).

A Chieftain may, if his prowess is legendary, unite all the tribes under his Warlord banner for a short time to accomplish a specific goal. This goal need not involve invoking the horde but may be something like constructing a trading post so the tribes can deal with outsiders.

Benefits

Extra Attack: While the horde is invoked, barbarians gain an additional Rage attack per day. Rangers and druids can rage once per day.

.Heightened Senses: When the horde is invoked, members' senses are heightened by the thrill of battle. To reflect this, horde members gain a +1 per grade to all Spot and Search rolls. This bonus is lost once the horde disbands but returns when next the horde is summoned.

Reputation: The following die roll bonuses apply whether the horde is currently rampaging or not, as long as the character has been on at least one rampage.

- Chosen Ones gain a +1 bonus to all Charisma-based rolls when dealing with members of their own tribe.
- War Leaders gain a +1 bonus to all Charisma-based rolls when dealing with barbarians of other tribes and a +2 bonus when dealing with their own tribe.
- Chieftains gain the ability to generate a small income from trading with other tribes or outsiders. They make a 1d10 check once per month, modified by Craft if they have it. They gain a +1 bonus to all Charisma-based rolls when dealing with druids and rangers, +2 when dealing with other barbarians, and +4 for their own tribe. They can call a council of chieftains and attempt to summon a horde. While this should be roleplayed, it may involve one or more Diplomacy rolls using the above bonuses in addition to any other modifiers.
- Warlords gain a +2 bonus to Charisma-based rolls when dealing with druids and rangers, +4 when dealing with other barbarians, and +6 for their own tribe.

Summon Horde: A Warlord can summon a horde for a maximum of three days or for one specific task (refer to table 1.2). The size of this horde is dependent on a Diplomacy roll, and the +4 bonus above applies, as do any other modifiers. Any penalties for being a barbarian do not apply, as these are applicable only when dealing with nonbarbarians. A Chieftain can attempt to summon a horde as well, although the DC for him to do so is increased by 5.

These numbers may be modified to suit the population base of your campaign. 2,500 should be the upper limit of any nomadic assembly, no matter how populated the world might be. Beyond this number, people tend to settle and build towns and cities rather than remain nomadic.

Disadvantages

Hostility: Barbarians are at a social disadvantage at the best of times. When the horde is invoked, any member who is captured can expect to be pilloried in the stocks before being executed (if he is lucky), sold into slavery, or (if it fits the campaign) thrown into the gladiator arena for the amusement of the masses. In any event, the character is out of the campaign unless his fellows can effect a rescue.

Affiliations

Almost none. Barbarian hordes are shunned and feared by everyone else. Only druids and rangers will freely associate with them, and only as individuals, not at an organizational level. Druidic cabals fear the destruction wreaked by a horde merely passing over the territory between them and their objective.

Wargames

Every few years, if there hasn't been an outside threat to deal with, the nomadic tribes get together for mock battles and tests of strength, stamina, and speed. To begin the festivities, each tribe puts on one or more performances depicting past victories (this is where characters get to use their Perform skills) while the onlookers feast on roast beast and drink too much mead and ale. The following day, the events begin in earnest. The first event is a test of speed, where the representatives of each tribe (no more than three per tribe) race from a standing start to a tree some 200 yards away and snatch a pennant from the tree. To win this event involves six opposed Athletics checks. Each +1 is a one-yard lead per check, so the lead can change several times over the event. The winner is the character with the most bonuses after the last roll.

The next event is a test of strength. Each tribe fields a team of up to six individuals with a combined Strength score of not more than 72. Each tribe also fields up to two

Table 1.1 – Barbarian Horde Advancement

Grade	Prerequisites	XP Cost	Benefits
Fodder (1)	1 level in Barbarian, Ranger, or Druid	0	Extra Attack, Heightened Senses
Chosen One (2)	Defeat three opponents in one battle	500	Extra Attack, Heightened Senses, Reputation
War Leader (3)	Lead at least two other barbarians against a superior force and survive, 5 levels in Barbarian	1,000	Extra Attack, Heightened Senses, Reputation
Chieftain (4)	Soundly defeat an opposing force, Leadership	1,500	Extra Attack, Heightened Senses, Reputation, can call a council meeting and attempt to summon a horde
Warlord (5)	10 levels in Barbarian, Diplomacy 2 ranks	2,000	Extra Attack, Heightened Senses, Reputation, Summon Horde

Table 1.2 – Summon Horde

Warlord DC	Chieftain DC	Size of Horde
10	15	20
15	20	50
20	25	100
25	30	300
30	35	1,000
35	40	2,500

individual contestants. The object of the exercise is for each individual contestant to engage in a tug of war with another tribe's team. The team makes opposed Strength checks using its highest Strength added to all other Strength modifiers. Each contestant has only his own Strength, or appropriate skill, to pit against the team. Each point of difference in the die rolls is one yard of distance pulled toward the higher roll. The tug of war is over when one side has been pulled 10 yards. While contestants are not expected to win (although sometimes it happens), the idea is to last as many rounds as possible and to be the last contestant to lose.

The last event is one of stamina. A race over five miles, with obstacles to overcome, has been set up by the chieftains. Depending on the terrain, these obstacles may include running through dense undergrowth, fording a fast-flowing stream or river, leaping over loose rock (scree), hurdling fallen trees, or climbing a sheer cliff. The winner is the first one to cross the finish line. He receives the accolades of all present, no matter which tribe they are from.

XP awards: Award 30 XP per test, with a bonus 20 XP for any test a character is triumphant in.

Leaving the Horde

With Permission: Once the threat has been dealt with, the horde disbands and the individual tribes go their separate ways until the next threat materializes.

Without Permission: Rangers and druids who abandon the horde before the threat has been neutralized are considered enemies of all the nomadic tribes unless they somehow redeem themselves. They will not be able to receive any kind of aid or shelter and may be killed if they are caught by the tribes.

Tribal members who abandon the horde during the conflict are considered outcasts and are not welcomed at any fires. This is effectively a sentence of death by starvation, by freezing, or as a meal for a denizen of the wilds and is far more cruel than a swift axe stroke would be.

Nomad Chieftain

Grorg the Red: Male half-orc Barbarian 6: CR 6; Medium-size humanoid (half-orc); HD 6d12 +6; hp 53; Init +1, Spd 30 ft.; AC 15 (touch 11, flat-footed 14); Atk +9/+4 melee (1d8+2/x3, masterwork battleaxe) or +7/+2 (1d8/x3 longbow); SA Rage; SQ horde abilities, half-orc abilities, barbarian abilities; Al CG; SV Fort +6, Ref +5, Will +2; Str 15, Dex 12, Con 12, Int 8, Wis 11, Cha 8.

Skills and Feats: Craft (trapmaking) +2, Diplomacy +2, Jump + 5, Listen +2, Ride +4, Sense Motive +2, Swim +5, Wilderness Lore +3; Leadership, Lightning Reflexes, Power Attack.

Possessions: masterwork battleaxe, longbow, chain shirt.

Grorg the Red is so called because of the trail of blood he tends to leave in his wake. He does not have the red hair normally associated with the appellation. Grorg is the head of his clan but is not always comfortable in the role. He is aware of his responsibilities to the clan members and does not relish the way these obligations tie him down. His soul is that of the wanderer, the nomad, and the responsibility of leadership drives him to distraction on a regular basis.

Fortunately for Grorg, there is an outlet for his tension. There is always a rival clan or band of marauding monsters invading the clan lands, so Grorg spends as much time as he can manage (and as clan leader that's quite a bit) leading war parties in defense of their territory.

Despite not enjoying his clan leader duties, he does take them seriously when he's not off fighting a battle. The sanctity of life, particularly that of clan members, is paramount to him. He therefore does what he can to ensure there is food to eat, shelter for warmth and protection, and a shaman to ward off evil spirits and diseases.

Grorg is fierce in combat, preferring to close with his opponents and split them with his battleaxe. His towering bulk makes him a frightening sight for would-be enemies, and the axe he swings only adds to the visage.

Grorg is just 25 summers, and his 250-pound frame towers almost 7 feet over the ground. His blond hair and blue eyes, combined with his preferred garb of tanned skins, would have him referred to as a Viking in some places, but he has no knowledge of traveling over water.

Negotiating with Grorg can be time-consuming and difficult. He isn't comfortable with fancy talk and would prefer to negotiate most deals with an arm wrestle. He is friendlier (+2 reaction) toward those who arm wrestle him than to those who are scared off by his bulk. It doesn't matter to him who wins the arm wrestle, just that someone is willing to participate.

As a nomad used to living off the land, Grorg is not one to kill for its own sake. He kills for food, for warmth, and to defend his clan from invaders. Even when going to council to raise a horde, Grorg only does so if he believes the clan lands are threatened in some way.

Your Campaign

The barbarian horde is a very loose and unpredictable force. It is rarely invoked, but when it is, it can come out of nowhere and change things forever. Unless your party contains barbarians, this is probably the best way to use the horde, as an element of fortune or misfortune, as the case may be. The horde can sweep into your campaign unannounced and then disappear just as fast, creating all manner of situations.

If you have barbarians in your party, the horde works well as a hook to draw the party into a new story. The barbarian characters are called to fight some previously unknown evil, and the party may decide to join them. It is also possible that the horde may cause a division in the party, especially if the horde is called to attack civilized lands.

Barbarian PCs who progress in grade may eventually be able to call up the horde themselves, thus providing impressive back-up for an adventuring party. See below under variations for a more permanent type of campaign centered around the horde.

Adventure Hooks

- The horde is invoked to rescue a captured chieftain from a border town. The characters may either help attack or defend the town.

- All of the nomads in a large area have disappeared. Supposedly the horde was called, and all of them marched away and never returned. What has happened?

- The party is trapped in the wilderness by a much more powerful group of creatures. The characters' only hope for survival is to incite the local barbarians against their enemies. Of course, this is easier said than done.

- A town has recently been attacked by a barbarian horde, and a number of the townsfolk were carried off. Can the party track down the scattered nomads and free these slaves?

Variations

Global Conquest: Probably the most successful barbarian in recorded history was the Mongol leader Temujin. Better known as Genghis Khan, he set out to conquer the known world—and very nearly succeeded.

To run an epic campaign of the scale of Genghis Khan's ravaging hordes, the goal becomes world domination, and the horde is held together by the force of the Khan's will. As this is a powerful character, the Khan should be an NPC, giving specific missions to the PCs as part of the global picture. Look at the rescue mission in Adventure Hooks for an idea about what might be an appropriate mission.

Druid's Cabal

Shrouded in the damp mist, the barely discernible figures shuffled around a stone altar, chanting in a language that had been lost to the civilized races for many centuries. Chained to the altar, unconscious, its tail and head dangling from either end and resting on the damp ground, was a dragon more than 20 feet long. Its huge wings were folded but still hung to the ground; its color was impossible to tell in the gray vapor. As the chanting rose in volume the dragon awoke with a start and began to struggle. But it was too late. The figures surrounding it turned inward as one and raised their arms to the stone pillars, forming an unseen circle some 50 feet away. With a rumble that quickly became a roar, the altar cracked open and sucked the wyrm into its gaping maw. Within seconds the dragon had disappeared and the altar lay bare in the midst of the cowled druids. One of them spoke, her voice barely above a whisper. "My sisters, as long as the pillars stand the dragon Garex will remain trapped in the womb of the earth. Its magical life force will power our most potent rituals and spells, and Mother Earth herself will hold Garex frozen in time, neither aging nor thirsting, nor tiring until the pillars be sundered. So let it be for all eternity." "So let it be for all eternity," replied the other druids in response to the mantra. They all turned away and vanished into the mist, to return to their stone circle when next the moon was full.

Purpose

Protection/Sharing: Druids are naturally shy, loner types. However, as priests of nature they sometimes have the need to perform rituals or great magic, or defeat a mighty foe, tasks that are beyond the abilities of any one individual. For this reason druids build stone circles, consecrate groves of trees deep in forests, or select some other focal point for their power and a place to meet. A secret organization is then created to guard and utilize these sites, and on important occasions the members gather to work their strange rituals.

Membership

Profession: A druids' cabal is fully open to druid characters. Rangers and barbarians may become members if circumstances warrant it, but their membership benefits are limited.

Joining the Guild

Application: Any druid who feels the need to be part of a larger whole may apply for membership in a cabal, if he can find one. Cabals don't advertise their existence to outsiders.

Invitation: From time to time, the cabal may need more members and will invite druids and perhaps rangers and barbarians to join them. This is usually in the lead-up to an important festival or ritual, where the cabal requires more magical energy than its present members can generate.

Test/Examination: However a character joins a cabal, he must first prove his worthiness to be a member. For invited members, this demonstration of faith requires the expenditure of 1,000 XP and nothing more. For prospective members who apply to join, the first test has been passed — they found the cabal. Each cabal has its own initiation requirements for applicants, ranging from the swearing of an oath to the ritual shedding of blood, to a more strenuous ordeal involving up to a week of fasting and meditating with little or no sleep allowed. However the rites are administered, the 1,000 XP must also be expended.

Size and Scope

Cabals are small in size, numbering no more than 20 in all but the largest groups. Their ranges are usually limited to a specific natural feature such as a forest, mountain range, prairie, river delta, or some other easily defined area.

Guild Structure & Advancement

Graded (Merit): A druid's cabal consists of six grades of initiates: member, friend, naturalist, enervator, circle, and high druid. Advancement is based entirely on merit and how well a druid is able to learn the talents of his profession. As a member's grade rises within the guild, the more he becomes trusted, and the more secret information he is allowed access to. A druid's grade reflects how much secret power and knowledge he has accrued within the cabal. The cabal is led by a single figure, called the High Druid. The High Druid makes all the decisions regarding when the cabal will meet and what rituals it will perform. The High Druid is the leader for life of the cabal. If he ever dies or steps down, a successor is elected from among the grade 5 members. The election is held at a cabal meeting, and all members are allowed a single silent vote. Voting is done by placing colored stones corresponding to the candidates into a slot in a sealed coffer.

Benefits

Access to Skills: Since the cabal is a secret organization, all members have Bluff, Sense Motive, and Innuendo as class skills.

Bonus Skills: Each time a member advances in grade he receives one additional skill point. These skill points reflect the shared knowledge that the cabal affords a character.

Bonus Spells: By being a member of the cabal, a druid gains access to secrets that improve his magical abilities. These secrets are reflected in bonus spells. Each time a member advances in grade, he gains one additional spell of the level equal to his new grade. These spells should be chosen as appropriate to the purposes of the cabal. Additionally, at first grade, a bonus 0-level spell is gained.

Call Order: The High Druid can call the cabal to order at will, and all members are expected to attend.

Fraternity: Members of a cabal are dedicated to helping one another protect the wilderness, and if one member comes up against a force that is too powerful for him, he can call on his brethren to assist him. Typically, one to two druids will come to help per grade he has achieved, assuming that the cause is a good one. These brethren are typically within four levels of the druid's own.

Disadvantages

Attendance: Cabal members are expected to attend the rituals of their group, usually dictated by the phases of the moon. Attendance is compulsory unless the High Druid has given leave. Absence without leave on more than one occasion is grounds for expulsion. For campaigns where time is tracked, a druid must spend 12 weeks (or whatever time units you use) per year attending ritual gatherings.

Fraternity: Druids are often asked by their fellow members to assist in fighting off unnatural forces. PCs may be called upon at any time to help or to attend rituals. Such calls are not mandatory unless they come from the high druid.

Secrecy: Members of a cabal must keep their membership secret, even to the point of requesting permission to invite a potential new member into the group. This dates back many centuries to when druids were fond of sacrificing local children to appease the nature gods. While most druids no longer practice those rituals, race memory is long and secrecy is safety.

Affiliations

None. A cabal is a secret organization.

Table 1.3 – Druids' Cabal Advancement

Grade	Prerequisites	XP Cost	Benefits
Member (1)	2 levels in druid, test/exam	1,000	Access to skills; bonus skill, bonus spells (0, 1st), Fraternity
Friend (2)	Diplomacy 2 ranks	1,500	Bonus skill, bonus spell (2nd)
Naturalist (3)	6 levels of druid	2,000	Bonus skill, bonus spell (3rd)
Enervator (4)	Innuendo 2 ranks	2,500	Bonus skill, bonus spell (4th)
Circle (5)	10 levels in druid, Diplomacy 4 ranks	3,000	Bonus skill, bonus spell (5th)
High Druid (6)	12 levels in druid, Sense Motive 2 ranks, Leadership, Available position; election.	3,500	Bonus skill, bonus spell (6th), Call Order

Note: Druid prestige classes count in determining druid levels.

Leaving the Cabal

With Permission: A druid who leaves a cabal with the blessing of the high druid loses all the benefits of membership, with the exception of bonus skill points and class skills. Should the druid ever wish to rejoin the same cabal, a new initiation and an additional 1,000 XP will be required, but the druid will then be reinstated at the grade he was when he left.

As druids are solitary by nature, it is not uncommon for druids to leave when the strictures of membership are seen to be stifling the druid's individuality.

Without Permission: Those who leave the group without the blessing of the High Druid suffer the same results as those leaving with permission, but rejoining later is not possible.

Expulsion: Druids who break the secrecy of the organization may be expelled from the cabal or reprimanded, depending on the severity of the transgression. Druids may also be expelled from a cabal for offending against nature. Such a crime is considered so serious the druid will most likely be put to death in a manner appropriate to the crime.

High Druid

Celeste Alstian: Female elf Druid12: CR 12; Medium-size humanoid (elf); HD 12d8+12; hp 75; Init +3 (Dex), Spd 30 ft.; AC 21 (touch 17, flat-footed 18); Atk +11/+6 melee (1d8+1/x3, long spear +1) or +10/+5 (1d6/x2 quarterstaff) or +16/+11 ranged (1d4+3/19-20/x2 sling +3); SA spells; SQ druid abilities, elven abilities; Al N; SV Fort +9, Ref +7, Will +11; Str 11, Dex 16, Con 12, Int 10, Wis 17, Cha 16.

Skills and Feats: Animal Empathy +8, Concentration +5, Craft (trapmaking) +4, Diplomacy +8, Handle Animal +7, Heal +9, Knowledge (nature) +9, Profession (herbalist) +11, Search +3, Sense Motive +4, Spellcraft +3, Spot +4, Swim +4, Wilderness Lore +7; Brew Potion, Craft Staff, Improved Critical (sling), Leadership, Track.

Druid Spells: (6/6/5/5/3/3/2): 0—*create water, detect magic, detect poison, guidance, mending, resistance;* 1st—*animal friendship, detect snares and pits, entangle, faerie fire, obscuring mist, pass without trace;* 2nd—*animal messenger, barkskin, flame blade, heat metal, summon swarm;* 3rd—*neutralize poison, protection from elements, snare;* 4th—*dispel magic, flame strike, spike stones;* 5th—*summon nature's ally V, tree stride.*

Animal Companion: Vernon, medium viper, AC 16, HP 10, Atk +0 (1d4–1 bite), Speed 20.

Possessions: Sling +3, longspear +1, leather +2, *ring of protection +4, ring of free movement, staff of healing, staff of the woods.*

Celeste Alstian is a solitary elf who dwells mostly in the forest, in a hut made primarily of twigs and moss. Her hut is alive and its life offers her some degree of privacy from the outside world, as her presence is hard to detect among the living plants that make up her home.

She is slight and has dusky skin, perhaps indicating some drow blood in her lineage. Her hair is raven, her eyes emerald green.

Celeste cares little for the affairs of mortals, unless their business affects "her" forest. She can be persuaded (if she can be found) to aid in any cause which defends nature against incursions. She has little interest in anything else.

Your Campaign

A druids' cabal can easily work either for or against your party. The cabal may be a bonded group of adversaries, determined to track down and destroy the party, or a band of brethren who can help druid characters who get into trouble. The cabal can also simply provide an excellent background for an adventure. What happens, for example, if the dragon mentioned in the intro to this guild is released? The cabal might approach the party and ask for help in recapturing and rebinding the dragon, or that cabal might be long dead, and the dragon becomes free to wreak havoc on the countryside. You also may want to use the secrecy to the cabal to give a campaign a mysterious flair. Maybe a number of distinct and unrelated events are all the work of the cabal, and point toward some sinister hidden purpose that the party must decipher.

Adventure Hooks

The cabal is a secret group, concerned with the well-being of the natural order. A number of things may disturb the natural order and require action:

⚔ A band of undead has invaded the area and is causing havoc among the populace. This isn't of concern to the cabal, but what is of concern is the damage being done to the environment by the undead hordes and the fleeing common folk. The undead must be stopped, even if that involves enlisting aid from cabal nonmembers

⚔ A PC is asked to join the ranks of a cabal. If he refuses, he may be hunted down so as to project the secrets of the guild.

⚔ The druids are concerned about the encroachment of "civilization." This is not something that can be fought directly and provides an opportunity for characters to use their skills to negotiate a solution to the balance between an expanding population needing somewhere to live and farmland to provide sustenance, and the need for nature's creatures to have a habitat in which they can survive. The cabal

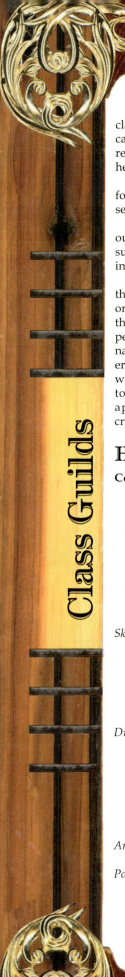

should be played as environmentalists in this situation, but not rabid ones. They are intelligent enough to know that they cannot halt the march of humankind. They simply want to promote the concept of biodiversity. The PCs in this situation should ideally be the deal-brokers between the cabal and the local townsfolk who are expanding the town limits.

- A ritual has gone horribly wrong, and the members of a druids' cabal have all become tainted with evil magic, creating overnight a very powerful, and very sinister, secret organization.

Other Druid Guilds

Some cabals might not be as secretive and may even advertise their services to local farmers experiencing a bad season or plagued by locusts. Druids must be careful in taking such assignments, as the natural order of things demands the odd plague and a drought every so often.

Golden Blades

The guild of the Golden Blades was formed more than a century ago in a small out-of-the-way kingdom as a means of controlling rambunctious young nobles. At the time, many younger children with few responsibilities were left with little to do but fight and cause trouble. Duels were common and deaths were numerous, resulting in feuds among noble families.

At the king's decree, it was ordered that an academy be formed to channel the energies of these young fighters into a more controlled and constructive form. The intent was to instill a sense of discipline into these unruly brawlers and perhaps shape them into a useful group of combatants for the realm.

The academy proved to be a considerable success, beyond the expectations initially considered. Not only were the wild antics of the young curbed and their arguments controlled and confined, but under the tutelage of royally commissioned instructors the skills of the academy students improved dramatically. Soon others were applying to enter the academy, not only from within the realm but from other countries as well. Not only noble scions were sent to the academy; patrons would send men-at-arms and other warriors in their service to improve their skills.

The renown of the academy spread far, which attracted not only students but also masters wishing to increase their own reputations from association with the school, by now known as the Golden Blades. This only improved the quality of training available, as well as further sharing of combat techniques from a variety of realms and cultures.

In addition to the finest fighter training available, members of the Golden Blades gained access to a wide range of contacts, particularly among the upper echelons of a number of societies, and became part of a larger fraternity of skilled fighters. It brought the cream of the crop together in one place, allowing prospective patrons to choose skilled warriors to employ and giving talented fighters access to said patrons, whose attentions might otherwise be unattainable.

From its origins as a form of detention for squabbling brawlers, the Golden Blades has now become a prestigious association with a reputation for producing highly skilled warriors. Membership in the Blades opens doors, and many members are highly valued men-at-arms, bodyguards, and instructors.

Purpose

Control: Young nobles of the realm are still sent to the Blades as a means of instilling discipline and forging a sense of fraternity and patriotism. The academy also allows the realm to have better knowledge of fighters from other places, as a gauge of potential allies and rivals.

Sharing: Within the Golden Blades, the intent is also to improve on skills and to develop and learn new combat techniques. Members are encouraged to share their skills, suggest new ideas, and experiment.

Membership

Profession: Membership is primarily by class, as the bulk of members are fighters, paladins, and rangers. Barbarians are usually not accepted, though some more urbane members of this class have been within the ranks of the Blades at times. Monks and militant clerics are also found, as well as the odd rogue or bard proud of his combat skills.

Alignment: Most members of the Golden Blades are Lawful or Neutral in outlook. Very few Chaotic members last for long, though there are those with the presence of mind to recognize the benefits and the willpower to curb their disorderly natures.

Number Limit (Optional): No more than two hundred members will be present at the Golden Blades academy at any one time, though actual membership is considerably higher.

Joining the Guild

Application: Most members request membership within the Golden Blades. Such an application may be made by the prospective member or by a patron. The individual must then meet the rules for qualification listed below.

Edict (Optional): All members of the nobility of the academy's home realm who are of a martial class (fighter, paladin, ranger, monk, barbarian) must join the academy if they have no family duties to take up their time. The GM may choose to use this rule to assist a character in joining early or to provide some background campaign color.

Invitation: Certain individuals might catch the eye of the Golden Blades and be invited to join. A GM might decide that the actions or talents of a particular PC warrant an unsolicited invitation by the Golden Blades. Generally such PCs should be of a martial class and have Strength and Dexterity ability scores each at 14 or higher, as well as a Lawful nature. They must also meet the minimum requirements detailed below.

Number Limit (Optional): At any one time there may be only 200 members at the academy. To determine if there are available slots, the GM should roll 1d20. On a result of 1 all slots are full and the applicant must wait 1d12 months before one becomes available. A GM may choose to use this option should he wish to make the Blades have a more controlled and exclusive membership.

Qualification: All members of the Golden Blades, barring those local nobles recruited by royal edict, must meet the following requirements:

- Base attack bonus +1 or higher

- Strength or Dexterity 13+
- Of stable character (Lawful or Neutral alignment, or Chaotic characters with Wisdom 12+)
- Pass the test detailed below

Test/Examination: An applicant's worth is determined by sparring with a member of the Golden Blades. The details of this combat are:

- **Golden Blades Entry Test Opponent:** Human Fighter Level 2, 15 hp; AC 15 (Dex, leather armor, Dodge); longsword (+4;1d8+1); Str 13, Dex 15, Con 14, Int 10, Wis 12, Cha 10; Feats: Dodge, Feint, Weapon Focus (longsword).
- The applicant has 10 rounds of combat with practice weapons (subdual damage) against the tester. The applicant must win or still be fighting at the end of the 10 rounds.
- The tester will taunt and provoke the applicant, who must make a Will save each round (DC 12) or become enraged for the round. Each round that the applicant is enraged he has a penalty of –1 to initiative and to AC.

Wealth or Payment: All members must pay an entry fee of 100 gp to join the Golden Blades. This fee covers equipment and training expenses. New members need not pay the fee themselves, however—a patron might do it for them.

Size and Scope

There are several thousand members of the Golden Blades spread across a number of countries. They can be found in most civilized areas, often in positions of importance. A large number, of course, are in the academy's home realm. At any one time there may be no more than 200 members at the academy itself.

Guild Structure & Advancement

Graded (Merit): There are five grades within the Golden Blades: novice, fellow, blade, master, and high master. Advancement within the Blades is by merit, members rising in station through increased martial ability and personal discipline. In charge of all is the High Master, a single individual acknowledged as having the greatest martial accomplishments of any within the Blades.

External rank is ignored within the Golden Blades. Members are treated by, and are expected to treat, other members based on internal hierarchy. Within the academy grounds a common-born blade or master has precedence over novices, even those of royal blood. Common courtesy is expected, of course, and dignified and polite behavior is demanded.

Outside of the academy such interaction is still observed. Members are expected to accord respect and fraternity to one another. Thus even a king may show deference to a lowly man-at-arms should both be Golden Blades members and the man-at-arms is of acknowledged higher standing. Social and alignment considerations might stop real camaraderie between members, but relations will usually be at least polite and respectful between known members.

The requirements for advancement through the ranks are thus:

Benefits

Access to Feats: Golden Blades members have access to the Feint feat (see Appendix B for details). This is not a free feat, but it becomes available for selection through normal advancement..

Access to Items: Golden Blades members receive a 10% discount on purchases of weapons or armor of up to masterwork quality.

Access to Prestige Classes: In a campaign where prestige class membership is restricted, it is recommended that Golden Blades members have access to the following types of prestige classes: bodyguards, duelists, gladiators, and weapon experts.

Table 1.4 – Golden Blades Advancement Table

Grade	Prerequisites	XP Cost	Fees	Benefits Gained
Novice (0)	Meet entry requirements	0	100 gp entry	Entry to guild, access to skills, access to feats, access to items, access to prestige classes, patronage
Fellow (1)	Complete a 3-month novice period	500	50 gp/year	1st Combat Bonus, Fraternity, Good Reputation
Blade (2)	Base attack +4, Str or Dex 14+, Feint, Weapon Focus, Diplomacy 2 ranks, challenge*	1,000	100 gp/year	2nd Combat Bonus
Master (3)	Base attack +8, Str or Dex 15+, Leadership, Weapon Focus (in at least 2 weapons), Diplomacy 4 ranks, challenge*	1,500	500 gp/year	3rd Combat Bonus
High Master (4)	High Challenge**	2,000	500 gp/year	+4 bonus to all Cha rolls involving other Blades

*__Challenge__: To advance, a character must defeat a fellow member one level higher than him in a formal nonlethal combat.
**__High Challenge__: To advance a master must challenge the standing high master to a duel, which must be approved by at least half of all current masters. Such duels are usually nonlethal, though some in the past have been to the death.

Access to Skills: Golden Blades members are trained in manners and etiquette as well as in martial skills. Thus Diplomacy and Sense Motive become class skills for members of the Golden Blades.

Combat Bonus: Due to their intensive training, members of this guild are superior in pressing or avoiding attacks. Upon reaching the grades of Fellow, Blade, and Master, members may choose between a +1 insight bonus to either their attacks <u>or</u> their armor class. If applied to attacks, this bonus increases all pluses, should the character have multiple attacks. The armor class bonus applies at all times, except in situations where the character would lose his Dexterity bonus. The bonuses achieved at different grades may be applied in whichever way desired and are cumulative if applied to the same score twice. A character cannot choose the same type of bonus three times. Thus at Master grade, for example, a character might have a +2 attack bonus and a +1 armor class bonus. Once achieved, these bonuses remain with the character, even if his membership within the Golden Blades ends.

Fraternity: Membership in the Golden Blades makes a character part of a fellowship, a separate community of fighters who see themselves as a cut above the rest. To achieve entry into the Blades means that each member is therefore a person of some worth. Such is the instilled sense of community and loyalty that members support each other even beyond the confines of the academy. A member can count upon fellow Blades for such assistance as small loans of money, an extra blade in a fight, acting as a second for a duel, testimony as a character witness, and so on.

The chance of there being fellow Golden Blade members in a specific settlement depends upon its size and on how many and what levels they are, as detailed below.

Fraternity works both ways, and there is a chance that a PC will be called upon for help by a fellow Golden Blades member. More detail can be found in the disadvantages section.

Good Reputation: Members have a reputation as fighters of the highest caliber. Excepting those groups with enmity toward the Blades, members will receive a favorable reception from NPCs familiar with the guild. This results in a +1 situation bonus to Charisma-based skills.

However, members are expected to live up to this reputation, and breaches of accepted behavior can result in punishment and even ejection from the Blades. More detail is provided in the disadvantages section.

Patronage: The Golden Blades look after the interests of their members, endeavoring to see them reach their potentials and ensuring that they are placed in positions of some prestige. It is suggested that the chances of a player character Blade gaining employment in a martial role be increased by at least fifty percent due to the reputation and backing of the Golden Blades. To determine the chance of finding a higher-level or more influential Blade in a settlement, the GM should use the table for Fraternity and reduce the chances as he feels is appropriate.

Patronage works both ways, and a PC is expected to look after the interests of other Golden Blades members whenever possible. More detail can be found in the disadvantages section.

Disadvantages

Apprenticeship: Upon being accepted into the Golden Blades, a character must undergo a period of intensive training and indoctrination as a novice at the Golden Blades academy. This requires three solid months of the character's time, during which nothing else can be done. At the end of this period, the character is a Fellow and applies the benefits and disadvantages of Golden Blades membership.

Enemies: The Golden Blades have no single organization with which they maintain any degree of enmity. However, the repute of the Blades earns envy and resentment from other martial practitioners. Known Golden Blades members are therefore constantly faced with challenges from those hoping to belittle the Blades and to increase their own renown. The GM should refer to the encounter table; there is a chance equal to half that listed for each settlement that a challenge will be made. Generally the challenger should be no more than 1d4 levels in difference from the character, though the GM may deem circumstances dictate otherwise. Likewise, the GM should determine whether the combat will be lethal or not; most often it should not.

Fees: In addition to the initial entry fee paid by novices, there is an annual fee. This fee is 50 gp for Fellows, 100 gp for Blades, and 500 gp for Masters. Failure to pay this fee will result in a lapse of membership, though a character may call upon fraternity or patronage if needed. Continual failure to pay the fee will see a character ejected from the Golden Blades, as deemed appropriate by the GM.

Fraternity: As noted previously, the tradition of fraternity can act as a disadvantage to the character. Fellow members of the Blades may call upon the character for assistance. Such assistance might take the form of a request for help in a fight, a loan of money, or a character reference. The GM should consult the encounter table and halve the chance of an encounter occurring to determine if a fellow member makes a call for help. In such a case, the member calling upon the character should usually be no more than 1d4 levels in difference from the character.

Patronage: As with fraternity, a character may be called upon to help a junior member of the Golden Blades. The same chance of such a situation occurring exists as listed above, but the junior member will be 1d6 levels lower than the character. Such a request for patronage might entail a character reference, a loan of money, assistance in finding employment, and so on.

Reputation: The character's actions reflect upon the reputation of the Golden Blades as a whole. Thus members are expected to maintain a disciplined and commendable lifestyle, by the standards of the guild. This means acting in a generally lawful manner, as well as avoiding acts of unnecessary evil. (Note that there are evil members of the Blades.) The GM should always consider the actions of any character with Golden Blades membership and determine if that character is maintaining generally conventional behavior.

A character whose actions are constantly bringing himself, and thus the Golden Blades, into disrepute will be ejected from the guild.

Time: In addition to the initial three months of the character's novitiate, further time must be spent undergoing training and maintaining superior martial skills. A character must sacrifice one month of his time each year, though this need not be one continuous allotment of time.

Golden Blades

Affiliations

Apart from the link to the crown of its academy's home region, the Golden Blades organization has no formal ties to any single group, whether as an ally or an enemy. However, the Golden Blades place their members with any number of organizations, as deemed appropriate for each member. They have links with mercenary groups, smaller fight schools, gladiatorial academies, noble houses, and so on.

Leaving

Generally, membership within the Golden Blades is for life. Leaving the guild is usually not an option. Even members who have suffered debilitation through age or injury and can no longer fight are still considered members and accorded the respect owed to them.

When a member leaves the Golden Blades, he retains any bonuses already accrued but loses all other benefits and disadvantages. Assuming that any issues resulting in a character's membership lapse are resolved, he can rejoin the Blades by succeeding in an advancement combat examination appropriate to his old grade, and a payment of 50 gp plus annual fees. He will then be restored to his old grade within the Golden Blades and recover all advantages and disadvantages.

With Permission: A member may voluntarily leave the Blades because he can no longer afford the time or the money, or because of commitments (such as to other guilds) that mean he is barred from continuing membership. In such circumstances, departure is likely to be amicable and there are no implications from the departure.

Expulsion: A member might be ejected from the Blades for continual failure to meet the time and fee requirements or for acting in a disreputable manner. Characters who could not meet the time and money requirements will be condescended to and sneered upon at worst, and their reputation will suffer (apply a –1 modifier to Charisma-based skill tests when dealing with people who regard the Golden Blades highly).

Should the character have been ejected for disrepute, however, things are much worse. Any Golden Blades member encountered who knows of the character will likely challenge him on sight. In addition, the character is seen to have betrayed the trust of the Blades and his reputation suffers even more (apply a –2 modifier to Charisma-based skill tests when dealing with people who regard the Golden Blades highly).

High Master

Sir Gart Ouveron, High Master of the Golden Blades: Male human Fighter 20: CR 20; Medium-size humanoid (human); HD 20d10+40; hp 156; Init +5, Spd 30 ft.; AC 29 (touch 23, flat-footed 21); Atk +27/26*/22/ 21*/17/12 melee (1d8+9+1d6, 1d8+8*/15-20/x2, +5/+3* longsword) or +30/22*/17*/ 12* ranged (1d4+5,1d4+2*/19-20/x2, +3/ +0* dagger); SA none; SQ Golden Blades abilities; Al LN; SV Fort +14, Ref +11, Will +9; Str 15, Dex 21, Con 15, Int 15, Wis 17, Cha 14.

Skills and Feats: Appraise +3, Climb +7, Craft (weapon repair) +12, Diploma-

cy +17, Handle Animal +7, Intimidate +17, Jump +7, Knowledge (weaponry) +17, Listen +8, Ride +15, Sense Motive +13, Speak Language (Elven), Spot +8, Tumble +10; Alertness, Ambidexterity, Blind-Fight, Deflect Arrows, Dodge, Expertise, Feint, Improved Critical (longsword), Improved Disarm, Improved Unarmed Strike, Improved Two-Weapon Fighting, Leadership, Mobility, Spring Attack, Two-Weapon Fighting, Weapon Focus (longsword), Weapon Focus (dagger), Weapon Specialization (longsword), Whirlwind Attack.

Special Qualities: Spell Resistance 19, Golden Blades abilities (+2 bonus to AC, +1 to attack rolls)

Possessions: *+3 dagger*, 4 daggers, *+4 glamered leather armor of spell resistance*, *+5 keen longsword of shock*, *+3 keen weightless longsword*, *ring of protection +5*.

Second cousin of the king of the realm, the High Master of the Golden Blades is a fighter *par excellence*. A member since he was fourteen, Sir Gart has devoted his life to the improvement of martial ability, both his own and that of the Golden Blades.

Now in his mid-forties, Sir Gart is a handsome man standing a shade over six feet, with short-cropped hair and a neatly waxed moustache. He is known for his fine taste in fashion and is always immaculately dressed. He is an austere fellow whose tendency to keep close counsel has led to accusations that he has no sense of humor. This is untrue, though there is little doubt that a smile from Sir Gart is a rare sight.

The High Master enjoys instructing students himself and will occasionally delegate administrative tasks to other masters to allow himself time to personally teach even the lowliest of novices. This is considered quite an honor among the membership of the Golden Blades.

Sir Gart has the king's ear and is much trusted by his cousin. The High Master is responsible for selecting the king's personal bodyguards, usually themselves members of the Golden Blades. This degree of trust has made the High Master a very influential person at court. The fact that he remains a bachelor also means that he is considered quite a prize by the unattached ladies of the realm. Sadly for them, Sir Gart has no time for marriage, as he considers his responsibilities to the Golden Blades and the Crown of the utmost importance.

Table 1.5 - Golden Blades Fraternity

Settlement Size	Chance to Find Member	Number of Members	Level
Thorp	1%	1	1d8–1
Hamlet	2%	1	1d8
Village	5%	1d2	1d8+1
Small Town	10%	1d4	1d8+2
Large Town	20%	1d6	1d8+3
Small City	50%	2d6	1d8+4
Large City	75%	2d8	1d8+5
Metropolis	100%	2d20	1d8+6

*Average Fellow is 1st–3rd level fighter; average Blade is 4th–7th level fighter; average Master is 8th+ level fighter.

Your Campaign

A GM should determine where in his own campaign the academy for the Golden Blades is located. It is suggested that this be in the capital city of a small nation, preferably neutral and out of the way.

Adventure Hooks

- ⚡ A martial-class character witnesses or takes part in a duel with a Golden Blades member, thus introducing the guild.
- ⚡ A PC who is a member of the Golden Blades has been assigned as a bodyguard to a bumbling fool of a noble who thinks that he too should join the Golden Blades.
- ⚡ A renowned personal weapon stolen from a senior Blades member has been found in a party member's possession.
- ⚡ A party member has recently won a nonlethal combat with a higher-level challenger and discovers that a fellow Golden Blades member drugged the challenger before the fight.
- ⚡ The High Master personally selects a party member (and possibly his associates) to help guard an important visiting dignitary who has assassins determined to kill her.

Other Fighter Guilds

Guilds that suit fighters and other martial classes come in many forms. Some other possibilities are:

- **Back-street Bravos:** A low-class organization of thugs, a fight club if you like, who gather together to beat the heck out of one another. Survival means growing stronger and more skilled.

- **Those who are about to die…:** The classic gladiatorial group, where for the mere bother of putting your life constantly on the line, wealth, fame, and prestige can be yours—not to mention the attractive fans clamoring for your attention.

- **For the cause:** A conspiratorial group of warriors dedicated to a cause, be it social, political, religious, or otherwise, who hone their skills for the chance to fight for what they believe in. Even death may hold no fear because of the glory that it brings in dying for the cause.

- **A horse and a lance:** The professional jousters guild, which controls entry into tournaments around the country or a collection of countries. Starting as squires, warriors may work their way up the grades to become rich and famous.

- **Off with his head:** The guild of executioners. It's a dirty job with a bad reputation, but someone has to do it. Members may take pride in their skills, as they're trained to do the job well. Anyone can take off a head, but can they do it with one swing so as to cause as little suffering as possible? Much like a circuit judge, a traveling executioner could be a useful sideline job for an adventurer on the go.

One Reed School

The One Reed Warrior Monk's School is found in the rural Two Rivers Monastery. The teachings and philosophies of the One Reed School prize discipline over action and emphasize meditation, body control, perception, mental self-control, ki, and the more mystical elements of the monk's arts.

Purpose

Sharing: The primary purpose of the school is to instruct in and share a philosophy of monastic life that emphasizes discipline and charity above all else. This training is delivered through a martial art that develops and trains minds, bodies, and spirits to the peak of perfection.

Goal: As part of the philosophy of the One Reed School, the school's disciples are required to defend and provide assistance to the region's farmers, villagers, peasants, and other good folk against brigands, outlaws, monsters, raiding soldiers, and acts of the gods. The monks will quickly respond to any news of attacks or disasters. The disciples have no requirements to assist the people of the region's more urban towns but often do so.

Membership

Location: The monks of the One Reed School are mostly from the Two Rivers and immediate regions, though the school's fame has drawn disciples from more distant lands.

Profession: All disciples of the One Reed School are monks.

Joining the Guild

Application: Entry into the One Reed School is only by application presented in person. See the Test/Examination section below.

Alignment: All disciples of the One Reed School must be Lawful Good or Lawful Neutral in alignment.

Membership Limit: The One Reed School never has more than 54 members, of which there are never more than 10 disciples in the lowest (Novitiates) grade. If this entry grade is full, a supplicant must wait for a vacancy to appear. If more than one supplicant exists at one time, the Masters continue the meditation test in the courtyard (see next section) until only one supplicant remains. The remaining supplicant is granted the next vacancy.

Test/Examination: A supplicant must travel to the Two Rivers Monastery, repose himself in the courtyard, and enter a state of deep meditation. The supplicant will be observed. If he shows any sign of a lack of self-control or a lack of mastery over his meditation, he is rejected. Otherwise, after a period of time (anything from 12 hours to several days), the supplicant will be approached and advised that he may enter the school.

Size and Scope

The One Reed School exists only in the Two Rivers Monastery and has influence only over the Two Rivers region. Nevertheless, disciples of the One Reed School can be found further afield as they travel and test their mastery.

One Reed

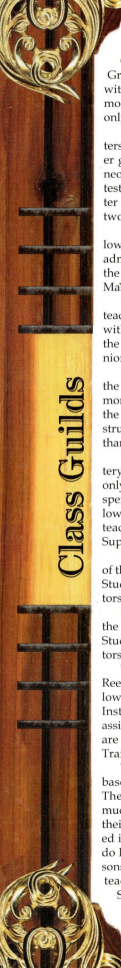

Guild Structure & Advancement

Graded (Merit): The senior member of the school is the Grand Master. The Grand Master has absolute authority within the school but usually delegates most teaching and most administrative duties to the Masters. There is always only one Grand Master.

The **Senior Masters** are the deputies of the Grand Masters and, though they rarely participate in teaching the lower grades, they often provide instruction through spontaneous testing of the disciples, irrespective of grade. These tests can be trivial or quite grueling. Only the Grand Master teaches the Senior Masters. There are never more than two Senior Masters.

The **Junior Masters** sometimes provide instruction to lower grades but are mostly involved in testing and in the administration of the school. Only the Senior Masters teach the Junior Masters. There are never more than three Junior Masters.

The primary responsibility of the **Senior Instructors** is teaching the disciples. They also help the Junior Masters with school administrative issues. Only the Masters teach the Senior Instructors. There are never more than four Senior Instructors.

The **Junior Instructors** assist the Senior Instructors with the teaching of the three Student and lower grades. They monitor exercises, discipline wayward students, and run the basic classes. Only the Junior Masters or the Senior Instructors teach the Junior Instructors. There are never more than five Junior Instructors.

The **Superior Students** have demonstrated their mastery of the school's teachings and philosophies and so need only minimal teaching from the Instructors. Senior Students spend as much time assisting the Instructors in teaching lower grades as they do being taught. Only the Instructors teach Superior Students. There are never more than six Superior Students.

The **Senior Students** and **Students** have mastered all of the basic lessons of the school. Only the Instructors teach Students, though Senior Students may assist the Instructors. There are never more than seven in the Students grade.

Inferior Students have begun to master the basics of the school's teachings. Only the Instructors teach Inferior Students, though Senior Students may assist the Instructors. There are never more than eight Inferior Students.

Trainees have begun to learn the lessons of the One Reed School. This grade, more than any other above or below, requires the most effort from its disciples. Only the Instructors teach Trainees, though Senior Students may assist the Instructors. There are never more than nine Trainees.

The **Novitiates** are the base grade of the school. These disciples spend as much time demonstrating their skills and being tested in their abilities as they do learning their basic lessons. Only the Instructors teach Novitiates, though Senior Students may assist the Instructors. There are never

more than ten Novitiates.

The school may have several **Supplicants** who have passed the meditation test but are awaiting vacancies in the Novitiates grade. There is no maximum to the number of Supplicants in the school.

Whenever a vacancy occurs, the disciples in the grade below who wish to contest the vacancy submit their request for trial. First the contesting disciples undergo a series of martial contests in a variety of scenarios. The winner of these then submits himself for the next test, a trial by meditation. The disciple must meditate in perfect stillness within the grounds of the monastery for a number of days equal to the grade of the vacancy. Masters and Instructors will attempt to distract the meditating disciple, who must not display any imperfection.

Many monks with high character class levels who join the school will advance quickly through the grades. However, advancing in grades means increased responsibilities with less time for personal pursuits such as adventuring. For this reason, some high-level monks choose never to advance beyond the grade of Junior Instructor.

Benefits

Bonuses: Due to the philosophy, training, and special instruction, a disciple of the One Reed School receives:

√ One bonus rank in Knowledge (martial arts) at 1st, 4th, 7th, and 10th grades.

√ +1 to Wisdom for every two grades he has in the school.

√ Through superior discipline and ki mastery, a disciple of the school develops enhanced toughness and receives a bonus of 4 hit points at 5th and 9th grades.

Fraternity: The members of the One Reed School are all brothers and sisters. An offense against one is an offense against all. In some circumstances, the entire 53 remaining members of the School may respond to help a lone disciple.

Good Reputation: In the Two Rivers region, the monks of the One Reed School are revered and respected by the people of the villages and farms. Whenever a monk travels through the region, he is regularly offered food, drink, shelter, and other goods and services.

Immunity to Fear: On reaching 3rd grade in the school, through rigorous mental control, a disciple receives complete immunity to fear (magical or otherwise).

Shelter: All disciples of the school, unless permission for temporarily leave is granted by a Master, live in the Two Rivers monastery.

Table 1.6 – One Reed School Advancement

Grade	XP Cost	Benefits
Supplicant (0)	0	Entry to guild, Shelter
Novitiate (1)	500	Good Reputation, +1 Knowledge, Fraternity
Trainee (2)	1,000	+1 Wisdom
Inferior Student (3)	1,500	Immunity to fear
Student (4)	2,000	+1 Wisdom, +1 Knowledge
Superior Student (5)	2,500	Bonus hit points
Junior Instructor (6)	3,000	+1 Wisdom
Senior Instructor (7)	3,500	+1 Knowledge
Junior Master (8)	4,000	+1 Wisdom
Senior Master (9)	4,500	Bonus hit points
Grand Master (10)	5,000	+1 Wisdom, +1 Knowledge

Disadvantages

Apprenticeship: While a disciple has the grade of Novitiate, he may not leave the premises of the Two Rivers Monastery, and his every waking moment is at the command and service of the other monks. This restriction is eased once the disciple advances to Trainee grade.

Enemies: Brigands and outlaws in the Two Rivers region despise the monks of the One Reed School. These outlaws will attempt to ambush any lone monk they find outside of the Monastery.

Exclusions: The rules of the One Reed School impose strict behavior upon its disciples. A disciple of the school must restrain from excessive vocalization and maintain a demeanor of politeness, submissiveness, and quietude. A disciple may not eat meat and must grant all respect and deference due to any authority. A disciple must spend as much time in stillness and meditation as he spends in energy and activity, to maintain balance. A disciple must face all danger with courage and calmness and must not flee if an innocent remains in danger.

Experience Cost: The experience cost of grade advancement is as in the Advancement Table above.

Fees: 50% of all wealth a disciple receives or finds must be donated to the One Reed School.

Regulations/Traditions: At some time, once every month, a disciple of the One Reed School must devote a long stretch of time to meditation. The length of this meditation is a number of days equal to one half the disciple's grade, rounded up. If this meditation is interrupted for any reason, it must be started again. Further, every day a disciple must spend one hour at sunset or sunrise meditating.

A disciple must never reveal the teachings and philosophies of the One Reed School outside of the Two Rivers monastery. Doing so is the most reviled of all sins in the school.

Time: Once a disciple reaches the grade of Trainee, he may request permission from a Master to leave the monastery for personal business. However, he must return to spend time in the school learning and, if of higher grade, teaching. A disciple must spend a number of months equal to his grade at the school each year or risk expulsion. Further, he must have spent the preceding months, equal in number to a vacant higher grade, at the school to be eligible to advance to that vacancy (after having met all other advancement requirements).

Affiliations

The One Reed School is on good terms with Lawful and Good churches of the Two Rivers region. Its members are deeply respected by villages and farming communities. Though combined operations of the school's disciples and the men-at-arms of the region's earl have attempted to eradicate outlaw bands in Two Rivers, the school is viewed with distrust by the earl as he cannot command them, only request assistance.

No disciple of the One Reed School may be a member of another guild.

Leaving

A monk must request permission from the Grand Master to leave the school. Regardless of the circumstances, when a monk leaves the strict regime and teachings of the school, he loses the bonus Wisdom points and special immunity to fear power. He retains the bonus hit points and Knowledge skill.

With Permission: Leaving with the Grand Master's permission grants the monk the right to apply for reentry at a future date.

Without Permission: Failure to obtain permission before leaving results in the monk being declared renegade, and he will never be permitted to rejoin the school.

Expulsion: Due to the intensive application process that weeds out those with undisciplined minds, monks are rarely expelled from the One Reed School. Occasionally, students who are disobedient to the point of being disruptive to the school are asked to leave. Generally this is a friendly break, and the monk may apply again after a year if he so desires.

Grand Master

Marron: Male human Monk 20: CR 20; Medium-size humanoid (human); HD 20d8; hp 88; Init +11, Spd 90 ft.; AC 37 (touch 29, flat-footed 34); Atk +15/+10/+15 melee (1d4/19-20/x2, dagger) or +22/+17/+12 ranged (1d4/19-20/x2, throwing dagger) or +15/+12/+8/+6/+3 (1d20, unarmed); SA none; SQ monk abilities, immunity to fear (magical or otherwise); Al LG; SV Fort +12, Ref +19, Will +18; Str 10, Dex 17, Con 10, Int 14, Wis 26, Cha 12.

Skills and Feats: Balance +22, Climb +12, Concentration +15, Diplomacy +11, Escape Artist +17, Hide +27, Jump +18, Knowledge (arcana) +5, Knowledge (martial arts) +8, Knowledge (philosophy) +5, Listen +15, Move Silently +17, Perform +7 (poetry), Speak Language (Elven), Speak Language (Halfling), Spot +10, Swim +5, Tumble +17; Ambidexterity, Dodge, Expertise, Improved Disarm, Improved Initiative, Mobility, Spring Attack, Whirlwind Attack.

Special Qualities: All monk abilities, immunity to fear (magical or otherwise).

Possessions: Belt, monk's outfit, *bracers of armor +8, manual of quickness in action +4* (used), *necklace of adaptation, ring of protection +3.*

Grand Master Marron was born the third son of simple farmers. He would have led a simple farmer's life except for a retired soldier living in the local village when Marron was a child. Marron was fascinated by the soldier's mastery of combat skills, especially unarmed maneuvers. The old soldier recognized that Marron had talent and self-control and so persuaded Marron's parents to release their child to pursue his destiny. The soldier sent Marron to a retired warrior monk who accepted Marron as an apprentice and taught him the mysteries and skills of the warrior monk's way.

After completing his apprenticeship, Marron wandered the realms studying in various monk schools and under old masters until he came to the One Reed School. For five decades Marron has studied and taught in the One Reed School and has risen to the venerable position of Grand Master.

Grand Master Marron is a gentle, wise, silver-haired old man. He is loved by children and dogs and respected by adults. He is wiry and agile but looks rather frail—a dangerously incorrect assessment. Few outside the school are aware of his great power and skill.

Your Campaign

The One Reed School can be transplanted to any rural location in your campaign and become a source of law and order in that region. Your party can form an alliance with the monks against Evil outlaws and monsters or, if the party is predominantly Chaotic, may even become the monk's opponents. If the party's monk requires further training he can attempt to join the school. Perhaps he originated from the school and would like to reapply for reentry.

Adventure Hooks

- The school hires the party to track down, apprehend, and return a renegade disciple.
- The party comes upon a monk under attack by brigands, or the party finds the monk bound and captured in the brigand's camp. Either way, the school would reward the party for rescuing its disciple.
- The party, retreating swiftly after raiding a monster's lair, encounters some monks who are on their way to eradicate the same monsters.
- It's a miserable, sleeting day and night is rapidly falling. The only shelter around is a monastery. The party will be granted shelter for the night and in staying there may witness some wondrous acts by the disciples in training.

Other Schools

- **The School of Iron** teaches that all real achievement must be through pain and that its disciples must struggle to be the supreme warriors by dominating others. The monks of this school are all Lawful Evil.
- **The Invisibles School** emphasizes in its teachings the ability to be unseen and unnoticed.
- **The White School** emphasizes the monk's martial skills in a war environment. Many disciples of this school serve in local lords' armies.

Paladin Orders

An order is a common organization for lawfully aligned paladins which unites the influence of many individual paladins toward a common holy martial goal. Orders are hierarchical organizations, with a blending of monastic and martial rules guiding the lives of all its members in their duties and daily routines.

Orders are always formed with a specific holy purpose in mind—*e.g.*, destroy evil, protect the weak, maintain order—and each order has its own name and colors—*e.g.*, the Order of the Blue Pennant in *azure* and *argent*, the Order of the Burning Sword in *or* and *argent*, and the Order of the Helping Hand in *gules* and *azure*. By joining an order, a paladin agrees and declares that he believes the order's specific purpose to be primary above all others. All the member paladins bear the insignia and colors of their order upon their surcoats.

A paladin does not have to spend all his time on his order's business. He may leave, with his superior's permission, to pursue personal pursuits, but when his order calls he must return immediately or be declared renegade. As a paladin advances in rank and responsibilities within an order, he has less and less time to pursue personal missions.

Purpose

Many orders exist. Some are small, with only a handful of paladins in membership and having only limited or specialized influence and very little fame. Some are large, with hundreds or even thousands of paladins in membership, and influence and fame stretching over multiple kingdoms. Whatever their size, the orders all fall into one of the three following categories:

Protection: *Protective orders* have the mission of protecting the sick, the weak, the righteous, and the holy and of guarding the resolute against evil. The members of these orders may guard holy buildings and individuals such as temples and priests. They may guard and treat patients in secure hospices or travel with pilgrims to protect them against brigands and barbarians. They may undertake to maintain the public peace in turbulent times. They may patrol civilized highways, rural tracts, and wilderness trails, protecting all travelers, and may operate fortified inns along well traveled but dangerous routes. Some orders even operate warships along shipping routes or coastlines to protect against pirates, sea barbarians, or the navies of evil nations. The most common prestige class in protective orders is the Hospitaler.

Control: *Crusading orders* see their mission as primarily martial, to engage in holy wars to eradicate evil and chaos and to defend order and justice. A crusading order may fight a war on its own, assembling and committing its entire membership to a just cause with holy zeal. In small numbers or even individually, members of these orders may join secular forces to help fight a just war with the *visiting* paladins, never very numerous, forming a *corps d'élite* which carries the great mass of knights and common soldiers into battle, often bearing battle pennants to rally and inspire the troops or claiming the most perilous posts, alternately holding the van and rear guards. Crusading orders receive many requests for assistance from desperate or ambitious leaders, governments, and high priests but rarely respond in exactly the way requested. Crusading orders may commit to long-term campaigns or short-term combat, but either way they cannot be swayed from their holy mission. There are few things more wonderful (or terrifying) than seeing the massed ranks of a crusading order charging fearlessly into battle. The most common prestige class in crusading orders is the Templar.

Goal: The members of *questing orders* see themselves as champions of just causes. These paladins are usually seen traveling individually or in small groups as they seek out evil or search for the lost. Once news of evil reaches a questing order, one or sometimes several members are sent out to search for its source or lair and to challenge and destroy the evil, *e.g.*, demons, evil wizards, evil priests, and undead. Sometimes, if the evil is large or numerous, such as an evil temple or an adult chromatic dragon, a company of paladins may be sent forth to combat it. The paladins of questing orders are also dispatched to redeem captives and the unjustly imprisoned. A questing order paladin may assemble or join an adventuring party to further his mission.

Membership

Belief/Code: All members of an order are paladins who have committed themselves, their lives, and their honor to the objectives of the order. They have bound themselves to a sacred oath and may not break their oath without dire consequences.

Profession: Only paladins can be members of the orders.

Joining the Guild

Only members of the Paladin class may join a paladin order. There are two ways in which a paladin may enter an order.

Application: The paladin, after long prayer, thought, and meditation, may decide to apply to join one of the famed orders whose mission most closely matches the paladin's own worldview. This is never undertaken lightly, as it is a serious and holy commitment, usually for life. The paladin must petition the Grand Master of the order he wishes to join and, when recognized, present himself for examination and testing.

Invitation: A paladin may be invited by the Grand Master to join an order if the paladin's famed deeds demonstrate that he would be a fitting brother within the order. The paladin may refuse this invitation without insult, dishonor, or penalty.

Foundation: A paladin may eventually create an order himself. This is never an easy decision, as it carries a very strong danger of the sin of pride. However, the paladin may sense a calling to start an order to meet a holy need and, after prayer and meditation, proceed to do so. Sometimes the valorous or saintly acts of a great paladin may attract others in his footsteps. As these new paladins set out to emulate the deeds of the first, an order evolves as the paladins cooperate in their efforts. However an order comes into being, it must start with at least one stronghold, even if only a simple wooden motte-and-bailey.

Test/Examination: No paladin is granted easy entry into an order, for his spirit must be tested to see if it is truly suitable. Before the Grand Master, Commanders, and Captains of the order, the paladin must stand for seven days and with magic and words be examined. The paladin is questioned on his faith, his goals, and his strength. If the paladin is found to be apposite for the order, he is granted the grade of Postulant and set a deed as a test of strength and commitment; a hard quest in which only the resolute and faithful will succeed. If the paladin fails in this deed, he may not apply again to enter any order until he has reached another level as a paladin.

Deed: If the paladin succeeds in his allotted deed, whether taking one day or ten years, he is permitted full entry into the order. In the great hall of the order's main stronghold, with the assembled paladins in attendance, covered with only simple rags and prostrate before the Grand Master, he swears a great oath binding himself to the order until released by the Grand Master or by death.

Size and Scope

Paladin orders vary greatly in size and fame. Their membership and influence may spread over multiple kingdoms or exist in only a single location. Some evil nations ban their existence, while good nations encourage their work. An order may own only a remote lonely keep or may own dozens of castles and thousands of manors spread over a continent.

Likewise the membership of an order varies a great deal. Some orders which have suffered great attrition from evil foes, have very specialized purposes, or have lost the confidence of the population may have only a handful of members. On the other hand, orders with wide responsibilities and with heroic reputations can have memberships in the hundreds or even thousands. An order prospers or falls on the strength of its membership and the support of good nations.

An order must have at least one stronghold, even if it is just a wooden motte-and-bailey. Over time, with monies and treasures recovered or rescued by its members and with the many donations and bequests from grateful citizens and leaders, an order can grow immensely wealthy in land and treasure. A wealthy order will have many keeps and fortresses in strategic locations and own many manors, estates, and other properties. The headquarters of a wealthy, powerful order and the residence of its Grand Master may be a great castle dominating the surrounding land and seas. In some cases, the Grand Master of a powerful order is also the sovereign temporal lord of the castle headquarters and its surrounding lands and a true ecclesiastical principality.

Whatever its size, an order's stronghold is part monastery, part barracks, combining the obedience of the soldier with the piety of the religious, living shoulder to shoulder in brotherly union, commander and subordinate. A paladin order surpasses, in that cohesiveness which is the ideal of every military organization, all other military forces. The stronghold also includes shrines to the gods and other divine forces of goodness, stables for the paladins' horses, a hall for the assembled members of the order, and a cemetery to which all members of the order are returned no matter where they fall.

Rarely are the member paladins the only inhabitants of an order's stronghold. Though the pious paladins are usually willing to work at the many simple chores and drudgery needed to maintain the stronghold and its inhabitants, often their training and duties leave little time for these necessary chores. To perform this work, many servants are employed in the strongholds. Further, for many reasons, secular noble knights and common soldiers often serve in an order's forces and billet in the strongholds. These knights and soldiers have dedicated themselves to the order's cause and swear an oath of obedience and loyalty to the Order's Grand Master.

Guild Structure & Advancement

All paladins, the world over, recognize each other as brothers. Paladins respect authority and order and in doing so recognize the authority of any paladin of high grade from any order.

Graded (Elective): Paladin orders have a hierarchical, monastic-martial structure, as follows:

At the summit is the **Grand Master** of the order. The Grand Master is the supreme temporal lord to whom all paladins and other martial forces of the order owe their allegiance. The Grand Master commands the order's primary stronghold. Within all of the order's strongholds and other properties, and in pursuit of the order's goals, the Grand Master's authority is absolute. An order's Grand Master is usually 10th level or higher as a paladin. A Grand Master is fully occupied with the order's business and never has any time to pursue personal missions or adventuring.

Below the Grand Master are the commander of the order's other major strongholds, the **Paladin Commander**, and the heads of the order's brigades. The heads of the brigades are the military commander, known as the **Marshal of Paladins**; the head of religious duties and rites, known as the **Master of Chaplains**; the head of hospices and care, known as the **Master of Infirmarians**; and the administrator of the order's worldly affairs, its logistics, and the servants, craftsmen, and bailiffs needed to operate the order's strongholds and estates, known as the **Seneschal**. The commanders are usually of 9th level or higher and have little time to pursue personal missions or adventuring. In any time period, at the GM's discretion, roll 1d10. Only on a roll of 9 or higher is a commander available for these personal pursuits. The individual strongholds of a large order will also have individual paladins, usually of lower levels, assigned these duties for the stronghold's territory. At any time, a paladin of this grade may command up to ten paladins of lower grade to cease whatever they are doing and assist or follow him until he releases them.

Below the commanders are the order's senior officers, the **Paladin Captains**. These paladins command a squadron of the order's forces in battle, command minor fortifications belonging to the order, or head missions assigned by the commanders. Captains are usually 6th level or higher. Captains pursue personal goals or adventure occasionally. In any time period, at the GM's discretion, on a roll of 5 or higher on 1d10 the Captain is free. At any time, a paladin of this grade may command up to three paladins of lower grade to cease whatever they are doing and assist or follow him until he releases them.

The grade below the Captains is the junior officers, the **Paladin Bannerettes**. These paladins are usually 3rd level or higher. In war, they command secular men-at-arms or bear the pennants and battle insignia of their order or the

Table 1.7 – Paladin Order Advancement

Grade	XP Cost	Benefits Gained
Postulant (0)	0	Fraternity, Good Reputation
Brethren (1)	500	Entry to guild, first 2 bonuses, Shelter, access to items
Sergeant (2)	1,000	Gain first domain
Bannerette (3)	1,500	Command Paladins
Captain (4)	2,000	Gain second domain, Greater Command
Commander (5)	2,500	Greater Command, third bonus
Grand Master (6)	3,000	Command Order

secular force they have joined. Bannerettes may also be commissioned by a higher grade to lead missions that do not require a Captain. Bannerettes pursue personal goals or adventurers occasionally; in any time period, at the GM's discretion, on a roll of 4 or higher on 1d10 the Bannerette is free. At any time, a paladin of this grade may command one paladin of lower grade to cease whatever he is doing and assist or follow the Bannerette until he releases him.

The grade below the Bannerettes is that of the **Paladin Sergeants**. These paladins are usually 2nd level or higher. The Sergeants accompany the officer grades and ensure all officers' orders are implemented. The Sergeants are also assigned to protect senior officers and usually make up the sharp lead and the critical end points of a military formation in battle. Sergeants are almost as free to pursue personal goals or adventure as are the Brethren. In any time period, at the GM's discretion, on a roll of 3 or higher on 1d10, the Sergeant is free.

The majority of paladins in an order are of the grade of **Paladin Brethren**. Brethren are the freest of all grades to pursue personal goals or adventure. In any time period, at the GM's discretion, on any roll other than a 1, the Brother is free. In an order's hierarchy, secular knights and nobles who have sworn themselves to the order are associated with this grade.

The **Paladin Postulant** is the grade of the novices pursuing assigned deeds to prove themselves worthy of full membership in the order. Postulants are free to pursue personal goals or adventures anytime, though doing so may delay the accomplishment of their set deeds. Postulants do not receive the benefits or suffer the penalties of full membership in an order. Common soldiers and other men-at-arms, as well as the chief bailiffs and heads of servants, are associated with this grade in the order's hierarchy.

Sometimes, if a paladin excels at his assigned missions or if he has a great and holy purpose to fulfill, he will never be promoted above the grade of Brethren within the order, no matter how high a level he achieves as a paladin, as his talents are better utilized out in the field than in the stronghold. This is rare, however, as Lawful paladins understand the requirement of service to further the order's goals.

Promotion in an order requires opportunity, seniority, achievement, and the favorable judgment of superiors. When a vacancy occurs within an order, usually through death or promotion and very rarely through the Grand Master releasing a paladin from his oath to the order, the most senior paladins (by both level and length of service) are examined by the Grand Master and Commanders. The achievements, valor, and skills of the candidates are studied and, guided by prayer, one of the candidates is chosen for the vacant position. Even if a paladin does not desire the promotion, he may be commanded to accept it by his superiors, and refusal can result in expulsion from the order.

Benefits

Membership in an order brings stability, certainty, and support to a paladin's life and holy mission. Through the organized structure of an order the member paladins can more successfully help the sick, weak, or oppressed, root out and smite evil, and bring order to their lands. When one paladin falls, another brother is there to take his place or to succor his fallen comrade. An order amplifies the influence of its individual members.

Access to Items: In some orders, the vaults of the main stronghold(s) may contain powerful holy items. If in dire need and if he has proven himself to be exemplary in honor, duty, and valor, a member of the order may be permitted access to one of these items.

Bonuses: Through the intense prayer, training, and support a paladin receives within an order, he receives a number of bonus special abilities. These benefits depend on an order's holy mission, *i.e.*, whether it is a crusading, protective, or questing order:

Bonuses of a Crusading Order
- *Immune to fear* starting at 1st grade, regardless of the paladin's class level.
- Extended *Aura of Courage* starting at 1st grade. Allies in a 30' radius gain the +4 morale boost for saves against fear effects.
- At 5th grade, the paladin automatically gains the Leadership feat.

Bonuses of a Protective Order
- Any member of grade 1 or above receives a +1 to his Charisma bonuses for determining how many hit points he may cure in a day through *Lay On Hands* ability.
- Any paladin in a protective order receives the *remove disease* ability at 2nd level in the paladin class rather than 3rd level. This ability still improves every three levels but is calculated from 2nd level, *i.e.*, *remove disease* once a week at 2nd level, twice a week at 5th level, three times a week at 8th level, and so on.
- At 5th grade, the paladin gains the ability to call a second paladin's mount.

Bonuses of a Questing Order
- When any paladin in a questing order uses his *detect evil* ability, he cannot be stunned by overwhelming evil unless the strength of the evil is three times the level of the paladin.

- *Smite evil* starting at 1st grade, regardless of the paladin's class level.
- At 5th grade, the paladin's empathetic link with his mount (if he has one) extends to 5 miles.

Command Order: An order's grand master is the supreme temporal lord to whom all paladins and other martial forces of the order owe their allegiance. Constrained only by morality and canon law, a grand master may command one, several, or all paladins in his order to perform any duty or achieve any objective he sees fit.

Command Paladins: At any time, a paladin bannerette has the absolute right (above and beyond his order's normal, martial, chain-of-command authority) to direct and command one other paladin of lower grade (Sergeant, Brethren, or Postulant) to cease whatever he is doing and immediately assist and follow the Bannerette until released, *e.g.*, "Water this horse," "Guard that tower," "Join me as I destroy the ogre mages of those mountains and recover their treasure hoards," "Follow me as I attack the entire Nine Hells," etc. Refusal to obey is grounds for expulsion from the order. This authority may be countered only by another paladin of higher grade than the bannerette. At any time, no more than one paladin may be so commanded by a bannerette.

Fraternity: All paladins within an order will always assist any other member of the order whenever a call for aid is made.

Good Reputation: Within Good or Lawful nations where his order is active or where his order's fame and good name have spread, a recognized paladin enjoys respect and a good reputation. The common folk and craftsmen will offer the paladin gifts and ask for blessings. The taverns and inns may treat the paladin to free meals, drinks, and lodgings. The mayors, city councilors, and guildmasters of the towns and cities will tend to be forthright and helpful with the paladin.

Greater Command: Paladin captains and paladin commanders also have the Command Paladins membership benefit, at increased force. A captain may so command three paladins, of Sergeant grade and lower, at any one time. A commander may so command ten paladins, of Captain grade and lower, at any one time.

Shelter: As a member of an order, a paladin receives free lodging and assistance from any stronghold, manor, or estate of his order.

Spell Domains: Upon reaching 2nd grade, the paladin gains access to a single cleric spell domain. The paladin may prepare any of his spells from this domain if he wishes. As a cleric, the paladin gains one bonus spell from the domain per spell level to which he has access. At 4th grade, the paladin gains access to a second cleric spell domain. Paladins must choose their bonus domains from the following list:

√ **Crusading Order:** Good, Law, War
√ **Protective Order:** Healing, Law, Protection
√ **Questing Order:** Good, Healing, Protection

Disadvantages

Fees: A paladin must tithe to his order 10% of all treasures, monies, and gifts he wins, finds, or receives. Failure to do so is grounds for expulsion from the order.

Regulations/Traditions: There is one holy day every year specific to each order in which all the paladins must gather together in the order's strongholds for prayer and review. If a paladin is absent from this gathering without the Grand Master's consent and does not offer an acceptable reason, he will be expelled from the order. Further, whenever a paladin away on personal business is commanded to return to his order and fails to do so, he will be expelled if he cannot offer an acceptable reason.

When a paladin of an order commits an act or violation that requires *atonement*, he must always first perform special acts of penance as set by his order for the *atonement* to work.

Time: The higher the paladin's grade in an order, the less time he has to spend on personal business. The grades' descriptions above describe this.

Affiliations

An order often forms alliances, or at least understandings, with the Lawful or Good churches in the lands where the order maintains a presence. The clerics of these churches can often be found in residence at the order's strongholds or traveling with the order's paladins on a mission for the order or the church.

Paladin orders are brother organizations. They cooperate with each other; heeding a fellow order's call for assistance, even when their goals are dissimilar. When their goals are complementary, they work together assisting each other for as long as their paths cross. When their goals conflict, they gather in council and discuss and pray until they reach a mutual agreement. On those few rare, tragic occasions where orders briefly clash on opposing sides of a conflict, wisdom, honor, and forgiveness guide their actions until the mistake is rectified.

Paladin orders often cooperate with virtuous and honorable secular orders of knights. They may pursue joint missions, provide rest and succor for each other, answer calls for assistance, and organize temporary postings of the other order's members.

Paladins of lower grades may be members of another guild, though it is uncommon (those of Command grade and above never have the time).

If a paladin joins another guild, it is usually a fighter's school or an ecclesiastical council. The fighter's school must be an orderly school with respect for authority. The ecclesiastical council must be of a Lawful or Good alignment. It is also not uncommon for the lower grades of the order who still have time for adventuring to be members of an adventurer's guild.

Less frequently, if a paladin in an order is multiclassed he may also be a member of a wizard's academy or a warrior monk's school. Through historical ties or a specific mission, a paladin in an order may have membership in a trading, craft, town, family, or even social guild.

The Lawful paladins of an order never join bardic colleges or sorcerer's schools. They also can never join and are usually opposed to thieves' guilds, barbarian hordes, and mercenary companies.

Leaving

Once a paladin joins an order, that order is forever his only means of advancing further levels as a paladin. Leaving an order is permanent. Once a paladin has left an order, he can never rejoin that or any other order. A paladin may be a member of only one order ever. The one exception to this last rule is if a paladin's first order no longer exists for some reason.

With Permission: If a paladin lawfully leaves his order with the permission of the Grand Master, he keeps all of his existing special abilities but loses access to the cleric domains of the former order and can never again advance in level as a paladin.

Without Permission: If a paladin leaves his order without the permission of the Grand Master, he has committed a serious violation of conduct and loses all his special abilities, spells, and the services of a paladin's warhorse. By an appropriate act of atonement, the paladin may regain his special abilities but may not rejoin the order nor ever advance again in levels as a paladin.

Expulsion: If a paladin is expelled from his order, he loses his special powers, spells, and the services of a paladin's warhorse until he atones. A paladin who does not make atonement for the usual violations and acts of misconduct described in the *Player's Handbook* will be expelled from his order.

Grand Master

Sir Bran Macasemes: Male human Paladin 17: CR 17; Medium-size humanoid (human); HD 17d10+34; hp 119; Init +1, Spd 30 ft.; AC 31 (touch 18, flat-footed 23); Atk +27/+22/+17/+12 melee (1d10+9/17-20/x2, sword, bastard) or +18/+13/+8/+3 ranged (1d10/19-20/x2, crossbow, heavy); SA none; SQ paladin abilities; Al LG; SV Fort +12, Ref +6, Will +7; Str 20, Dex 13, Con 14, Int 12, Wis 15, Cha 16.

Skills and Feats: Concentration +12, Diplomacy +8, Handle Animal +13, Heal +7, Knowledge (military) +11, Knowledge (religion) +11, Ride +21, Speak Language (Dwarven); Exotic Weapon Proficiency (sword, bastard), Improved Critical (sword, bastard), Leadership, Mounted Combat, Ride-By Attack, Spirited Charge, Weapon Focus (sword, bastard).

Special Qualities: Paladin abilities—access to Domain of Healing (9th-level caster for healing spells), access to Domain of Protection (protective ward power), Aura of Courage, Detect Evil, Divine Grace, Divine Health, Lay On Hands (68 hp per day), Remove Disease 6/week, Smite Evil, Special Mount, Second Special Mount, Turn Undead.

Paladin Spells (3+1/3+1/2+1/1+1): 1st—*bless, divine favor, magic weapon,* and either *cure light wounds* or *sanctuary* (domain spells); 2nd—*delay poison, resist elements, undetectable alignment,* and either *cure moderate wounds* or *shield other* (domain spells); 3rd—*dispel magic, heal mount,* and either *cure serious wounds* or *protection from elements* (domain spells); 4th—*dispel evil* and either *cure critical wounds* or *spell immunity* (domain spells).

Possessions: full plate armor +5, holy bastard sword +4, large steel shield +5.

Sir Bran Macasemes was born to a noble family and grew up pampered in his every whim. As a young man he learned the knightly warrior skills but not the knightly virtues, as he and his fellow miscreant scions of nobility indulged themselves in endless revelry, hunts, and abuses of their class and rank.

Eventually, young Bran grew restless and tired of his purposeless life. He rejected his former selfish and chaotic behavior and found his calling as a paladin. After years of service to the Good gods, he was offered membership in the Order of the Helping Hand, a protective order. Within the order, his selfless service was rewarded and he rose through the grades. After 30 years he is now Grand Master of the order.

Grand Master Sir Bran Macasemes is a strikingly handsome, tall, swarthy man. His hair is still very dark and his eyes are deep, penetrating, and black. Though he is compassionate and altruistic, Sir Macasemes is not a soft man. He is resolute, decisive, an excellent leader, and deeply devoted to his order and the holy powers. Though he shows due respect to rulers and royalty, he bows to no one, speaking as a peer to all lords, rulers, and those of noble rank.

Sir Macasemes' paladins can be found throughout the realm in holy or dangerous places, helping, guarding, and protecting. He receives many missives requesting, begging, even demanding that he send his paladins for several reasons, usually selfish. Sir Macasemes gives every request due consideration but sends the order's paladins only where they can do the most good.

Your Campaign

A GM should decide what orders of paladins exist in his campaign, their names, their purposes, and the locations of the primary strongholds of each order. He should also decide which of these orders are available for the paladin PCs to join. He can then populate his campaign with paladins from these orders, pursuing their holy goals and encountering the PCs.

Adventure Hooks

- A questing paladin hires the PCs to assist in seeking out and destroying an evil monster.
- The PCs mistakenly become the targets of a questing paladin.
- The PCs recuperate in a hospital run by paladins of a protective order.
- The PCs and some pilgrims join a caravan traveling through lawless or dangerous regions. One or two paladins of a protective order accompany the caravan to provide protection from outlaws, monsters, and barbarians.
- The PCs are caught up in a war zone and are brought before the commander of a squadron of a crusading order of paladins, where they must explain themselves (and possibly choose sides).
- A paladin PC wishes to join an order and is set a deed to prove himself. His fellow PCs accompany him on his deed.
- The PCs find an evil too great for them to defeat and too dangerous to just leave. When (or if) they escape, they may decide to track down a stronghold of a questing or crusading order, convince the commander that the evil is real, then lead a contingent of paladins back to engage and eradicate the great evil.

Specific Paladin Orders

- **Blue Pennant:** A questing order that seeks out and rescues, through combat and negotiation, the kidnapped, the enslaved, the unjustly imprisoned, and the lost. These paladins sometimes quest to destroy slaver organizations.

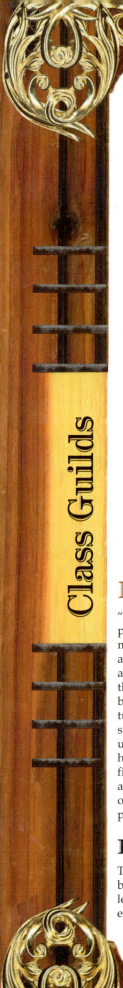

- **Burning Sword:** A crusading order dedicated to defending good nations and defeating evil nations, tribes, and monster hordes. The order is devoted to achieving its purpose through organized wars and battles. Sometimes the order conducts military campaigns on its own. Much more frequently, the paladins of this order are found assisting the secular military forces of civilized nations.

- **Golden Mace:** A questing order dedicated to the eradication of undead. These paladins tend to grow hard and bitter due to the countless horrors they witness and their never-ending mission.

- **Helping Hand:** A protective order dedicated to assisting and tending to the sick and the injured everywhere. The members of this order can be found in the midst of a war zone, in a city's poor neighborhood, and traveling across the open countryside. Wherever they go, they defend the weak and treat the sick.

- **Iron Gate:** A protective order dedicated to protecting temples and to patrolling highways in chaotic or dangerous regions. These paladins travel with caravans and other companies of travelers to provide protection. They build and operate watchtowers and fortified inns for the protection of travelers.

- **White Cloth:** A protective order dedicated to guarding VIPs and priests. Immune to bribery and fear, the paladins of this order can often be found guarding the high priests of Good churches. They are also much sought-after by kings, nobles, the rich, and the self-important. The order judges each request carefully but grants it infrequently. Once granted, however, the recipient is guarded for life or until he dismisses the order. Each time a guarding paladin falls, another is sent as replacement to continue the guard.

Rogues' Gallery

"Stop, thief!" The jeweler's shrill voice rang out amid the pedestrians at the crowded town square. As the city watchmen spun around, a cloaked figure darted into a narrow alleyway. "Fall in, men!" called the captain of the guard, and the soldiers took off running. The patrolmen pursued the rogue through the alley and out into a narrow street beyond. The frantic thief was now running full-tilt and turned sharply onto another street. Despite his initial head start, it was quite apparent the watchmen would soon be upon him. Again the figure darted down an alleyway, and, hot on his heels, the soldiers turned the corner, only to find…nothing. A plain black cloak lay on the flagstones of an empty courtyard. Baffled, the men made a quick search of the courtyard, took the cloak, and shuffled back to their post.

Purpose

The Rogues' Gallery exists to control crime within the boundaries of its influence. Not all crime is run by the Gallery, but woe betide anyone who gets a mind to go it alone, except for some one-time or minor crimes. While this may seem something that player characters should not be involved in, it's worth remembering that crime is whatever the authorities of the day say it is and that an oppressed people will often rise up against the tyranny of a corrupt regime. Robin Hood is probably the best known example of this, but he is by no means the only one.

Membership

Profession/Location: All thieves who live in the guild's area are required to be members of the Gallery or cease their thieving. Thieves who live elsewhere and are passing through or staying for a short time have a grace period before they are "invited" to join. Bards who have a leaning toward nefarious activities may also be invited to join the Rogues' Gallery.

Joining the Guild

Edict: The Rogues' Gallery invites all thieves and other criminals to become members. It is not an invitation that can be safely declined. If the membership limit has been reached, the prospective rogue is warned off any roguish activity until such time as a vacancy in the ranks occurs. This is normally not more than two weeks due to the high number of low-level thieves who get caught.

Invitation: Unlike thieves, bards who practice the thiefly arts are not compelled to join, but they will be warned off any activity the Gallery might see as competing with its interests if they choose not to join.

Size and Scope

Guild activities include protection, pickpocketing, burglary, and the occasional assassination, as well as highwayman roles on the outskirts of town. Begging, smuggling, gambling, loan sharking, and prostitution are also under the control of the Rogues' Gallery. The Gallery's influence rarely extends far away from a given town. Some of the Gallery's activities are undertaken at the behest of the authorities, who trade Gallery services in exchange for turning a blind eye to a crime like petty larceny or a brothel or other den of iniquity.

The Rogues' Gallery is limited in size by its very nature. As rogues are seen by law-abiding folk as criminals to be eradicated, it's not good business to grow too large, lest the organization be noticed. It is also a built-in self-protection mechanism to keep numbers low. If a member is caught by the authorities he can betray (willingly or by coercion) only the other members he knows, those members can betray only the members they know, and so on. The larger the organization, the greater the chance of a member being caught and the more other members he is likely to know. For these reasons, membership is typically limited to about 2% of the population of a given area. A typical town of 5,000 people would have a rogues' gallery of about 100 members.

Guild Structure & Advancement

The Rogues' Gallery is a tiered organization, and information about members in higher circles is highly protected. Revealing the name of any higher-ranking member of the Gallery to a nonmember is punishable by death.

There are seven circles in the Gallery, each with progressively fewer members. The seven circles are listed in the advancement table below. Advancement within the

Gallery requires great merit, and, within the higher circles, the death of an incumbent member. Given the nature of a Rogues' Gallery, death or incarceration are regular events that thin out membership, so the wait is seldom a long one. Table 1.8 shows how many positions typically exist at each level. Advancement also requires spending experience points. Bard members cannot advance past the third circle of the Gallery unless they also take at least one level in a Rogue class.

Advancement from circles one to two is automatic, as long as all Gallery membership conditions have been satisfied, after the rogue in question is deemed competent (reaching 4th level or above). Advancement to higher circles generally involves undertaking a special task for one of the high-ranking members of the Gallery. Such a task is invariably some sort of illegal activity, although the type varies greatly. A task could be to steal a particular object, to bribe a certain official, to assassinate an individual, or simply to burgle a certain amount of wealth in a given period of time. The higher one's circle, the more difficult and important one's tasks are. Sometimes a rogue is given several small tasks rather than one major task to complete. It is not uncommon for several rogues all to be given the same task, such as to bring a particular unique item to the guildmaster, pitting all who want to advance against one another in a race to succeed.

The first two circles of rogues are the foot soldiers of the organization, those who spend their time out on the streets committing most of the crimes approved by the organization. Rogues in the 2nd circle (sneaks) gain the responsibility to form small teams of lesser rogues to carry out more complex criminal activities. Once he has reached the 3rd circle (sharp), a rogue is expected to contribute significantly to the Gallery's income by overseeing the activities of a number of sneaks and their teams, as well as the occasional larger job in which he takes an active role.

Becoming a sharp requires at least three years of devoted service, putting at least an average of one week per month into Gallery business. As with previous circles, it also requires the performance of at least one special task. As sharps are only occasionally found on a job, they are not caught as often as lower-circle members, so turnover is not as frequent. Once a sharp, rogues are expected to devote all their nonadventure time to the Gallery. About 12% of the Gallery is composed of sharps.

The 5th grade (thief) is a highly exclusive position; there are generally no more than half a dozen members at this level, even in the largest of rogues' galleries. Galleries in small cities and towns may have only two or three rogues in this position. Thieves are engaged almost full-time in Gallery business and have no time to go adventuring. They almost always have a (semi) legitimate business that they use to launder money and to explain their wealth and status to the authorities, often a pawnshop which the Gallery uses to fence items that aren't too hot to handle. It is not unheard of for a 5th-grade rogue to be a member of the local government, as the majority of citizens are unaware of the rogue's true nature. Thieves are rarely directly involved in criminal activity, leaving the risk of capture to the lower members. An exception to this would be breaking into the city treasury or a similarly lucrative undertaking. Tier five members have the final call on whether jobs such as robbing the treasury are allowed to proceed, based on such factors such as how well planned the job is, what the likely reward will be, and the risk of failure and/or retaliation from the victim. Members of the 4th circle are also responsible for setting up safehouses and creating boltholes throughout the guild's area of influence. Around 6% of the Gallery is composed of thieves.

Rogues of the 5th grade and above are almost never player characters. To hold a position in the organization at this level requires that a character devote all his time to Gallery business, even if on the surface it appears he is doing something else. Advancement to the 4th circle is only by invitation from the current 4th-circle and higher members, and comes only when a rogue has been a part of the Gallery for at least seven years and a position becomes available. This can be a way for the GM to reward long-term roleplaying, by allowing a favorite character to retire from active adventuring but still remain a part of the campaign.

Members of the 6th grade (master thieves) are quite similar to those in the 5th, with the exception that they have direct contact with the Guildmaster. A guildmaster rarely

Table 1.8 – Rogues' Gallery Grade Advancement

Grade	Circle	Prerequisites	XP Cost	Benefits
Novice (1)	1 (Messenger)	Entry to guild	100	Equipment, Fence, Information
Cutpurse (2)	1	4 levels in a Rogue class	500	Safety, skill bonus
Sneak (3)	2 (Associate)	One or more special tasks 6 levels in a Rogue class	1,000	Skill bonus
Sharp (4)	3 (Businessman)	Vacancy, 8 levels in a Rogue class, 3 years guild service, at least one special task	1,500	Skill bonus, Compel Help (+2)
Thief (5)	4 (Faceless one)	Vacancy, 10 levels in a Rogue class, 7 years guild service, an invitation from at least half of all grade 5 and 6 rogues and the Guildmaster	2,000	Skill bonus, Compel Help (+3)
Master Thief (6)	4	Vacancy, 12 levels in a Rogue class, completion of a special task.	2,500	Skill bonuses, Compel Help (+4)
Guildmaster (7)	5 (Guildmaster)	Vacancy, 2 years in grade 6, and either selection by one's peers or by being the most successful participant in one or more selection tests	3,000	Command Gallery

has direct contact with the members of his guild. Many even keep their identities and whereabouts secret and communicate with the Gallery members only through their master thieves. Master thieves also are able to act as advisors to the Guildmaster and have a great deal of influence over the actions of the guild. 3% of the Gallery are masters.

The 7th circle of the Rogues' Gallery always has only one member, the Guildmaster, who must first be a master thief. This person is not necessarily the highest-level rogue in the vicinity, but is always someone who is able to back up his roguish talents with social and political skills. It is rare for a guildmaster to have a public profile; these people are shadowy figures known only to their immediate subordinates and perhaps a few select others within the Gallery.

To advance to Guildmaster, a rogue must have been a 6th-grade member for at least two years and the position must be available. It is rare for a guildmaster to retire; most hold the position until their deaths. Surprisingly, this is not always a violent death but can often be from old age. Depending on the thoughts of the senior Gallery members at the time, the new guildmaster may be chosen in one of several different ways. The position may be filled either by consensus among the 5th- and 6th-grade members or by having those members who wish to become Guildmaster undergo one or more tests, resulting in one finishing ahead of the competition. Such tests may involve the risk of death but are more often about stealth and cunning than about acrobatics or combat skills.

Benefits

Command Gallery: The Guildmaster has absolute say over the actions of the guild. He can plot and staff operations as he sees fit. If a member of the guild is asked to participate in a mission by the Guildmaster, he is expected to do so, at the risk of being declared a renegade.

Compel Help: Everyone has a skeleton in the closet, and the Gallery knows about most of them. A rogue in trouble with the law may be able to persuade an official that pressing charges would be a bad idea because of information that might come out at the trial. In game terms, this gives a sharp (Grade 3) a +2 circumstance bonus to the relevant skill roll (usually Diplomacy) to negotiate a release. Grade 4 members receive a +3 bonus, and so on. This bonus is in addition to any other bonuses for high Charisma, a bribe, or other factors.

Equipment: Specialized equipment such as thieves' tools is not something you can pick up at the general store. In areas where the Rogues' Gallery has tight control, such items can be obtained only through the Gallery unless they are found as loot in an adventure. Apart from lock picks and similar tools, cat suits and black silk ropes may also be available only through the Gallery and only to members. Where these items can be obtained in the local marketplace, Gallery members can get them from the Gallery at 10% less than market price.

Fence: Gallery members have guaranteed access to several trusted fences who will dispose of the proceeds of a robbery with no questions asked. The standard commission on sales of dubious assets is 20%, and the assets will normally be disposed of for 50% of book value. So the rogue gets 40% of book value but doesn't risk capture. Items which are unique or otherwise easily identifiable will not be accepted by the local fences and must be sent out of town to associate fences elsewhere (see "Affiliations" for more details).

Information: Bards in particular make a living out of trading information. The Rogues' Gallery is an information broker and has background or even detailed information on the whereabouts of valuable items, hordes of treasure, and the security measures in place around them. This information is traded for new information on important people's movements, new artwork brought into town, caravan movements and manifests, and any other information the Gallery sees as useful. In game terms, this gives members a +2 insight bonus to all Gather Information rolls made within the guild's sphere of influence.

Safety: There are always boltholes and even safehouses for members to use when the heat is on. They may take the form of secret rooms in the basement of a tavern or business, or even a private residence, and they provide a sanctuary for rogues who are being actively pursued or who just need a place to hide. In game terms, the safehouse provides a circumstance bonus to a rogue's Hide checks. It also forces those looking for the rogue to use Search rolls, not Spot rolls, to find him. Those not searching have no chance to find the rogue. This bonus varies on the rogue's grade in the guild and distance from his pursuers. The bonuses from grade and distance stack with one another.

Of course, in order to use a safehouse, a rogue has to know of its existence. Generally, the longer a rogue has been in the guild, the more safehouses he is aware of. If a rogue is in trouble, he is typically allowed a percentage change equal to ten times his grade to know the location of a safehouse within a eighth of a mile of his position. Characters who have successfully used a particular safehouse before may return to it without having to make a percentile roll.

Skill Bonuses: As a sneak, the rogue gains a +2 insight bonus to either Open Lock or Pick Pocket rolls. At cutpurse grade, the rogue gains a +2 insight bonus to either Move Silently, Perform, or whichever of the sneak grade skills was not taken. Upon reaching the grade of sharp, the character gains a +2 insight bonus to either Disguise, Gather Information, or any of the skills not chosen in the lower two bonuses. On reaching the grade of thief, the rogue may take a +2 insight bonus in any one of the above skills not already chosen. On reaching master thief status, the rogue can either take a +3 insight bonus in any one class skill, including one already chosen, or a +1 insight bonus to all Rogue class skills except for the four in which he took an earlier +2 bonus.

Table 1.9 – Chance of Using a Safehouse to Evade Pursuers

Pursuer is within	Bonus to Hide Roll*
20 feet	Nil**
40 feet	+1
60 feet	+2
100 feet	+4
200 feet	+5

More than 200 feet, or no active pursuit: +10
*Pursuers must use the Search skill to find the hidden rogue.
**Rogues who are being this closely pursued should not risk blowing the location of the safehouse by using it.

Table 1.10 – Safehouse Evasion by Grade

Gallery Grade	Bonus*	Safehouse**
Novice	Nil	Nil
Sneak	+1	20%
Cutpurse	+2	30%
Sharp	+3	40%
Thief	+4	50%
Master Thief	+5	60%
Guildmaster	+6	70%

*This bonus applies to the member's Hide roll. Pursuers must use the Search skill to find the hidden rogue.
**This is the chance that the member actually knows of a safehouse.

Disadvantages

Enemy: Members of the Gallery have the City Watch as a natural enemy. Known Gallery members will have a 5% chance each day they are on the streets of the city of being arrested on suspicion and held for 24 hours.

Time: Each member in the first circle is required to devote at least four weeks out of the year to Gallery tasks. At second circle this increases to eight weeks minimum, and as much as 12 weeks if the rogue wishes to advance to third circle. At third circle, rogues are expected to devote all their time when not adventuring to Gallery business, and this must be at least 20 weeks each year.

Exclusivity: Members of the Rogues' Gallery may not also be members of any other class-based guild. They may be members of a generic adventurer's guild and/or craft- or skill-based organizations.

Affiliations

Rogues' galleries seldom have associations with other organizations, unless it is with another rogues' gallery in a distant locale which can be used to fence stolen goods too "hot" to fence locally.

There is sometimes a loose association with local authorities, especially if those authorities are corrupt. It is much more palatable to have some rogues do your dirty work than to use the town guard. It is also a deniable association if the rogues are caught. In exchange for this kind of association, the Gallery always expects a certain level of petty crime to be tolerated.

Galleries typically have an affiliation with a number of legitimate pawnbrokers in other towns who fence items that are too hot to be disposed of locally. Naturally, the pawnbrokers expect a sizeable cut (usually 35% instead of the normal 20%) for providing this service.

Leaving the Gallery

With Permission: Occasionally, a rogue may wish to leave the Gallery to pursue other interests or another career. If the rogue has proven trustworthy in the eyes of the Gallery, permission to leave may be granted by the Guildmaster, with the condition that the rogue never discuss the Gallery with anyone—ever. Breach of this condition changes the status of the rogue to leaving without permission. Members at thief or master thief grade will never be permitted to leave the Gallery.

Without Permission: Any rogue who attempts to leave the Gallery without the permission of the Guildmaster will have a price on his head. The amount is 1,000 gp times the circle he was in when they left.

Expulsion: Nobody is expelled from the Rogues' Gallery. Any offense against the organization that would result in expulsion in a more gentle way of life results in death here.

Guildmaster

Burtip Tipple: Male half-elf Rogue 10/Bard 2: CR 12; Medium-size humanoid (half-elf); HD 12d6+24; hp 74; Init +3, Spd 30 ft.; AC 20 (touch 15, flat-footed 17); Atk +13/+8 melee (1d4+3/19-20/x2, dagger + 3) or +11/+6 ranged (1d8 + 2 x3 longbow +2); SA sneak attack; SQ rogue abilities, bard abilities, half-elf abilities; Al CN; SV Fort +13, Ref +5, Will +6; Str 10, Dex 16, Con 15, Int 14, Wis 10, Cha 14.

Skills and Feats: Appraise +9, Balance +8, Climb +5, Decipher Script +8, Diplomacy +12, Disguise + 8, Forgery +7, Gather Information +9, Hide +8, Innuendo +5, Intimidate +6, Knowledge (religion) +3, Listen +10, Move Silently +10, Open Lock +8, Perform (prestidigitation) +9, Pick Pocket +8, Read Lips +9, Scry +5, Search +8, Sense Motive +6, Speak Language (Draconic), Speak Language (Elvish), Speak Language (Infernal), Speak Language (Undercommon), Spot +6, Tumble +10, Use Magic Device +5, Use Rope +8; Dodge, Improved Critical (dagger), Skill Focus (gather information), Track, Weapon Finesse (dagger).

Special Qualities: Half-elf abilities—Immunity to *sleep* spells and similar magical effects; +2 saving throw bonus against Enchantment spells or effects; Low-light Vision; +1 bonus to Listen, Search, and Spot checks; Elven Blood.

Spells: (3/1): 0—*dancing lights, detect magic, flare, light, prestidigitation*; 1st—*charm person, cure light wounds*.

Possessions: Dagger +3, longbow +2, leather armor +3, ring of protection +2.

Burtip is a selfish, manipulative individual who has no visible redeeming features. He is a charmer, though, and that's how he often gets what he wants—flattery and bribery can work wonders, and Burtip is a master at both. He's also quite capable of blackmail if that's a better avenue to get his way.

Burtip rose to the position of Guildmaster by arranging for the assassination of his predecessor. He enjoys the power and intrigue of the Gallery and makes use of all members in the best ways to increase his personal profits. He cares nothing for the individual members and cares about the Gallery only because it is the source of his power and wealth.

He holds onto power by cultivating those from whom he can gain something, then arranging for their demise if they rise to the point of being potential threats to him. One or two rogues have worked this out and are careful to remain useful to the master without becoming threats. Good luck seems to follow Mr. Tipple and those close to him.

Physically, Burtip looks a little like a hawk, with the beak-shaped nose and sharp eyes of a bird of prey. He is 5'7" tall, 168 pounds, with brown eyes and black hair.

Your Campaign

Unlike most other guilds in this book, the inclusion of a Rogues' Gallery raises some ethical questions. Is it OK to encourage your players to engage in criminal activity, even if it is only make-believe? That's a decision each GM must make for his campaign, and if the answer is "no", then the Rogues' Gallery becomes an NPC organization to be feared, respected, or hunted down at every opportunity.

If the answer is "yes", the Gallery might be modeled along the lines of Robin Hood's Merry Men, robbing the rich to give to the poor and generally being a pain in the side of a corrupt government. The Gallery may still be an organization to be feared, respected, or hunted down at every opportunity, but this time the PCs are the foxes instead of the hounds.

Unless your campaign has a lot of rogues in it, the Rogues' Gallery should not be a major focus in the game. It serves a better purpose if it remains a shadowy organization, always watching the goings-on in the local area but seldom if ever being seen in return.

Adventure Hooks

- A rogue PC is approached by the local thieves' guild and requested to join up or stop his activities. This works best if it is backed up with stern threats.

- As a special task, a large number of thieves is told to steal an item from the party. Whichever

rogue manages to acquire the object gains a promotion to the next circle.

- A party member is framed for a robbery. While in custody (or in hiding) he is approached by a representative of the Gallery, who can clear matters up in return for the character's assistance in a certain matter.

- A number of churches, as well as many nobles, keep a golden chalice as a symbol of their wealth and influence. Some are simple designs, and others are covered with gold filigree and encrusted with gemstones. However they appear, a golden chalice has value both as a chalice and when reduced to its component parts. The PCs may take the side of the thieves, stealing a gem-encrusted chalice from the vault of a corrupt Lord Mayor. Or they may take the part of sellswords whose task it is to guard the ancient chalice of a visiting prince while his own guards are watching his royal personage.

Variations

Rural: In a rural area with small villages and farmsteads, the major activity is robbing merchant caravans and the like. The local gallery's territory may extend up to a day's ride in every direction. It is rare for a rural gallery to have more than 50 members. A rural bolthole might be located in a hayloft, under the floorboards of a barn, or perhaps in a hidden cave in the forest.

Large City: An urban rogues' gallery may have as few as 20 members (*e.g.*, a specialist assassin's cadre) or as many as 200 (*e.g.*, a street gang that "owns" a section of the city and runs petty street crime and burglaries). A large city may be informally divided into sectors, with each sector having its own rogues' gallery and the sector boundaries providing scope for many adventures between the galleries. A city may also be divided along an activity basis. One gallery may handle smuggling and be based around the docks, another handle burglaries, and yet another pickpocketing. Individuals who commit cross-over crimes may create conflicts between the guilds, giving rise to opportunities for many adventures.

Sacred Light Council

It's a huge, complex, dangerous world, and those clerics who share a common viewpoint or purpose find it beneficial to gather together to discuss problems, provide mutual assistance, or cooperate in achieving a goal. Lawful-aligned clerics may cooperate in bringing peace and order to a troubled city or land. Good-aligned clerics may cooperate in fighting a pandemic or a demon. Evil-aligned clerics may cooperate in order to prevent the destruction of their congregations in a hostile realm. An association of identically aligned clerics is called an **ecclesiastical council**, an organization of clergy for sharing resources, information, and assistance for the furtherance of a common holy goal. The Sacred Light Council is an ecclesiastical council of Chaotic Good clerics.

The Sacred Light Council was founded to advocate and protect the sacred spiritual gift of free will and to coordinate opposition to tyranny and slavery in all their vile forms. Though its members serve different gods, and preach the different theologies and ethics of these gods, all members find common cause in their opposition to oppression.

Purpose

The Sacred Light Council exists to oppose tyranny, slavery, and anything that denies an individual's free will. The members of The Sacred Light Council do not deny the role of law and order in a just and peaceful society, but they do not feel overly constrained by issues of temporal law if they feel it is necessary to break that law in pursuing their holy purpose. Sometimes the more energetic members of the Sacred Light Council earn the annoyance, and even the enmity, of law-abiding citizens and organizations.

Sharing: The Sacred Light Council shares the intelligence and the resources of its members in their fight against slavery, oppression, and tyranny. In addition to money and equipment, another resource shared by council members is an assembly of select volunteer lay members from member clerics' congregations (those proselytizing members who have congregations) who have sworn an oath to the Sacred Light Council and devoted themselves to furthering the goals of the council. Sometimes these lay members are not from congregations but have chosen to join the council because they believe in the council's work or for other personal reasons. e.g., slaves freed by the council's work. Further, where this does not conflict with the member's church's rules, the premises and assets of the member's temples are also available to council members as a resource.

Protection: The members of the Sacred Light Council cooperate in protecting each other, their congregations, and their assets against those who oppose the council's activities and the preaching of the council members. These enemies are usually slavers and other agents of tyrannical organizations or governments.

Goal: The members of the Sacred Light Council all share the goal of waging moral war against tyranny, slavery, and those who deny the right of living beings to choose their own destinies. The methods used by the council range from street preaching, sometimes in dangerous locations, to sponsoring direct action, e.g., sending in agents to expose or smash a slavery ring, or to wage guerrilla and propaganda warfare against a tyrannical government. The undertaking of all activities is voluntary, and the amount of danger a member must risk is always that member's choice.

Membership

Belief/Code: All members believe that any sort of tyranny or slavery is fundamentally, morally wrong and spiritually obscene. The members of the council not only believe in the basic right of enlightened liberty but also have usually experienced and suffered the destructive and depraved oppressions of slavery or tyranny.

Location: The Sacred Light Council should be placed so that its influence can extend over a number of sizable cities, possibly even in several different kingdoms. Council activities range across the continent but are mostly concentrated close to these cities and nearby slaver routes.

Profession: All full members of the council are clerics. The council also has an associated membership of laymen who need not be clerics.

Joining the Guild

Application: Any cleric may apply to join the Sacred Light Council. Once the cleric submits his application he must wait for a considerable length of time, anywhere from three to twelve months, while the application is considered. During this time, the applicant will be observed. If he does not show sufficient energy in opposing oppression in all its forms, whether petty or dramatic, he will be denied his application. If his activities are acceptable, the applicant will be invited to an interview with a committee of three members. If the committee finds the applicant acceptable, he need only swear an oath, by whatever he holds sacred, to be accepted as a member.

Invitation: The most frequent way a cleric enters the Sacred Light Council is by being approached by a council member, sounded out, and, once found suitable, asked to join. This is a gradual process, as the council usually observes a potential member for some time to ensure his morals and goals are compatible with the council's. If this proves to be true, a decision is made to approach and invite the potential member to join the council. Any questions from the potential member are answered in full so that his choice to join is open, freely given, and untainted.

Alignment: All members of the Sacred Light Council must be Chaotic Good in alignment.

Size and Scope

The chambers of the Sacred Light Council are best located in a large city, central to a populated area. These chambers serve as the headquarters and meeting rooms of the council and are situated on neutral premises independent of any church. The council believes it should oppose slavery and tyranny wherever it is encountered, but this is far beyond its strength and influence. The chambers maintain contact with and coordinate the activities of a membership that numbers in the hundreds and is mostly concentrated in nearby territories but is also spread thinly over the continent.

Guild Structure & Advancement

All policies of the Sacred Light Council are openly discussed among the membership and ratified by majority vote. Specific activities and missions are discussed and voted on by the available membership at the time. For urgent matters, the Council Eparch has the authority to make quick decisions but must explain his choices to the membership at a later date.

Graded (Elective): The Sacred Light Council has a fairly flat structure with only three grades. These grades have clergylike titles but bear no relationship to a member's rank within his own church; they relate only to the organization of the council itself.

Council Deacons: All new members join the council with the grade of Deacon, which is the grade held by the majority of the membership. They are the activists and implementers of council business. They are the ones to sermonize on the streets of towns and cities, to organize citizens' committees in opposition to slavery or in favor of human rights, and to travel to foreign lands on council missions. Deacons are the council members who implement physical action when it is called for.

Council Proctors: The Proctors are the council's organizing members. They research, plan, and coordinate the activities of Deacons and associated laymen. They gather intelligence, interview contacts, and interrogate captives. They negotiate with guildmasters, merchants, bureaucrats, ministers, diplomats, and other VIPs. Proctors are elected to the grade from among the Deacons, usually after serving many years. The election is through a majority vote of the membership. To be eligible for the position, a Proctor candidate must have bought at least one rank each in Diplomacy and Sense Motive, and have the Leadership feat.

Council Eparch: The head of the Sacred Light Council is the Eparch. The Eparch does not rule the council but rather leads. The Eparch has to be both diplomatic and decisive, with a clear vision of the council's mission. The Eparch is elected from among the Council Proctors by a majority vote of the council membership. To be eligible for the position, an Eparch candidate must have at least four ranks in Diplomacy and ability scores of 17 or better in both Charisma and Wisdom.

Benefits

The following are the benefits enjoyed by a member of the Sacred Light Council.

Fraternity: The council has created a network of clerics, churches, followers, homes, businesses, contacts, and sympathizers to help escaped slaves and refugees of oppressive regimes. This organization also helps council members in their actions opposing slavers and tyranny and in assisting council members in need of aid.

Good Reputation: Good-aligned or freedom-loving people, and anyone who opposes slavery or tyranny, hold the council in good regard. These people will usually offer assistance and shelter to council members if they can. Other people who do not particularly agree with a member's god or with some of the council's methods still respect the council's goals and will consider council members' requests in good favor.

Henchmen: The network of council laymen is a resource that any member may call upon at any time, as long as the member is within territory covered by the council's network. When a member requests assistance, a number of council laymen, equal to the member's Charisma modifier (to a minimum of one), will respond. If the member is a Proctor, double this number. If the Eparch makes a request for assistance, all available council laymen will respond.

Sense Motive Bonus: Through their dedication, training, and experience, all council members receive an insight bonus of +2 on all Sense Motive checks against all Lawful and Evil people or creatures.

Third Domain: While clerics remain members of the Sacred Light Council they receive access to a third domain. This domain must be either the Good or Chaos alignment domain. If the cleric already has these two domains, a third domain may be chosen, with the GM's approval, from the cleric's deity's other domains. If the cleric is not devoted to a particular deity, the third domain must be chosen from Luck, Protection, or War.

Disadvantages

Bad Reputation: Significant segments of society, the percentage varying from realm to realm, view the Sacred Light Council with feelings ranging from distaste through to hatred. Lawful people tend not to trust them particularly but do not revile them. Lawful Good folk may even admire the council's purpose but still treat council members cautiously. Tyrants, slavers, evil clerics, and those who benefit or profit from them despise the council.

Enemies: The Iron Hand slavery ring is an enemy of the Sacred Light Council. The slavery ring was nearly destroyed by the council 32 years ago and the fortunes of its operators and patrons wiped out. The ring has slowly rebuilt itself over the years and has a policy of murdering or enslaving any member of the council that falls under its power.

Experience Cost: The cost to join the Sacred Light Council and become a Council Deacon is 500 XP. It costs 1,000 XP to stand for election to the grade of Council Proctor (this

Table 1.11 – Sacred Light Council Advancement

Grade	Prerequisites	XP Cost	Fees	Benefits Gained
Deacon (1)	Approval as suitable member	500	100 gp/month	3rd Domain, Sense Motive bonus, Fraternity, Good Reputation, Henchmen
Proctor (2)	Diplomacy, Sense Motive, Leadership	1,000	100 gp/month	More henchmen
Eparch (3)	Diplomacy 4 ranks, 17+ in both Charisma and Wisdom	1,500	100 gp/month	More henchmen

XP payment is a one-time cost; the cleric may continuously stand for election until the Proctor grade is won without paying any more XP). To stand for election to Eparch costs 1,500 XP.

Fees: The operation and activities of the Sacred Light Council are expensive. To fund these activities, the Council receives donations from sympathetic people and organizations, but all members are also expected to contribute 100 gp per month.

Time: Council Deacons must arrange their personal and religious duties to free the time to spend three months of every year pursuing council business. Council Proctors must spend six months of every year on council business. The sitting Eparch has usually retired from formal activities in his church, as he is required to spend all his time administering the council.

Affiliations

The Sacred Light Council has many links to Good-aligned churches and other humanitarian organizations that view the council's work favorably. However, many clerics, even Good-aligned ones, frown upon the council members' dangerous dalliance with split loyalties, *i.e.*, between faith and the council.

Craft guilds and other societal bodies that depend upon long-term servitude (*e.g.*, apprenticeship) often find the council's preaching as annoying and some (*e.g.*, a few police forces) even view the members as potentially dangerous fanatics.

Occasionally, a council member may also be a member of an adventurer's guild, a fighter's school, a thieves' guild, or a social club. More rarely, a council member may also be a member of a sorcerer's fraternity, bardic college, barbarian horde, or town guild. A council member may never also be a member of a mercenary company, wizard's academy, druidic circle, paladin order, warrior monk's school, trading guild, craft guild, or family guild.

Leaving

With Permission: A member may leave the Sacred Light Council at any time, usually because of old age and, all too often, death. On retirement, the cleric loses access to all his guild benefits. He will, however, usually keep his contacts within the council's membership and network and his good reputation with council sympathizers. He may even be called upon occasionally as a layman to help the council with its activities.

Expulsion: Members are rarely expelled from the council. Typically this is only done if a member's alignment changes permanently, or if it is determined that the member is attempting to sabotage the council's efforts from within. Upon expulsion, all benefits are lost, and the member will never be allowed to rejoin the council.

Eparch

Bishop Alander Moy: Male half-elf Cleric 16: CR 16; Medium-size humanoid (half-elf); HD 16d8+48; hp 114; Init +0, Spd 30 ft.; AC 22 (touch 14, flat-footed 22); Atk +16/ +11/+6 melee (1d6+3/x2, mace, light) or +12/+7/+2 ranged (1d4/x2, sling); SA none; SQ half-elf abilities; Al CG; SV Fort +15, Ref +5, Will +18; Str 9, Dex 10, Con 16, Int 15, Wis 22, Cha 17.

Skills and Feats: Concentration +10, Diplomacy +19, Heal +10, Knowledge (arcana) +8, Knowledge (religion) +10, Profession (fisherman) +8, Scry +17, Sense Motive +12, Speak Language (Celestial), Speak Language (Gnome), Spellcraft +12; Endurance, Extra Turning, Great Fortitude, Iron Will, Leadership, Spell Penetration.

Special Qualities: Half-elf abilities—Immunity to *sleep* spells and similar magical effects; +2 saving throw bonus against Enchantment spells or effects; Low-light Vision; +1 bonus to Listen, Search, and Spot checks; Elven Blood.

Cleric Spells (12/11+1/11+1/11+1/10+1/10+1/9+1/9+1/ 8+1): 0—*detect magic* x4, *guidance* x2, *light*, *read magic* x2, *resistance* x3; 1st—*bane* x2, *bless* x2, *command* x2, *divine favor* x2, *doom*, *magic weapon* x2; 2nd—*aid*, *augury*, *calm emotions*, *endurance*, *enthrall*, *gentle repose*, *hold person*, *lesser restoration*, *silence*, *speak with animals*, *zone of truth*; 3rd—*bestow curse*, *daylight*, *deeper darkness*, *dispel magic* x2, *invisibility purge*, *prayer* x2, *remove curse*, *remove disease*, *searing light*, *water walk*; 4th—*control water*, *discern lies*, *dismissal*, *divine power*, *imbue with spell ability*, *restoration*, *sending*, *spell immunity*, *status*, *tongues*; 5th—*atonement*, *break enchantment*, *commune*, *dispel law*, *flame strike*, *greater command*, *hallow*, *healing circle*, *scrying*, *true seeing*; 6th—*animate objects*, *banishment*, *blade barrier*, *forbiddance*, *geas/quest*, *greater dispelling*, *harm*, *heal*, *word of recall*; 7th—*control weather*, *destruction*, *greater scrying*, *holy word*, *refuge*, *regenerate*, *repulsion*, *resurrection*, *spell immunity*, *word of chaos*; 8th—*antimagic field*, *cloak of chaos*, *discern location*, *earthquake*, *fire storm*, *holy aura*, *mass heal*, *symbol*; Cleric Domains—Chaos, Good, Strength.

Possessions: bracers of armor +8, crystal ball with see invisibility, +4 dispelling light mace, ring of protection +4.

Bishop Alander Moy, a 16th-level cleric, grew up in a fishing clan. As a young man he gained fame for the large hauls of fish he brought back from the sea and for the risks he would take in storms that no other sane fisherman would chance. Alander left his fishing boat to become a cleric after the storm god called him to serve.

When an empire conquered the small coastal kingdoms where Alander lived, including Alander's home village, he joined with other Chaotic Good clerics in the Sacred Light Council to coordinate their resistance to the empire. Eventually the overstretched empire was forced to withdraw, but Alander remained a member of the council. He even remained on the council after he had achieved the rank of bishop in his church, and, some years later, also accepted the duties of Council Eparch.

Eparch Moy is a small elderly man with graying blond hair and gray eyes. He moves and speaks quickly but efficiently with no wasted energy. He has an immense capacity for work and is a smart, devious, charismatic man; some say he could charm the crown off a king. He commands a vast network of council informants and collaborators throughout the local kingdoms, the empire, and beyond. Little happens that Eparch Moy does not eventually know about.

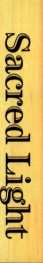

Sacred Light

Your Campaign

The Sacred Light Council is a useful tool to give your party (or a cleric PC) a purpose. The party can be a full advocate of the council's goal or just be caught in the middle of an ongoing war between the council and slavers or between the council and a tyrant. This war need not be fought with weapons but may be a battle of propaganda and influence.

Adventure Hooks

- A cleric is preaching on the street against the evils of slavery. The party sees him assassinated by a shadowy figure. The party may pursue this figure or may be approached by another cleric who hires the party to find and punish the shadowy figure. The shadowy figure is tracked back to a slavery ring.

- The party is hired to help a cleric rebuild an underground escape route for refugees from a tyrannical, evil kingdom.

- In the dungeon of a ruthless noble, the party encounters an imprisoned council member who promises to reveal the location of the noble's treasure if the party helps all the prisoners escape.

- A party cleric may join the Sacred Light Council and persuade the rest of the party to help the cleric with the council's activities.

Other Ecclesiastical Councils

- The **Golden Orb Council** is an ecclesiastical council of Lawful Good clerics dedicated to bringing evil criminals before justice.

- The **Peace Union** is an ecclesiastical council of Lawful Neutral clerics dedicated to restoring law and order in a strife-torn empire.

- The **Order of the Dragon** is an ecclesiastical council of Lawful Evil clerics dedicated to the conquest of neighboring island nations.

- The **White Society** is an ecclesiastical council of Neutral Good clerics dedicated to helping the sick and the poor.

- The **Silver Shield** is an ecclesiastical council of Neutral clerics dedicated to defending their territories from outside invaders.

- The **Black Hand Council** is an ecclesiastical council of Neutral Evil clerics dedicated to advancing the profits and pleasures of its member clerics.

- The **Assembly** is an ecclesiastical council of Chaotic Neutral clerics dedicated to getting together and having a good time.

- The **Union of Night** is an ecclesiastical council of Chaotic Evil clerics dedicated to resurrecting and controlling an ancient evil power.

Seekers

The Seekers were founded more than a hundred years ago to help those people, adults and children, whose talent in wizard, sorcerer, or bard magic has gone undetected and unfulfilled.

Sometimes nascent magicians fail to recognize and control the source of their power or have led lives of such ignorance that they can find no explanation or understanding for their manifesting abilities. Strange feelings awaken in them and bizarre events dog their footsteps. They are often cast out by their fearful families or villages, or sometimes are even locked away in building basements or hidden caves. Persecuted or not, having no understanding of their abilities, many of these people attempt to repress and deny their talent and its manifestations. This is rarely successful, and these unfortunate people drift closer and closer to the dark pits of fear, despair, and insanity. The Seekers refer to these people as the Lost.

Seekers are sworn to redeem these Lost. They prefer to use persuasion and reason to request the release of a Lost one into their care. However, if this fails or is not possible, a Seeker may resort to kidnapping if the situation with the Lost is dire enough.

Purpose

Sharing: The Seekers form a large network of rumor collectors and information gatherers. They communicate with each other through coded letters and face-to-face meetings, sharing the information and gossip they have uncovered or overheard. Of this, the most important subject is always information about the Lost.

Goal: The Seekers were founded with the goal of searching for the Lost and redeeming them. If the newfound Lost one has the talent of a sorcerer, he may sometimes be raised within the Seekers fraternity. Usually, the Seeker will take his charge to an appropriate person or institution for training, *e.g.*, a wizard's academy, bardic college, or master.

Membership

Belief/Code: All Seekers believe that every time a person fails to find his magical calling, to find his gods-given talent, it is a tragedy, an impoverishment of the world. They believe that their calling is noble.

Location: The Seekers should be loosely headquartered in a city major to the campaign. The members, those who can make it, gather in the city once a year in an inn, tavern, or some other venue chosen for the occasion, to report on their successes and failures, share information, execute fraternity business, swap stories, boast, and brag. After all fraternity business is over, the membership usually carries on with a celebration, partying into the night and often into the following morning.

Profession: The majority of Seekers are sorcerers, but bards are also permitted to join and so a small minority of members are bards. All Seekers must have at least one level in either the Sorcerer or Bard class. Seekers travel far and wide, through crowded cities, dark forests, and open countryside. They need skill with weapons, a quick wit, the ability to deal well with people, the capacity to travel light and usually quickly, and the indispensable advantage of magic without the time or burden of memorizing spells. Sometimes Seekers tour the lands with their purpose freely admitted. Often they travel with their objectives secret. They also travel under several different guises and assume many different jobs, even joining adventuring parties, while they search for the Lost.

Joining the Guild

Application: Anyone may apply to join the Seekers. Once he demonstrates that he meets the membership requirements, only a simple majority of a quorum of members, usually at an annual gathering, is all that is needed to confirm candidate membership.

Invitation: It is not unusual for a Seeker to invite a sorcerer or bard to join the fraternity. Either the Seeker has studied the person and considers him good membership material or perhaps just feels it would be a good idea. Once again, a simple majority of a quorum of members is all that is needed to accept the invitee into candidate membership.

Other Criteria

Alignment: No fraternity member may be Evil in alignment.

Deed: A candidate member must rescue his first Lost before he is confirmed in full membership.

Qualification: A candidate for Seeker membership must demonstrate command of six spells, of any levels, and have at least two ranks in Gather Information. This rule is not set in concrete, so, if the candidate seems fitting in other ways, it may sometimes be waived.

Wealth or Payment: All candidate members are required to demonstrate their commitment to the Seekers by donating something of value, usually money, to the frater-

Table 1.12 Seeker Guild Advancement

Grade	Prerequisites	XP Cost	Benefits Gained
Candidate (0)	6 spells, Gather Information 2 ranks	0	Bonus spell
Searcher (1)	Rescue 1 Lost	500	Entry to guild; increase Gather Information skill limit; Gather Information as a class skill; access to, skills, feats, and spells; Fraternity; Good Reputation; bonus spell
Quester (2)	Rescue 2 Lost	1,000	+1 Gather Information, bonus spell
Rescuer (3)	Rescue 3 Lost	1,500	Bonus spell
Liberator (4)	Rescue 4 Lost	2,000	+1 Gather Information, bonus spell
Deliverer (5)	Rescue 5 Lost	2,500	Bonus spell
Redeemer (6)	Rescue 6 Lost	3,000	+1 Gather Information, bonus spell
Seeker (7)	Rescue 7 Lost	3,500	Bonus spell

nity. For example, the donation may be some premises for the storage of fraternity records, a venue for an annual Seeker's meeting, or the funding of a post-fraternity meeting party.

Size and Scope

The Seekers usually roam the realms within a few hundred miles of the city in which they are headquartered. On a few occasions, members have traveled even further to seek the source of rumors of the Lost. In spite of these many hundreds of miles of territory covered, the Seekers rarely have more than 200 members. There is no rule limiting the Seekers' size. It's just that a group larger than 200 members tends to be too unwieldy. When the membership approaches 200, factions, arguments, and disagreements start to destabilize the organization and eventually one or more members or groups of members split away to pursue their own missions.

Guild Structure & Advancement

There is very little strict hierarchy in the Seekers' organization. The members tend to be highly individualistic and spend far too much time apart for any sort of administrative system to have any meaning. For this reason, the day-to-day organizational structure of the Seekers is effectively flat. Nevertheless, the fraternity has seven grades which reflect its members' reputations and experience.

Graded (Merit): A member advances in grade through rescuing the Lost. The more time and effort a member has spent, and the more people he has rescued, the higher his grade. A Seeker has the right to advance in grade once he has rescued a number of Lost at his current grade equal to the target grade. The longest-serving 7th-grade member has the right to assume the responsibilities of the fraternity's head, the master of the guild, titled the Moderator. The Moderator is always a famous Seeker who has rescued many, many Lost and then retired from Seeking to spend his time managing the fraternity's business. He organizes and chairs the fraternity's rambunctious annual meetings and coordinates, as much as is possible, the activities of members searching for the Lost. Further, a major responsibility of the Moderator is to protect the fraternity's members. He sends messages to warn them of dangerous locations and situations, organizes investigations into rumors of open acts of hostility toward members, and organizes rescue or justice missions for captured or murdered members. The Moderator occasionally appoints deputies from among members with the highest grades to help him with these responsibilities.

Benefits

Access to Skills, Feats, and Spells: The wide-ranging travels of Seekers and the sharing of discoveries and information among the membership gives Seekers access to, and intuitive understanding of, spells outside their normal spell lists. Whenever a Seeker advances a level in his spellcasting class he may select one spell, of a level he can cast, from any spell list, not just his class list, as one of the new spells learned at level advancement. Bards may choose a cleric, druid, paladin, ranger, or wizard spell for example.

Further, the large amount of shared information gives Seekers a benefit when they research original spells: Seekers gain one half of their grade, rounded down, as a bonus to the Spellcraft check for successfully learning a researched original spell. Lastly, sorcerer Seekers gain Gather Information as a class skill.

Bonus Spells: Every time a sorcerer or bard advances in grade he gains a bonus known spell. This bonus spell is always in the level equal to the new grade attained. A 0-grade Seeker can know one additional 0-level spell, a 1st-grade Seeker a 1st-level spell, and so on. The character must be able to cast spells of that level in order to utilize the bonus spell. Bards of grade 7 can choose any one spell level to apply their final bonus spell to.

Fraternity: Seekers' travels can take them into dangerous situations. As a consequence, it is a requirement for all Seekers to immediately respond and provide aid on hearing news of a fellow member's peril.

Gather Information Bonus: For every two grades of membership, a Seeker gains a +1 insight bonus to Gather Information checks.

Good Reputation: The Seekers usually enjoy a good reputation among fellow spellcasters and magic-friendly populations, who appreciate the rescue work of the Seekers.

Increased Skill Limit: Seekers are highly practiced information gatherers and may take their Gather Information skill rank up to Level + 3 + (1/2 Seeker grade).

Disadvantages

Bad Reputation: In some magic-unfriendly realms, and in villages and populations, the Seekers have acquired a bad reputation. Rumor and innuendo have labeled them as kidnappers, particularly of disturbed children. Some stories state that they are the source of curses which afflict their victims with mental suffering. In some locales, being identified as a Seeker can result in an immediate lynching.

Experience Cost: As with all guilds, advancement in grade requires expenditure of experience points (see the table above).

Time: A member must spend at least three months a year on Seeker business. The Moderator may approve a reduction in this time. Nevertheless, whenever a member is called to Seek, he must respond or risk expulsion.

Affiliations

The Seekers fraternity is a fairly easygoing guild with a good reputation with most other magical organizations. It has long-established links with many wizard's academies, bardic colleges, and other sorcerer's fraternities.

A member of the Seekers may also be a member of an adventurer's guild, a fighter's school, a bardic college, a thieves' guild, a trading guild, a craft guild, or a social club. Occasionally, a Seeker may also be a member of a wizard's academy, a druidic circle, or an ecclesiastical council. A Seeker is never a member of a mercenary company, barbarian horde, paladin order, warrior monk's school, town guild, or family guild.

Leaving

With Permission: A member may retire from the Seekers at any time as long as he has no outstanding business with the fraternity. After retirement, a member may no longer participate in the Seekers' sharing of information and loses all of the membership benefits, except for the bonus ranks in the Gather Information skill.

Expulsion: A member will be expelled from the Seekers if he abandons an assigned search, refuses an appointed search without a legitimate reason, or refuses to aid an imperiled fellow member. An expelled member may never rejoin the Seekers and is refused contact with all members. His reputation among fellow spellcasters usually suffers severely once the bards of the fraternity spread the news.

Moderator

Aleksa Barthum: Female human Sorcerer 18: CR 18; Medium-size humanoid (human); HD 18d4; hp 45; Init +2, Spd 30 ft.; AC 25 (touch 17, flat-footed 23); Atk +12/+7 melee (1d6+3/x2, quarterstaff) or +11/+6 ranged (1d4/ x2, dart); SA none; SQ Summon Familiar; Al CG; SV Fort +6, Ref +8, Will +12; Str 12, Dex 14, Con 11, Int 16, Wis 12, Cha 22.

Skills and Feats: Concentration +18, Diplomacy +24, Gather Information +10, Knowledge (arcana) +20, Knowledge (geography) +9, Profession (cartographer) +5, Scry +23, Search +8, Speak Language (Draconic), Speak Language (Elven), Speak Language (Halfling), Spellcraft +23; Combat Casting, Empower Spell, Extend Spell, Maximize Spell, Silent Spell, Still Spell, Spell Focus (enchantment), Spell Penetration.

Sorcerer Spells (12/12/12/12/12/12/12/12/11/9): 0—*daze, detect magic, disrupt undead, flare, light, prestidigitation, ray of frost, read magic, resistance*; 1st—*charm person, comprehend languages, hypnotism, magic missile, sleep*; 2nd— *flaming sphere, hypnotic pattern, invisibility, levitate, hideous laughter*; 3rd—*dispel magic, fireball, hold person, suggestion*; 4th—*charm monster, rainbow pattern, scrying, holy sword (paladin)*; 5th—*dominate person, prying eyes, seeming, teleport*; 6th—*legend lore, mass suggestion, veil*; 7th— *greater scrying, limited wish, prismatic spray*; 8th—*discern location, whirlwind (druid)*; 9th—*meteor swarm*.

Possessions: *bracers of armor +8, carpet of flying, ring of protection +5, rod of splendor, staff of the illusionist*.

Moderator Aleksa Barthum was born a bastard to a sorceress, Anatha of the Waters. Barthum grew up mostly neglected by her mother, who passed her from nanny to temporary foster home to nanny. Once her powers of sorcery were revealed, Barthum went in search of her mother and, when she was found, learned the ways of sorcery from her.

During the years that followed, Barthum traveled far and experienced much. Remembering her own childhood, she always went out of her way to help children, especially those who showed talent for magic. When she found the Fraternity of Seekers, she recognized an organization of sorcerers and bards of like mind. Barthum joined the Seekers and worked long and hard searching for the Lost. She traveled the continent and had many adventures, rising through the Seekers' grades as she rescued the Lost.

Moderator Barthum is a tall slender woman with a wicked sense of humor, a gift for conversation, and an interest in people. She takes pleasure in personally debriefing all returning and visiting members but prefers to delegate the more monotonous paperwork and trivial administrative matters to secretaries and deputies. The membership of the Fraternity of Seekers respects Barthum's moderatorship, and Barthum feels a strict loyalty to the membership in return. Whenever anyone threatens or harms any of her members, she ruthlessly pursues any rescue, if required, and inflicts a proportional response upon any and all perpetrators.

Your Campaign

The Seekers provide a source of information and adventures for any party with contacts or members in the organization. A Seeker may be encountered anywhere at any time—alone on the road, in a caravan, in an inn, in a market—and may approach party members for information and gossip they are willing to share or trade. A Seeker may also request assistance from adventurers or even to join the party for a period.

Adventure Hooks

- A Seeker hires the party to accompany him on a quest to find one of the Lost.
- A party sorcerer or bard joins the Seekers and requests the party's help in finding his assigned Lost.
- Someone begs the party's help in finding his child, kidnapped by a stranger (a Seeker).
- The party is hired to discover and retrieve some secret or arcane knowledge possessed by the Seekers.

Other Fraternities

- The **Dragonkin** members believe the legend that all sorcerers are descended from dragons. They seek to awaken other draconic powers within themselves.
- The **Mystic Delvers** are devoted to locating and researching new sorcerer spells.
- The Far Travelers are enthralled by the mysteries of distant lands and strange places. Individually and in groups, they explore faraway places and return to describe all that they have seen and done to the other members.

Seekers

Wizards' Academies

Wizards are a naturally gregarious lot. Wherever several wizards of similar inclination and interest reside within easy travel distance of each other, an association of mutual assistance soon arises. Frequently, resources and knowledge are shared, and eventually the wizards and their apprentices come together at a more convenient, mutually beneficial location. A wizard's academy is born, also known as a wizard's guild or college. Many wizard's academies can be found throughout the lands. They range from small associations consisting of less than a dozen member wizards and apprentices up to large, long-established institutions with hundreds of members.

An academy is both an association of wizards and a physical set of buildings. Within an academy, a wizard may securely study and pursue research with access to resources far beyond the reach of most individuals, as well as enjoy the experience, discussions, and cooperation of a community of like-minded scholars.

Wizard's academies tend to enjoy a privileged position in most of the towns or cities in which they reside because of the prestige and wealth they bring to the host town or city. In fact, an academy can be so lucrative for its host that the towns and cities may compete with tax breaks and legal benefits to become host for a new academy.

An academy is usually founded in a town or city where the member wizards can easily purchase appropriate resources for their work (parchment, ink, crystals, various rare metals), where they can be supported so that they may concentrate on their work (food, drink, cleaning staff), and where master craftsmen and fellow scholars can be found (a city rich in guilds, traders, and libraries). Occasionally, an academy that specializes in life or weather magic, or is located in a realm hostile to wizards, may be founded out in the countryside or even in the wilderness.

Although academies can come in all shapes, sizes, and construction materials, and usually reflect the host culture's architectural trends, many academies have some common physical features. One of these is the tendency of all academies to have at least one tall tower upon which astronomical observations can be made, weather magic be practiced, and other esoteric rites performed. Most academies have at least one great hall, a well guarded and secured communal library, and a warren of small chambers for students, apprentices, and serving staff.

Not all academies are publicly known. Some are secret societies or private institutes that do not advertise their presence. Some specialize in rare and dangerous magics and remain quiet behind tall walls. Some are dedicated to purposes contrary to or opposing the surrounding nations' or cultures' ethics or dominant alignments. Some academies just remain quiet so as not to arouse the passion of a magic-fearing populace.

Purpose

All wizard's academies share the common goal of expanding magical knowledge, cooperating in magical research, and teaching apprentices. Some academies also take on the goal of managing or controlling magic. Each academy specializes or excels in particular areas of magic, produces famous spells or famous wizards; therefore by saying to which academy a wizard belongs, he identifies himself to other wizards, as far as the academy's fame extends. When wizards meet, the first thing they exchange is their academy memberships. Academy wizards tend to look down on rustic individualist wizards.

Sharing: The primary purpose of an academy is to provide an environment in which its members can pursue well resourced research without interference in privacy and comfort, and to debate and discuss magical theory and personal discoveries. An academy is also an excellent environment in which to train apprentices. An academy provides facilities and recourses beyond anything that all but the wealthiest wizards can achieve. An academy's library is likely to have far more tomes than any individual wizard is going to ever see on his external wonderings, and in many academies a museum displays well guarded strange, unique, and legendary magic items and arcane paraphernalia.

Protection: Magic is a mysterious and powerful force that many rightfully fear, some to an excessive degree. Even the most powerful wizard cannot remain eternally vigilant and so, if alone, can fall victim to the ignorant and superstitious. A studious wizard quietly researching some spell in his country cottage can potentially find a mob of torch-wielding villagers ready to string him up in revenge for pestilence or a crop failure. A disease sweeping a city could see an individual wizard blamed and, if he's lucky, tarred, feathered, and run out of the city on a donkey.

By coming together in an academy, wizards find safety in numbers. While some wizards sleep, others can guard; while some wizards surrender themselves to deep study, others can remain alert. An academy is a wizard's corpora-

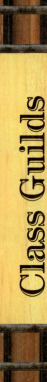

Table 1.13 Wizards' Academy Advancement

Grade	XP Cost	Fees	Benefits Gained
Associate (1)	500	50 gp/month	Bonus skill points, discount components, early wizard feats, Fraternity, Good Reputation, income, increased skill limits, Shelter
Bachelor (2)	1,000	100 gp/month	Bonus skill points, Spellcraft bonus
Tutor (3)	1,500	150 gp/month	Bonus skill points, increased skill limits
Master (4)	2,000	200 gp/month	Bonus skill points, Spellcraft bonus
Scholar (5)	2,500	250 gp/month	Bonus skill points, increased skill limits
Dean (6)	3,000	300 gp/month	Bonus skill points, Spellcraft bonus
Doctor (7)	3,500	350 gp/month	Bonus skill points, increased skill limits
Fellow (8)	4,000	400 gp/month	Bonus skill points, Spellcraft bonus
Professor (9)	4,500	450 gp/month	Bonus skill points, increased skill limits
Chancellor (10)	5,000	500 gp/month	Bonus skill points, Spellcraft bonus

tion. An academy can wield significant power, allowing the wizards to negotiate with kings, governments, and other guilds on an equal basis and protecting its members from arbitrary political or economic interference.

Lastly, an academy can be a secure location for the storage and guarding, by experts, of powerful or dangerous magical artifacts.

Control: Some academies are established to regulate magical research and control magical knowledge. These academies require all wizards within their territory to join and be subject to the authority of the academy. Sometimes these controlling academies are founded by cabals of powerful wizards with either noble or self-serving goals, *e.g.*, to protect innocents from the slavery of powerful spells or the horrors that can be unleashed by powerful spells. Mostly they are established by governments or other regimes to control or suppress the dangerous or chaotic powers of magic. Occasionally, an academy may be established to monopolize and regulate the availability of magic, increasing its economic value and forcing higher prices for wizards' services and magical products.

Goal: The primary activity of academies is the furtherance of magical knowledge through research and teaching. Within the academies, the wizards study ancient spells and musty old tomes, sometimes in quiet concentration, sometimes in energetic debates with their peers. They concentrate on magical and mysterious puzzles; pursue hints and rumors of new knowledge, spells, and unearthed arcana; and store and further the body of magical knowledge and wisdom through the accumulation of spellbooks, tomes, scrolls, librams, codices, treatises, magical items, and wizards' records of research and observation diaries.

Economic: An academy is also a central location for those with a need to request the services of a wizard. These applicants are usually quite wealthy, such as nobles, governments, guildmasters, and wealthy merchants. An academy with a good reputation is in a powerful position to negotiate substantial payments for such services.

As well as teaching magic, academies' reputations as sources of quality scholarship mean that they may also engage in the profitable service of teaching the children of the rich and powerful. The subjects an academy may teach include languages, history, natural history, arithmetic, geometry, and astronomy.

Membership

Belief/Code: The wizards who join an academy share a common belief in cooperation and mutual support.

Location: Each academy supports the wizards of a particular city, district, or region. Some academies have members from even farther afield but are particularly famed in an area of wizardry or are highly specialized.

Profession: All members of an academy are wizards.

Joining the Guild

Application: Usually, any wizard may apply to join any academy at the cost of 100 gp. The applicant wizard must take and pass an entry examination demonstrating his knowledge of magic. If he passes this test, the wizard is a member of the academy. If he fails, the wizard has lost his 100 gp and may not apply again until he has achieved another level as a wizard, or he presents to the academy for scrutiny a spell or a magic item of his own devising. Reapplication requires an additional 100 gp and retaking the test.

Foundation: A wizard of 10th level or higher with five ranks in Spellcraft may found an academy. The cost is five tomes on the subject of magic to seed the academy's library and 10,000 gp.

Alignment: Some academies with additional purposes beyond study and research have an alignment criterion for their membership. For example, an academy dedicated to developing magics with which to fight demons may require its members to be Lawful Good. An academy requiring total dedication to knowledge and magic above all things may require its members to be Neutral.

Number Limit: An academy must have at least three members. Although there is no theoretical upper limit to membership, it is rare for an academy to have more than thirty wizards.

Test/Examination: The entry examination to join an academy is a test of the applicant's Spellcraft skill versus DC 15. If he passes this examination, the applicant is admitted into the academy. If he fails, the applicant is declined and he may not apply again until certain conditions are met. (See "Application" above.)

Size and Scope

Except in the few rare cases where membership is limited to and mandatory for a region's wizards, an academy's membership reflects the range of its fame and reputation. As such, an academy's membership usually consists of local wizards, but a significant minority may be wizards who traveled from distant regions to study at the academy, attracted by the academy's reputation. An academy's fame may be small, known only in the local city or district, or it may stretch as far as other nations. Some few academies may be very large, with memberships approaching a hundred, with half or even more of the wizards from distant lands. However, the majority of academies have at most a dozen wizards, all from the local city or district.

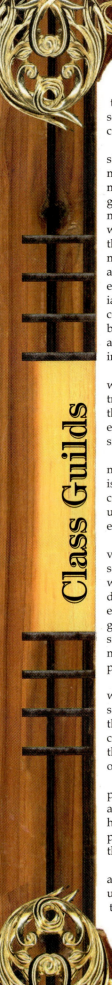

Guild Structure & Advancement

Nearly all academies broadly fall into two structure types: an association of equal scholars, dedicated to research and mutual assistance, or a hierarchy, dedicated to control. Most academies are a blend of these two structures.

Collective: Wizards, like most intellectuals, tend to hold strong opinions and enjoy robust debates. Nevertheless, most prefer to reach decisions by following the scholarly method of discussion and consensus. Although a wizard's grade in an academy measures his seniority, most academies customarily function as participatory democracies where many of the academy's decisions are reached through discussion and consensus. In these types of academies, all wizards of all grades are essentially organizationally equal. Such an academy usually has a ruling council elected by the membership to handle day-to-day and trivial affairs. The chairman of the council, the academy's Chancellor, is chosen by the council and approved by the membership. Candidates for the Chancellorship are usually wizards of great achievement and reasonable popularity within the academy's membership.

For standard decisions, the wizards (or at least those who can be bothered with what others consider administrative trivia) tend to spend days, even weeks, discussing the pros and cons until a basic consensus emerges. The academy council then adopts the consensus as a formal decision and passes it to the Chancellor for ratification.

For issues requiring a more serious decision or commitment, a general assembly of wizards is called and the issue discussed until a majority resolution emerges. The council, or the Chancellor alone, may make decisions for urgent matters but must seek endorsement from the academy membership as soon as possible.

In truth, no academy runs this smoothly. Behind the veneer of consensus and participation, cliques and factions soon arise on almost every issue. Most wizards are too busy with their studies and research and are uninterested in the day-to-day campaigning. Nevertheless, some wizards revel in the politicking; they are the organizers of the factional groups and the driving force behind many academy decisions. These wizards are the most influential in any academy and are sought after by those wishing to influence the particular decisions of an academy.

Graded (Elective): Those academies founded to control wizards and magic (as often for good as well as evil reasons) tend to be much more hierarchical in structure. In these academies, a wizard's grade reflects his authority. All control resides in the academy council, which consists of the wizards with the highest grades. The council makes all of the important decisions.

Each advancement in grade (see below) requires the approval of a wizard senior to the applicant. The senior wizard may sometimes require an oath from the applicant upholding the applicant's dedication to the academy's purpose, or some deed to prove his dedication to the art and to the academy.

Graded (Merit): An academy member is permitted to apply for grade advancement in each of three different situations. First, he may apply for grade advancement each time he improves in Class Level as a wizard. Second, he may apply any time he permanently delivers to his academy a magic item or a new, previously unknown, spell. Lastly, he may apply any time he creates a spell or magic item of sufficiently advanced design (a spell whose level is at least one half the target grade or a magic item whose cost is 1,000 x target grade in gp), whether original or not. In this last case, the academy will study his creation, record a copy for the library if it is a new spell, and return it to him.

The attempt to advance in a grade is an examination similar to the academy entry examination. This examination is determined by a Spellcraft check against DC 15 + the target grade. If the candidate fails this test he may not attempt it again until he delivers a new magic item or spell to the academy, or goes up a Class Level as a wizard.

Benefits

Membership in an academy provides many benefits to a wizard. It provides a quiet environment for study and research and a location of security and safety. It provides contacts with other wizards, places to stay while traveling, and an identity with which to introduce himself to other wizards. However, the most significant benefit to a wizard is the boost that membership gives the wizard's scholarly research and capabilities through access to the academy's libraries, other wizards' expertise and experience, and the other resources available in an academy.

Bonus Skill Points: Each time an academy wizard advances a grade in the academy he gains his Intelligence bonus in skill points (to a minimum of one point) which he may spend on any of the following skills: Alchemy, Craft (magic-item-creation related), Knowledge (a single magic-related area), Profession (one wizard-related profession, *e.g.*, apothecary, herbalist, scribe, engineer, etc.), or Spellcraft.

Discount Components: Through an academy's economic influence and scale, the component costs of item creation at the academy are one-third the cost of the item (rather than one-half).

Early Wizard Feats: An academy member is eligible to receive his Wizard class bonus feats one level sooner, i.e., at 4th level, 9th level, and so on, if and only if they are spent on Item Creation feats.

Fraternity: The wizard gains several colleagues at the academy. He may call upon these colleagues for assistance with a successful Diplomacy (DC 10) check. He may also gain assistance from fellow wizards in other friendly academies against DC 14.

Good Reputation: If the wizard's academy is one famed for magical skill or for service to the community, the wizard may gain benefits in dealings with wizards or other folk.

Income: While staying at the academy, a wizard may use his Craft or Profession skills to generate income while enjoying free room and board (as such costs are covered by the academy's membership dues).

Increased Skill Limits: A wizard at the academy is allowed to increase the maximum number of ranks he may put into the skills listed above under Bonus Skill Points. This increase is equal to half his grade at the academy, rounded up.

Shelter: An academy member can usually request rooms at the academy if he wishes to live close to his work or his students. Further, an academy member can usually request and receive food and temporary shelter from most other wizard's academies. He will be expected to be free with news of events and happenings in his home academy, in magic, and in the wider world. He will also be expected to make some small contribution to the host academy's storehouse of magical knowledge.

Spellcraft Check Bonus: All Spellcraft checks receive an insight bonus equal to half the wizard's academy grade (rounded down).

Disadvantages

Bad Reputation: While some academies have good reputations, others have bad reputations, whether deserved or not.. Although a wizard may be innocent of all wrongdoing, the revelation of his academy membership can sometimes be very detrimental to him. He may face anything from negative feelings through ostracizing to public beatings, and even execution.

Experience Cost: As with all guilds, advancing in grades requires expenditure of experience points.

Fees: A wizard must pay monthly dues of 50 gp times his grade per month for his academy membership.

Time: The higher a wizard's grade in the academy, the more time he must spend working in the academy. For every grade, the wizard must devote two weeks a year working full-time on academy business. During this time he is unavailable for any personal activities or adventuring.

Affiliations

Wizards, like scholars, tend to view each other as either comrades or rivals. Depending on their current relationship and history, two academies may view each other as friends or as adversaries. The meetings of wizards from two academies may range in attitude from cheerful welcome and offers of assistance to polite inquiry, or even to mistrust and suspicion.

It is rare for members of other guilds also to be members of a wizard's academy, mostly because of the significant time requirements academy membership places upon a character. Nevertheless, if all membership requirements are met, it is possible in a few instances as follows:

√ A member of a wizard's academy may also be a member of a family guild, town guild, or social club.

√ A member of a wizard's academy may occasionally also be a member of an adventurer's guild, a fighter's school, a thieves' guild, an ecclesiastical council, a warrior monk's school, a trading guild, or a craft guild.

√ It is very rare but possible for a member of a wizard's academy also to be a member of a druidic circle or paladin order.

√ A member of a wizard's academy can never also be a member of a mercenary company, sorcerer's fraternity, bardic college, or barbarian horde.

Leaving

With Permission: A wizard may retire from an academy at any time. As a consequence, he loses early access to wizard feats but keeps the ones he already has; loses his Spellcraft skill check bonus; loses the cheaper component costs benefit; and loses the Shelter benefit. The wizard keeps his bonus skill ranks and his good or bad reputation from being associated with the academy.

If a wizard leaves one academy and transfers to another, he keeps all his membership benefits.

Chancellor

Grett Austrimer: Male human Wizard 19: CR 19; Medium-size humanoid (human); HD 19d4+19; hp 57; Init +0, Spd 30 ft.; AC 23 (touch 10, flat-footed 23); Atk +12/+7 melee (1d4+3/x2, dagger) or +9/+4 ranged (1d4+1/x2, dagger); SA none; SQ Summon Familiar; Al LN; SV Fort +8, Ref +6, Will +13; Str 14, Dex 11, Con 14, Int 22, Wis 15, Cha 16.

Skills and Feats: Alchemy +31, Appraise +13, Concentration +22, Craft (jewelry) +15, Craft (metalwork) +15, Craft (woodwork) +15, Diplomacy +7, Knowledge (arcana) +31, Knowledge (commerce) +17, Knowledge (history) +11, Knowledge (nature) +10, Knowledge (nobility and royalty) +12, Knowledge (politics) +17, Knowledge (the planes) +26, Profession (teacher) + 19, Scry +29, Sense Motive +6, Speak Language (Celestial), Speak Language (Draconic), Speak Language (Dwarven), Speak Language (Elven), Spellcraft +36; Brew Potion, Craft Magic Items and Armor, Craft Rod, Craft Staff, Craft Wand, Craft Wondrous Item, Forge Ring, Leadership, Scribe Scroll, Spell Penetration.

Wizard Spells (13/13/13/13/13/ 13/13/13/12/12 per day): 0—all; 1st—*animate rope, comprehend languages, identify, magic missile, magic weapon, magic aura, undetectable aura, floating disk, unseen servant;* 2nd—*arcane lock, detect thoughts, invisibility, knock, locate object, magic mouth, obscure object, see invisibility, web;* 3rd—*dispel magic, explosive runes, fly, illusory script, keen edge, lightning bolt, tongues;* 4th—*bestow curse, detect scrying, minor creation, polymorph other, polymorph self, remove curse, scrying;* 5th—*major cre-*

ation, permanency, sending, stone shape, teleport; 6th—analyze dweomer, contingency, guards and wards, legend lore, true seeing; 7th—greater scrying, limited wish, spell turning, vision; 8th—binding, demand, polymorph any object, symbol; 9th—foresight, wish.

Possessions: bracers of armor +8, dagger of souls, ring of wizardry (I), robe of the archmagi, tome of clear thought +3 (used).

Master Grett Austrimer, a 19th-level wizard, was born into a large, wealthy merchant family. He had the best education that money could buy, and when he showed talent for spells, his parents bought him entrance into a wizard's academy. Intellectually gifted and with a keen interest in the arts, Austrimer did very well in his academy, completing his apprenticeship in record time. After traveling and working for many years, including periods as a court wizard and a merchant wizard, Austrimer joined the River's Head Academy with the intention of leading a quiet life of research, study, and teaching. After twenty years of membership, Austrimer was recently honored by voted being Chancellor of River's Head Academy.

Chancellor Austrimer is a large, but not particularly overweight, man. He enjoys brisk walks twice a day and is careful with what he eats. He has a deep and quiet voice, with a special resonance that travels far and a modulation that makes listening to it a pleasure. He is willing to give anyone a few minutes of his time and is very popular with the students and apprentices. However, Austrimer loathes cheats, swindlers, and shoddy workmanship, so the merchants and craftsman of the surrounding city treat him with fearful respect, especially after a few well known duplicitous craftsmen overcharged the academy for incompetent work and then disappeared. Anyone who counted toads would have noticed an increase in numbers at that time.

Your Campaign

Wizard's academies can be anything ranging from mere magic universities to secretive Illuminati-style organizations. Perhaps examples of both may populate your campaign. Many wizards spend their apprenticeship years in an academy. A party wizard may have fond or foul memories of his years in an academy, which can give the GM many hooks for storyline development. The founding of an academy can be the basis of a new campaign. The party assists in the search for an appropriate location, participates in negotiations with local governmental and guild authorities, and helps the first wizards travel from their former homes to join the new academy.

An academy is also a good place to retire party wizards from adventuring. They may join an existing academy to pursue a quiet life of research and study, or if they're high enough level as a wizard they may settle down and found their own academies. If they have significant fame from their adventuring days, they may attract quite a few fellow wizards very quickly.

Adventure Hooks

⚡ The party meets a venerable scholar fleeing with his spellbooks under his arms. He is being hunted by a hostile force—an enemy of his clan/town, an anti-magic crusade, etc. He hires the party to escort him to an academy of which he has heard, where he hopes to find protection and a new home.

⚡ A wizard in the party has joined an academy and wishes to retrieve a legendary magic item for the academy. Of course, this would also mean the wizard may attempt to advance a grade in the academy. The wizard persuades the rest of the party to hunt for the magic item with him.

⚡ The party is in a city where a new academy has been founded. It seems that all wizards in the city and surrounding district are joining this new academy or, as has happened to openly vocal opponents of the academy, disappearing.

⚡ The party is hired to protect a new, small academy that has just been founded.

Variations

All wizard academies are similar in structure and purpose. An academy is usually named after the city or region in which it is located.

Ye Merry Olde Companye of Fools

Popular opinion would have it that bards are merry wanderers, light-hearted souls with songs on their lips and heads full of wondrous tales. But not every bard has benevolent motives. Some of them aren't very nice at all. On the surface, Ye Merry Olde Companye of Fools appears to be a rather nice bunch of minstrels and storytellers. Scratch the surface, though, and something more sinister is revealed. Here is a bardic group with a less than pure heart.

The Fools found their origin in the black heart and warped mind of a former court jester. This woman had become too close to her master, the king. Too close, indeed, for the queen's peace of mind. Cast out of the kingdom by the queen's men and ordered never to return on pain of death, the former jester was shamed and infuriated. No matter that she was a woman scorned. More importantly, she was a bard scorned.

Gathering other bards around her, fellow discontents like herself, she plotted her revenge. Her weapons were song and prose, the words hers, the voices those of her disciples. Subtle innuendo and scathing satire soon ruined the reputation of the queen, driving her to take her own life. Her loyal followers fared no better as they were made laughing stocks or reviled villains in turn.

Expectant victims pleaded with the jester and her cohorts, offering money, services, land, anything to be left alone. This was a revelation to the Company of Fools, as they had mockingly titled themselves. Now they gave serious consideration to the power their talents gave them. With the jester as their chief they became feared far and wide and few dared to cross them. With their ability to ruin someone without ever facing him, the Fools were a force to be reckoned with.

Eventually, of course, their downfall came about. Long after the jester's death, those who followed her became even more corrupt and far less careful. Their enemies, and there were many, pounced at the right moment. The Company was almost totally destroyed, but there were survivors.

For some time these survivors remained hidden, concealing their links to the Fools and passing themselves off as ordinary minstrels, taletellers, or perhaps good-natured bards. In secret, however, they recruited apprentices and passed on their secrets and their convictions.

In current times, the stories of the Company of Fools are long forgotten, or perhaps remembered as silly tales told by superstitious ancestors. The Fools have resurfaced, calling themselves Ye Merry Olde Companye of Fools. To the outside world they appear little more than a guild of traveling entertainers, clowns, and jokers. They are welcomed as cheery bringers of fun and laughter, carriers of news from the outside world. Little do people suspect the real goal of the Fools: to bend others to their wills and to toy spitefully with others' lives.

Purpose

Goal: The Fools aim to insinuate themselves into society, making themselves appear as innocuous as possible, so that they may control and manipulate those they actually appear to be entertaining. Though not necessarily evil in outlook, the Fools are certainly selfish in the extreme.

Membership

Profession: Membership consists almost completely of bards, although multiclassed rogues with levels in either wizard or sorcerer may find their way into the Fools.

Alignment: All members of the Fools are of the following alignments: Neutral, Chaotic Neutral, Neutral Evil, and Chaotic Evil. By nature the Fools are self-serving and manipulative, so Good and Lawful alignments are completely inappropriate.

Joining the Guild

Invitation: The Fools are a secretive group and keep their true nature closely guarded. Prospective members are carefully scrutinized to determine if they are made of the right stuff. Only then will a character be approached and offered entry into the Fools' ranks.

Should a player wish his PC to join the Fools, the player and the GM should work together to plot the process by which the character is enlisted. Alternatively, the GM may wish to maintain the air of secrecy and bar players from reading about the Fools, unleashing them when best suits his campaign.

Deed: Members must prove themselves in order to be accepted into the Fools. The senior member judging the character will identify a person whom the potential member must manipulate in some form or another. This could involve duping another person, seducing him, or perhaps publicly ridiculing him. Whichever is chosen, the action will

not be to the benefit of the victim and should require some cunning on the candidate's part. The character being tested need not necessarily know why he is being asked to do the deed. He may think it is just a challenge or a bet from a new colleague.

The deed is designed to determine whether the candidate is skilled, cunning, and ruthless enough to join the Fools. The GM should set up a situation involving the character using one or more appropriate skills (Bluff, Diplomacy, Gather Information, Innuendo, Intimidate, Sense Motive). Once the skill choice has been made, the test should involve a DC approximately 15 higher than the character's skill rating. It is recommended that good or bad roleplaying on the part of the player may modify the DC. Here are some suggested deeds:

- Convince a dignitary that his spouse is secretly having an affair when in reality this is not true.
- Ruin the camaraderie between a pair of long-time friends.
- Frame an innocent person for a random crime.
- Seduce a virtuous cleric.
- Frighten off some tough rowdies without ever directly attacking or ensorceling them.

Qualification: All members of Ye Merry Olde Companye of Fools must meet the following requirements:

- Charisma 15+
- At least two ranks in Bluff
- At least two ranks in Diplomacy
- Candidate must perform the deed described above.

Size and Scope

The real size of the Fools is not known to any one member. In other words, the GM can choose the numbers in the ranks to suit his campaign. It is recommended that there shouldn't be many more than a few hundred members, and one individual character shouldn't directly know more than a few dozen fellow members at most. The Fools are spread across the world, appearing in the most obscure places.

Guild Structure & Advancement

Graded (Merit): Advancement through the Fools is through skill, merit, and defeating senior members to prove one's worth. This is measured by a character's Charisma score, the number of ranks he has in a variety of skills, and his success at the Fool's Duel. To rise to any grade above the first, a fool must defeat a higher-ranking member of the guild at a special battle of wits called the Fool's Duel. Additionally, to advance past the 1st grade, a character must be able to cast arcane spells (typically by taking a level in the bard class).

Table 1.14 – Fools' Guild Advancement Table

Grade	Requirements	XP Cost	Benefits
Pretender (1)	Cha 15+, Bluff 2 ranks, Diplomacy 2 ranks, entry deed	500	Skill bonus (Bluff), Skill bonus (Diplomacy)
Faker (2)	Duel, arcane spells, Bluff 4 ranks, Intimidate 2 ranks	1,000	Barbed Wit, Skill bonus (Intimidate)
Imposter (3)	Duel, Bluff 6 ranks, Innuendo 2 ranks	1,500	Skill bonus (Innuendo)
Counsel (4)	Duel, Cha 16+, Bluff 8 ranks, Diplomacy 4 ranks	2,000	Scorn
Confidant (5)	Duel, Bluff 10 ranks, Intimidate 4 ranks	2,500	Demoralize
Mask (6)	Duel, Cha 17+, Bluff 12 ranks, Innuendo 4 ranks	3,000	Fool's Curse

Fool's Duel

Sometimes two rivals may not wish to resort to martial prowess to determine who is the superior of the two. Some might choose to engage in a battle of wits, letting words be their weapons and suffering no physical wounding, instead taking damage to their egos. The Fool's Duel provides a means by which a formalized war of words may be resolved, in a fashion similar in dynamics to melee combat.

To determine the abilities of appropriate opponents for advancement duels, the GM should craft bards whose skills and levels are 1d4 higher than the challenger's. Ability scores should be randomly generated or chosen to suit the GM's purpose. Choosing lower ability scores is one way for the GM to give a PC a fair chance of defeating his opponent.

Each participant needs to work out the equivalents of his attack modifier, armor class, hit points, and initiative modifier before starting the duel.

In place of an attack modifier, the character uses an appropriate interaction skill, chosen from Bluff, Diplomacy, Innuendo, Intimidate, and Perform.

Rather than hit points, a character has a Self Esteem score, equal to the total of his Intelligence, Wisdom, and Charisma attributes (not modifiers) plus his total level.

Instead of armor class, the character has a Pride rating equal to 10 plus his Will save modifier.

Initiative is based on the character's Intelligence modifier. The Improved Initiative feat does not apply.

To begin, each character involved in the duel must roll initiative, the order of which remains the same for the length of duel and otherwise follows normal initiative rules.

Each round, a combatant in the duel may do one of the following:

- **Press an attack:** Choosing one of the attack skills listed above, the character rolls 1d20 and adds the skill. A hit is struck if this total equals or exceeds the opponent's Pride. A successful hit deals (1d6 + attacker's Charisma modifier) points of damage to the opponent's Self-esteem. The attacker may choose to use different skills each round.
- **Search for weakness:** The attacking character may make a Sense Motive (DC 20) roll to search for a chink in the opponent's ego. Success gives a +2 bonus to the character's next attack. This action may be continued over several rounds to build a cumulative bonus.
- **Build a defense:** A character may also use the Sense Motive skill (DC 20) to predict an attack and gain a +2 bonus to Pride against the opponent's next attack. This bonus may be used against only one attack, though the defender chooses when to use it, allowing him to accumulate a bigger bonus over several rounds.
- **Take a round of normal actions:** At any time in the duel, a character may opt to take normal actions such as spellcasting, movement, and melee attacks. An attack on the opponent through spells or combat is considered a concession of defeat, and the attacking character has lost the duel.

The duel ends when one combatant concedes defeat, attacks the opponent as detailed above, or is reduced to 0 Self-esteem. Should a character be reduced to 0 Self Esteem, he operates with a –2 morale penalty for the next twenty-four hours, until some pride has been restored.

Benefits

Barbed Wit: Upon reaching Faker grade, Fools may use this spell-like ability to cause real damage with their words. The Fool may use this ability a number of times a day equal to his grade. To use Barbed Wit, the bard unleashes a stream of invective at the victim, who must make a Will save (DC 10 + Grade + Fool's Charisma bonus). Failure results in the victim taking 1d4 per grade plus the Fool's Charisma bonus hit points damage.

Demoralize: At Confidant grade, the Fool has learned how best to use a few choice words or gestures to undermine the confidence of other people. The Fool can affect a number of people within appropriate range (line of sight for mime, hearing for words, etc.) equal to the total of a Perform test. Each victim must make a Will save (DC 10 + Grade + Fool's Charisma bonus). Failure means that the victim is totally demoralized and suffers a morale penalty to all skill, attack, and saving throw rolls equal to the Fool's Charisma bonus. Failure by more than 10 means the victim's morale is shattered and he will flee in fear and shame. This effect lasts for (1d6 + Fool's Charisma bonus) minutes. The Fool may use this ability a number of times a day equal to his grade.

Fool's Curse: Upon reaching Mask grade, Fools may call down a terrible curse upon an unfortunate victim. The Mask must form the curse into an appropriate medium, be it music, verse, or another form of art. This requires a Perform (DC 30) test to compose the curse successfully. The victim must then make a Will save against a DC equal to 20 plus the Mask's Charisma bonus.

The effects of the curse are particularly cruel. First, the victim suffers a –2 penalty to all skill, attack, and saving throw rolls. Additionally, he suffers a 10% reduction in all XP awards. Finally, all NPC reactions are automatically one level worse than would be normal.

Removal of the curse is as though it were applied via a *bestow curse* spell. The Fool who laid the curse can lift it at any time. Additionally, another Fool with the Fool's Curse ability may counter the curse. This requires the second Fool to make a Perform (DC 30) test to make a countercharm to lift the curse. The Fool may use this ability once per day.

Scorn: At Counsel grade, the Fool has learned how to carry such an air of unimpressed and confident superiority that foes are less able to affect him. This ability lasts for (1d6 + Fool's Charisma bonus) rounds and may be used a number of times a day equal to the Fool's grade plus Charisma bonus. This ability allows the Fool to add his Charisma bonus to armor class and Will saving throws for the duration. The armor class bonus should be treated as increasing the Dexterity modifier for the purposes of determining when and how it applies. The Scorn ability does not work against creatures immune to mind-affecting attacks, such as undead.

Skill Bonuses: At Pretender grade, Fools become so skilled at hiding behind a friendly guise that they gain a +2 competence bonus to all Bluff checks.

Also at Pretender grade, Fools need to put on a diplomatic front so often that they gain a +2 competence bonus to Diplomacy.

At Faker grade, Fools are able to project their personal confidence and derision of the world to such a degree that they gain a +2 skill bonus to Intimidate.

At Imposter grade, Fools are so familiar with more subtle arts of conversation that they enjoy a +2 competence bonus to Innuendo.

Disadvantages

Enemies: The Fools have earned the enmity of more benevolent bardic groups and have a very adversarial relationship with them. Generally speaking, should a bard of Good alignment learn a member's true nature, he will do all he can to thwart and defeat that member. Members of the Fools should be particularly vigilant in areas where there are established bardic colleges or a strong tradition of good bards.

Competition: Advancement within the Fools is not an automatic process. Before a member can advance to the next grade, he must defeat a fellow member in a Fool's Duel. That other member must be a Fool at the grade the advancing member wants to attain. If the challenger wins the Fool's Duel he may expend the necessary XP and advance to the next grade, receiving the appropriate benefits. If he loses the duel, he loses 1,000 XP and remains at the old grade. If the senior Fool loses the duel he remains at his grade but does lose the 1,000 XP.

There is a chance that a PC of Faker rank or higher will be challenged to a Fool's Duel by an ambitious fellow member. The chance of this happening in any given month is one tenth of that listed in the Encounter Table. In such a situation the challenging NPC will be one grade below the member and 1d4 levels lower.

Should a PC wish to make a challenge to advance, the chance to find an appropriate opponent is half that listed on the Encounter Table. The opponent will be one grade higher and 1d4 levels above the PC.

In both cases the chance of an opponent appearing can not drop below 1%.

Affiliations

The main affiliation that the Fools have is their enmity with other bardic groups. Many are long-time adversaries and no love is lost. Fools should always be on the look-out for other bards seeking to ruin them.

Individual Fools have insinuated themselves into all sorts of influential positions. Members of royalty and nobility and other wealthy patrons often see it as vital to have a jester or other such entertainer in their employ. Few realize just how much influence their supposedly loyal retainer might have over them. The Fools make good use of these connections to further their own insidious ends and to satisfy their twisted senses of humor.

Leaving

Without Permission: As with any conspiratorial group, Ye Merry Olde Companye of Fools does not like people to leave its number breathing. Even the most trusted member will be viewed with suspicion if he tries to leave the guild. As there are no dues to be paid and no deeds to be done in the Fools' service, there is no good reason to leave. Simply put, a member cannot voluntarily leave the Fools in good favor.

Should a member decide to leave regardless, he has put themselves at odds with the Fools. They are now his enemies, with all the baggage that brings. The Fools will actively hunt the former member, using their skills of influence to destroy the renegade's reputation as much as possible. The renegade at least has the advantage that the Fools will endeavor to maintain their aura of secrecy.

Expulsion: It is unlikely that the Fools would ever eject a member. They are far more likely to kill the person instead. This would happen when a member has become a threat to the Fools' existence, whether through disruptive habits or perhaps by revealing the group's secrets to the wider world. It is recommended that the GM should warn a PC member that his actions warrant expulsion should such appear imminent.

Once a member has left the Fools he can never rejoin. Good relations may somehow be restored, but the character's membership is forever gone.

All benefits accrued up to the point the member leaves are retained. The GM should decide whether the Enemies disadvantage pertaining to normal bards remains, but the character certainly should now have a formal Enemies disadvantage relating to the Fools.

Senior Mask

Franco DeVoron: Male halfling Bard 17: CR 17; Small-size humanoid (halfling); HD 17d6+17; hp 68; Init +3, Spd 20 ft.; AC 19 (touch 19, flat-footed 16); Atk +17/+12/+7 melee (1d6+1/19-20/x2, small longsword) or +15/+10/+5 ranged (1d4/x2, sling); SA spells; SQ bard abilities, halfling abilities, Fool abilities; Al CN; SV Fort +7, Ref +14, Will +15; Str 8, Dex 16, Con 13, Int 17, Wis 15, Cha 22.

Skills and Feats: Bluff +30, Decipher Script +4, Diplomacy +30, Disguise +14, Gather Information +22, Innuendo +30, Intimidate +18, Perform (lute) +24, Sense Motive +16; Iron Will, Skill Focus (bluff), Skill Focus (diplomacy), Skill Focus (innuendo), Skill Focus (perform), Weapon Finesse (small longsword).

Special Qualities: Halfling abilities—+4 Hide; +2 Climb, Jump, Listen, and Move Silently; +1 to all saving throws; low-light vision; +2 bonus to fear saving throws; +1 attack modifier to thrown attacks; Small creature attack modifiers. Fool abilities—Barbed Wit, Demoralize, Fool's Curse, Scorn, skill bonus (Bluff, Diplomacy, Innuendo, Intimidate).

Bard Spells (10/10/10/10/9/9/7): 0—*dancing lights, daze, detect magic, ghost sound, prestidigitation, read magic*; 1st—*cause fear, charm person, hypnotism, sleep, ventriloquism*; 2nd—*detect thoughts, enthrall, invisibility, suggestion, undetectable alignment*; 3rd—*bestow curse, emotion, fear, remove curse*; 4th—*detect scrying, dominate person, legend lore, modify memory*; 5th—*dream, greater dispelling, mind fog, nightmare*; 6th—*geas/quest, mass suggestion, repulsion*.

Possessions: *hat of disguise, ring of protection +5, small flute sword, vest (cloak) of charisma +6*.

Franco is an ordinary-looking middle-aged halfling whose only remarkable feature is an extremely engaging smile. Thrown out by his own people for being a troublemaker in his youth, he has harbored a grudge against society for some considerable time. He is a selfish little creature whose friendly demeanor hides the fact that he cares for no one but himself.

Becoming a traveling wit and minstrel, Franco was naturally suited to Ye Merry Olde Companye of Fools and soon joined their ranks. Advancing through the grades with ruthless efficiency, Franco made a point of befriending as many Fools as he could. This has proved to be advantageous to him in later years, as he has used his contacts to keep a close watch on potential rivals and allies.

Unlike other Fools, Franco does not directly associate with known influential figures. Instead he pulls the strings of fellow Fools, having them do his bidding indirectly. He thus has considerable influence in many places without anyone knowing that he is the puppet master.

Franco is a sly enemy who strikes at his foes from a distance with subtlety and malice. Few realize how powerful he is, and some of his victims never even know they have made an enemy of him. In short, Franco is a sneaky, nasty little piece of work.

Your Campaign

A GM should choose whether to allow the Fools to be available to PCs in his campaign. As a group they are far from heroic, and if the campaign is based around generally good activities they may be more appropriate as enemies. Should the GM decide to allow PCs to become Fools, he needs to consider best how to introduce them into the campaign. It is suggested that an NPC mentor or associate be introduced to monitor and guide a PC toward eventual membership.

Adventure Hooks

- The PCs are hired by a Fool to spy on a prospective target and gather details of that NPC's private life.
- A PC who is a member of the Fools is instructed to ruin or laud an NPC whom the guild has its eyes on.
- An NPC bard is hunting down Fools. Depending on the nature of the PCs' involvement, they may be allied or opposed to the bard.
- A disgruntled Fool has gone rogue and is being hunted by the guild. The PCs are either among the hunters or helping the renegade Fool.
- A Fool decides to ruin a PC or group of PCs. A campaign of propaganda ensues that starts to badly affect the reputation of the PC(s). The Fool must be stopped or countered.

The Lorekeepers

Ye Merry Olde Companye of Fools is designed more as an organization to thwart and provide a foil for your PCs. Most PCs will not be able to join the Companye due to their alignments. If you would like to present your bardic PCs with a guild of their own you may decide to create your own guild. The rules in Chapter 5 will walk you through the process. The most common good bardic guild is the Lorekeepers, a loose brotherhood dedicated to sharing information, stories, cultures, and histories. The guildhouse of the Lorekeepers is typically a school with a large library. Most members roam the land singing songs and telling stories, and when they meet others of their kind, they trade what they have learned. The higher-ups in the guild teach younger bards at the school and maintain the library. If you decide to craft the Lorekeepers, feel free to make use of this sample advancement table. Characters may join at either level 0 or 1, depending on their level of experience.

Accountability: Members are required to document their exploits and send a quarterly report of what they learn back to the guild. All such documentation is read by the historians and stored in the school library.

Bonus Spell: Due to access to the guild and library, a member gains the ability to know one additional spell each time he advances in the guild. The level of the spell gained is equal to the bard's grade in the guild. Members who skip grade 0 gain both a bonus 0-level level and a bonus 1st-level spell upon joining.

Brotherhood: All guild members are dedicated to sharing knowledge and to helping one another. Members may call upon other members for assistance, shelter, and good reference when needed.

Fame: By grade 3, the character has made a name for himself as a performer. All rolls made to influence the attitude of an NPC gain a +5 bonus.

Guildmaster: The Keeper is the master of the guild and must spend nearly all of his time at the school managing the place. The Keeper cannot adventure for more than one month a year, but he has the power to send others on missions of import.

Instruction: Higher-grade members are required to spend some of their time teaching students at the guildhouse. Instructors may spend as much time as they like but must meet the minimum time requirements. Dues need not be paid for those months in which the character serves as an instructor.

Knowledge: Gain an insight bonus to all Bardic Knowledge and Knowledge (any one) checks.

Library Access: Members may access the school's library in order to do research. When using the library, a member's Knowledge bonus (above) is doubled. Library use requires one hour of study for every 2 points of the check's DC. A member needs to be physically at the library in order to use it himself, although he may also send a written request to have someone research something for him. Such requests are usually performed by historians, and a response is generally sent in about a week's time. Average historians make Bardic Knowledge checks at +20 (10th level, 14 Int, +8 library bonus). If a member requests research, an additional fee, equal to 2 gp per DC of the check, is added to his next dues.

Library Access, Greater: Historians have access to the restricted area of the school's library, where powerful artifacts and dangerous books are stored. Members at this grade can also borrow items from the library for personal use.

Oath: Guild members are required to swear an oath upon joining, saying that they agree to uphold the principles and goals of the guild.

Ransom: At grade 2, a member may take out an emergency loan from the guild, usually as ransom for his own life if he is ever captured. The guild will pay ransomers up to 1,000 gp per level of the kidnapped member. Once freed, the bard must pay the money back, optionally over a several-year payment plan, with interest. A member cannot get a second loan until his first is fully paid off.

Other Bard Guilds

Further possibilities for bard guilds are:

- **Words of passion:** Not everyone can write a good love letter or come up with a flowery romantic speech. Much like Cyrano de Bergerac, a guild of bards might assist those unskilled in the ways of romance, gaining money and favors along the way. In time members would be skilled manipulators.

- **The world is a stage:** A band of traveling entertainers might gather together to share skills and expand their repertoires.

- **Listen and learn:** A more enlightened realm may have a group of professional educators, and who better than bards? By teaching they build their contacts and must also expand their knowledge skills, which may gain bonuses.

- **Digging up the past:** Consider a group of crusading historians who actively seek lost secrets from history. They might become very skilled at reading auras of old objects, as well as at observation skills.

Table 1.15 – Lorekeepers' Guild Advancement Table

Grade	Requirements	XP Cost	Costs	Benefits
Fledgling (0)	Cha 12+	0	100gp per month tuition	School, library access, bonus spell
Minstrel (1)	1 level in Bard, Perform 2 ranks, Oath	500	10gp per month, Accountability	Knowledge +1, Brotherhood, bonus spell
Troubadour (2)	Perform 6 ranks, Gather Information 4 ranks	1,000	20gp per month, Accountability	Knowledge +2, Ransom, bonus spell
Fellow (3)	Perform 10 ranks, Knowledge (arcana) 4 ranks	1,500	30gp per month, Instruction (min 3 months per year), Accountability	Knowledge +3, Fame, bonus spell
Historian (4)	10 levels in Bard*, Gather Information 8 ranks, Knowledge (history) 4 ranks	2,000	40gp per month, Instruction (min 6 months per year), Accountability	Knowledge +3, bonus spell, greater library access
Keeper(5)	Position available, win guild election	2,500	Full-time service, Accountability	Knowledge +5, Guildmaster, bonus spell

*Bardic prestige classes count toward this total.

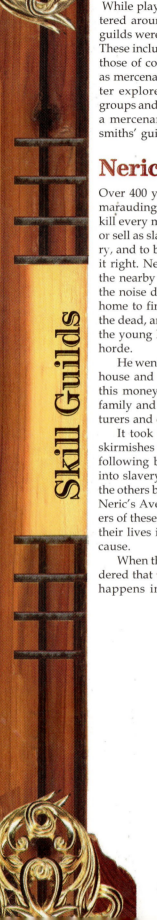

Skill Guilds

While player characters are most likely to join guilds centered around their classes, the vast majority of historical guilds were actually based on specific professions or skills. These include the wide variety of craftsmen guilds, such as those of cobblers or wagonwrights, and also such groups as mercenary companies and merchant unions. This chapter explores the roleplaying possibilities of skill-based groups and provides three model guilds for immediate use: a mercenary company, a trading guild, and a weaponsmiths' guild.

Neric's Avengers

Over 400 years ago, a village was all but wiped out by a marauding band of barbarians. The barbarians intended to kill every man and kidnap every woman and child to keep or sell as slaves, to steal everything of value they could carry, and to burn the village to the ground. They almost had it right. Neric the Younger was returning from a hunt in the nearby forest and heard the commotion. He hid until the noise died away, then snuck into what was left of his home to find only corpses and smoking ruins. He buried the dead, and on the grave of his father — Neric the Elder — the young hunter swore an oath of vengeance against the horde.

He went to a hidden basement under his now-destroyed house and took the family treasure, a mere 350 gp. With this money, and the story of what had been done to his family and village, Neric found some out-of-work adventurers and enlisted their aid in fulfilling his oath.

It took Neric and his Avengers two years and many skirmishes to whittle the horde down to size, all the while following behind and rescuing those who had been sold into slavery, recruiting those who had skills, and sending the others back to their homelands. During those two years, Neric's Avengers financed their war by relieving the buyers of these slaves of some operating capital, and indeed of their lives if they resisted the request to contribute to the cause.

When the Avengers finally trapped the horde, Neric ordered that the barbarian leader be left to him, but as often happens in the heat of

battle, one of the mercenaries ran his sword through the barbarian's chest before he realized whom he was facing. To his credit, Neric did not punish the soldier but rewarded him with the captaincy of the newly formed infantry company.

Purpose

Neric is long dead, and the modern-day company which bears his name no longer loots as it pursues its goals. They do however take appropriate spoils of war if circumstances permit. Neric's Avengers exist solely to pursue military and quasimilitary operations for which they are paid handsomely up front. They are not particular about whose money they accept, but they do insist on at least some military aspect to their task. They will not engage in butchery or mistreatment of innocent noncombatants under any circumstances. This restriction does not apply to any races which are considered monsters in the local region.

Membership

Location: Neric's Avengers are headquartered in a solid keep built over the ruins of the town where Neric grew up.

Alignment: All members of Neric's Avengers must be of Lawful alignment, although no distinction is made between Good, Evil, and Neutral. The Avengers view these traits as a question of perspective rather than of absoluteness.

Level-based: Characters must be a minimum of 2nd level to be eligible to join Neric's Avengers.

Joining the Avengers

Application: Any character of at least 2nd level and of Lawful alignment may apply to join Neric's Avengers. Neric's Avengers do not distinguish between male and female characters, nor is racial stock important.

Invitation: Any Lawful character of at least 2nd level may be invited to join Neric's Avengers by a member of Cap-

Table 2.1 – Neric's Avengers Advancement

Grade (Rank)	Prerequisites	XP Cost	Benefits Gained
Private (1)	2nd-level character, deed, Lawful	0	Fraternity, Income, Upkeep
Senior Private (2)	3rd-level character, survive one battle or assignment	500	Bonus feat
Corporal (3)	4th-level character, Diplomacy, Leadership	1,000	Skill point
Sergeant (4)	6th-level character	1,500	Prestige class
Warrant Officer (5)	8th-level character	2,000	Bonus feat
Lieutenant (6)	10th-level character, Diplomacy 4 ranks, Leadership	2,500	Skill point
Captain (7)	12th-level character, successfully leading troops	3,000	
Major (8)	14th-level character	3,500	Bonus feat
Lt Colonel (9)	16th-level character, at least two classes	4,000	Skill point
Colonel (10)	18th-level character, Diplomacy 8 ranks	4,500	
Brigadier (11)	20th-level character, appointment to position	5,000	Bonus feat

Structure of an Army

A group of three or four soldiers makes up a squad. Three squads make up a section; three sections make a platoon. A platoon has one or two additional members in command of the rest. Four platoons make a company, again with some additional people in command and support functions. A company is about 140 soldiers. Four companies make a battalion, again with additional staff in the command post. Three battalions make a brigade, around 1,700 people including all the command and support staff. Beyond that, three brigades make a division and three divisions make an army (around 16,000 people).

tain rank or above. This will normally be as a result of observing the potential member performing an heroic deed during a combat in which the Avengers are involved. The character may even have been fighting for the other side.

Deed: Any character who applies for membership must back up his application by providing the tale of at least one heroic combat in which he took part. He does not need to have been on the winning side, merely to have excelled individually. The tale must be verifiable. Characters who are invited to join do not need to provide this information, as their nominators will do so.

Size and Scope

Neric's Avengers go where their work takes them, and they can be found anyplace, at any time. The group is the size of a modern-day brigade (around 1,700) and is large enough that it can, and does, take on more than one assignment at the same time. There is only one rule—at least one company (150 people) must be kept in reserve at the keep.

There are seven basic cadres in the Avengers. The first, and largest, is the infantry; known as Neric's Swords, they are all skilled warriors in close combat. The Swords may number up to 600 at any time (four overstrength companies), but not more than 150 of them will be found on the same assignment. Paladins and fighter characters who specialize in melee combat are suited to this cadre. Many of Neric's Swords began their adventuring careers as Golden Blades (a guild detailed earlier in this book).

The next largest cadre is the archers. Neric's Barbs are all skilled in the longbow, shortbow, and crossbow, as well as the use of larger weapons of war such as catapults. There are up to 300 Barbs at any time, but never more than 75 (two overstrength platoons) in any one place unless they are at the keep. Fighter characters who specialize in ranged combat are suited to this cadre.

Of similar size to the Barbs is the support cadre, Neric's Angels. There are no noncombatant members of the Avengers, so the Angels all have some fighting skills. Their primary role, however, is to provide medical aid, deliver messages to and from the battlefront, do the cooking, shoe the horses, sharpen swords, mend armor, repair or replace broken weapons, and keep the Barbs supplied with arrows and other missile weapons. There are eight overstrength platoons in the Angels, and at least one platoon deploys with any other Avengers unit on active duty. Of particular in-

terest to the other cadres, the Angels are also the paymasters for members on active duty. Priests, druids, and ex-bards are suitable character classes for this cadre, as are any characters who have the appropriate skills to be of use.

The Avengers' magical cadre, Neric's Arcane, are all combat wizards. They have few defensive spells and are best used to deliver ranged attacks into the enemy ranks in the form of multiple *fireballs* or *lightning bolts*. As wizards, they are not involved in the frontline fighting and are always protected by a number of infantry in the event the Avengers' position looks likely to be overrun. There are up to 200 Arcane at any time, formed into two slightly understrength companies. It is rare that more than two platoons (50 wizards) are deployed to the same battle. Character wizards may join the Arcane if they satisfy the level and deed requirements.

Neric's Eyes are the scouts of the Avengers. Alone among all the cadres, the Eyes are not formed into large units but operate in squads of no more than five. They mostly operate in threes, and occasionally alone. The Eyes set up forward observation posts, spy on enemy positions, sneak into enemy camps, and carry out assassinations of enemy commanders. There are up to 200 Eyes in the Avengers, commanded by a lieutenant colonel. There are eight light platoons, each platoon made up of eight squads of three and a lieutenant. Normally only one platoon will be present on any single assignment. The Eyes are an appropriate cadre for rangers, rogues, and monks.

The Avengers' cavalry regiment is known as Neric's Wings because of its speed into battle. The Wings are a small cadre of elite horsemen and more. Four understrength platoons make up a light company, although their elite status has led to them calling themselves a regiment. Two of the platoons are light horse, fast cavalry who use horsebows and light lances to harry an enemy force from the flanks. One platoon is heavy cavalry, riders of heavy warhorses with barding, who generally charge into the thickest concentration of enemy forces, with heavy lances and the weight of their mounts providing the impetus to smash a break in the line for the Swords to exploit. The fourth platoon is highly specialized, consisting of one section each of pegasus, griffon, and hippogriff riders. These flying units are used to strike behind enemy lines, into the heart of the command posts and other rear-echelon positions. Due to the nature of the different winged beasts, the airborne sections never deploy together, and rarely with the other platoons. It's one thing to have your griffon tear apart an enemy's horse for its supper but quite another to have it salivating over a companion's pegasus, or even a regular cavalry horse. With up to 100 members at any time, the Wings are a suitable cadre for fighters with riding skills (light or heavy cavalry), rangers or druids (light cavalry), or paladins (heavy cavalry). Other characters may join if they have the appropriate skills.

The elite of Neric's Avengers are the Blitz: two platoons of battle-hardened mercenaries whose job is to go in, smash the enemy, and either get out or hold the position for no more than half a day until other units arrive to take over. Members of the Blitz are at least 10th-level characters with a minimum of two classes. One of those classes must be fighter, ranger, or paladin. Most Blitz members have some magical ability, and some are specialist assassins. Members of the Blitz are

selected from within the ranks of the other cadres, never from new recruits. The minimum rank in the Blitz is warrant officer, the highest is major. Blitz members often refuse promotion, as it would mean they may have to move to another cadre. As the Blitz is open only to existing Avengers, it is left to the GM and players to decide which characters are suitable for this elite unit.

Table 2.2 – Avengers' Income

Grade	Monthly Wage	% per Person*	% per Rank
Private	5 gp	0.02	20
Senior Private	10 gp	0.05	15
Corporal	15 gp	0.06	10
Sergeant	20 gp	0.13	6
Warrant Officer	25 gp	0.16	9
Lieutenant	30 gp	0.20	13
Captain	35 gp	0.33	4
Major	40 gp	0.42	5
Lt Colonel	45 gp	0.58	3.5
Colonel	50 gp	0.83	2.5
Brigadier	55 gp	2.00	2
Avengers War Chest	n/a	n/a	10

*Although the percentage is small, the actual amount may be significant if an enemy castle or ship is captured, as these can be worth thousands of gold.

Guild Structure & Advancement

Neric's Avengers is structured as any combat unit of brigade strength. The commander of Neric's Avengers is a one-star general, or brigadier. Below the general are three full colonels, each of whom commands a battalion, but the make-up of the battalion varies from assignment to assignment. Each colonel has two lieutenant colonels to assist in planning and executing operations. Company commanders are majors, with a captain to help out. Platoons are led by lieutenants or sometimes warrant officers, with a sergeant as the second-in-command (2IC). Sections are led by corporals and squads by senior privates.

All new recruits to the Avengers start as privates, no matter what level character they are. Advancement is a combination of survival, skill acquisition, and spending XP. The requirements are summarized in the table below; the stats listed are minimums. Advancement may not always be available, even if a character satisfies all the requirements. It is possible to have a 20th-level character who is still a corporal, and members of the Blitz may choose not to be promoted above major as they don't wish to move to another cadre. On the other hand, all the promotion requirements can be adjusted to allow lower-level characters to fill high positions if the Avengers take such heavy casualties in a battle that no remaining members qualify for promotion.

Promotion to senior private is automatic upon reaching 3rd level and on successful survival of the first major battle (field promotion), or first assignment if there are no major battles for the recruit to be involved in.

Making corporal requires survival of a major battle or significant assignment, at least one rank in Diplomacy, and at least four levels in total.

Sergeant's stripes come with experience in battle. To be promoted to sergeant, an Avenger must have at least six levels in total.

The warrant officer is the most senior of the noncommissioned personnel. Warrants are issued by the brigadier when a sergeant makes 8th level and the character spends the required XP.

Lieutenant's bars are the indication of a junior officer, who may represent the Avengers from time to time in negotiations. Lieutenants are authorized to accept assignments on behalf of their cadre and must therefore have at least four ranks in Diplomacy. As leaders they must have taken the Leadership feat. Lieutenants are minimum 10th-level characters.

Captain's pips are earned by leading the troops into battle and bringing at least most of them out alive. This experience is demonstrated by the character being at least 12th level.

The major's crown is the penultimate step for most members, there being few positions above this rank. It requires the attainment of 14th level.

The Silver Sword is the symbol of the lieutenant colonel, of which there are only six at any time. This is the highest rank that any member should ever expect to reach, as there are only four members with higher rank. To reach these dizzying heights a character must have at least two classes and 16 levels or more, and there must be a position available. Given the nature of battle, the last requirement is usually not long in coming.

The Crossed Swords of a full colonel represent the officers who lead major forces in all-out wars. These three exalted personages are seldom seen at minor skirmishes such as the cleaning out of a nest of orcs or goblins. They have general control over 500 or more troops and use their years of experience to plan battle strategies to maximize the chance of success and to minimize their own casualties. Full colonels must have at least eight ranks in Diplomacy and be 18th-level characters. Colonels are authorized to enter into any contract on behalf of the Avengers. There must be a suitable vacant colonel's position for the member to fill.

The full weight of command falls on the brigadier. In regular military service, promotion to this level is at the discretion of the politicians. In a mercenary outfit this is clearly not the case. Neric's Avengers are all Lawful characters, which makes selecting the brigadier less difficult than it might otherwise be. When the current brigadier wishes to retire, the brigadier and the three colonels meet to reach consensus on who will succeed to the command position. If the vacancy is as a result of the death of the brigadier, the three colonels decide among themselves.

Benefits

Bonus Feats: Due to the intensive training regimen of the Avengers, members become quite skilled at performing special maneuvers in combat. At the level of senior private and every three ranks after that an Avenger gains a bonus feat. These feats should bear a relation to the character's cadre: Swords may choose combat feats, Wings riding feats, and so on.

Fraternity: Since members of the Avengers rarely travel alone, any Avenger who is cornered in a bar fight or dark alley, or who needs assistance of any kind (including on the battlefield), can call for aid, which will arrive in 1d3

rounds of combat. The number of Avengers who arrive to help is two times the member's grade in the outfit.

Income: There are eleven grades in Neric's Avengers, each corresponding to a military rank. Members are paid 5 gp times their grade per month as a base salary and also receive a percentage of the spoils of war from all battles the Avengers are in. These amounts are shown in Table 2.2.

Prestige Class: On reaching the rank of Sergeant, a character has the option of taking the prestige class of Avenger (see Appendix B for details).

Skill Points: When not engaged on a mission, Neric's Avengers can be found at the keep, where they practice their skills for six to eight hours a day, six days a week. As a result of this rigorous training, Avengers receive an extra skill point at each third grade (Corporal, Lieutenant, Lieutenant Colonel), which must be spent on a skill appropriate to their training regimes. Neric's Avengers often spend these points in Diplomacy, which they have learned to use in battle to better command troops. See Appendix B for details on using the Diplomacy skill in this manner.

Upkeep: As long as a character is a member of Neric's Avengers, his upkeep is covered from consolidated funds and need not be paid out of the character's pocket, other than alcohol and entertainment. This upkeep includes equipment repairs and/or replacement and all healing magic, as well as *remove curse* and *remove disease* if required. For officers, it also includes one *raise dead* per year. It does not include *resurrection*. For cavalry members, it includes nonexotic mounts.

Disadvantages

Exclusivity: Members of Neric's Avengers may not join any other organization while they remain members of the Avengers. If they are already members of another organization, this membership must be terminated when they join the Avengers. The only exception to this is the family unit, where membership is by blood and is for life. Avengers may decline to participate in an operation, direct or indirect, against their own family units but must otherwise do as ordered.

Neutrality: All Avengers are, and must be seen to be, totally disinterested in any racial, national, or political activity that may be behind their current assignment.

Affiliations

None. Neric's Avengers are professional soldiers who work for the person paying the bills. Long-term affiliation with any organization is bad for business.

Leaving the Guild

With Permission: A character who wishes to leave Neric's Avengers may submit his resignation to the brigadier, endorsed by his cadre commander with a recommendation to accept or reject the resignation. If the resignation is accepted, the character turns over the Avenger's tabard, receives any payments owed, and is sent on his way. All benefits of membership except for extra feats, skill points, and Avenger prestige class levels are lost to the character when he leaves. Characters cannot advance in the Avenger class if they are not active members of the Avengers. The member's rank is transferred to the reserve list and he may re-

join the Avengers at a later time if he so chooses. If he was a commissioned officer (lieutenant or higher), he may not be able to rejoin at his old rank if there are no positions available, and may have to accept a lower rank in this case.

Without Permission: If the resignation is not accepted or the member simply leaves without asking, all benefits of membership except those gained from the Avenger class and extra feats and skill points are lost and the character is listed as a deserter. If the deserter is ever captured by the Avengers, a court-martial is sure to follow. The best the character can hope for is dishonorable discharge with forfeiture of accumulated pay. If the desertion was during a battle, the sentence will be death. A dishonorably discharged character can never rejoin the Avengers.

Expulsion: Expulsion from Neric's Avengers is unlikely, but possible. If a character undergoes an alignment change, willing or not, that makes him no longer Lawful, he cannot remain in the outfit. If the change is the result of a curse which the Angels cannot remove, membership may be suspended for up to one year while the character attempts to have the curse removed.

Members may also be expelled from the Avengers for gross insubordination or other breaches of military etiquette. Since only Lawful characters can join in the first place, disobeying an order or being insubordinate to a superior is going outside alignment restrictions. A court-martial followed by dishonorable discharge is the likely outcome. This means the ceremonial shredding of the member's tabard and forfeiture of accumulated pay. Expelled Avengers can never rejoin.

Avenger Profiles

Brigadier Gareth Silvier - Male human Fighter 14/Cleric 4/Rogue 2: CR 20; Medium-size humanoid (human); HD 14d10+4d8+2d6+60; hp 176; Init +2, Spd 20 ft.; AC 28 (touch 14, flat-footed 27); Atk +26/+26/+16/+11 melee (1d8+9/19-20/x2, long sword +4) or +21/+16/+11/+6 ranged (1d8+1/19-20 x2, repeating crossbow +1); SA spells; SQ none; Al LG; SV Fort +16, Ref +12, Will +9; Str 16, Dex 14, Con 16, Int 11, Wis 12, Cha 17.

Skills and Feats (ability mods included): Climb +10, Concentration +6, Craft (Armorsmith) +2, Craft (weaponsmith) +4, Diplomacy +11, Gather Information +6, Handle Animal +7, Intimidate + 5, Jump +6, Knowledge (religion) +4, Listen + 8, Move Silently + 3, Ride + 13, Search +9, Spot +10, Swim +8; Alertness, Blind-Fight, Cleave, Combat Casting, Combat Reflexes, Endurance, Great Cleave, Improved Bullrush, Improved Critical (longsword), Leadership, Lightning Reflexes, Mounted Combat, Power Attack, Ride-By Attack, Track, Two-Weapon Fighting, Weapon Focus (longsword), Weapon Specialization (longsword).

Cleric Spells (5/5+1/3+1); Deity God of Justice/War/Valor; Domains War, Law: 0—*detect magic, detect poison, light, read magic, virtue;* 1st—*bless, command, invisibility to undead, magic weapon, protection from evil, remove fear;* 2nd—*bull's strength, hold person, lesser restoration, spiritual weapon.*

Possessions: Repeating crossbow +1, full plate +3, spiked gauntlet +1, longsword +4, ring of protection +2, small steel shield +3.

Brigadier Silvier is a serious-looking man in his mid-forties. He has blond hair and piercing blue eyes.

that seem to cut right through whatever they are focused on at the time. He has a lot of weight on his shoulders as commanding officer of the Avengers, and although he tries to keep a neutral expression at all times, it's hard to do when so many lives are in your hands. The Brigadier is a tall man with "presence." He automatically takes the center of attention wherever he is, just by his personal magnetism.

He cares about only a few things in life and nothing else. First is the destruction of tyranny and oppression wherever he finds it. These are things associated with chaos and must not be tolerated. Second are the mercenaries under his command. He feels each and every casualty as though the death were his own, and he cares very much for the well-being of his people. His third priority is his successor. He really wants to be Gareth Silvier, husband and father (he has a wife and two children whom he seldom sees), but he is concerned that Cromarty might become Brigadier, and Cromarty cares little for the well-being of his troops. Brigadier Silvier has decided to remain in the job until he is convinced Cromarty won't sacrifice people needlessly or that one of the other colonels will get the top job.

Fighter (Sword) Colonel Cromarty - Male dwarf Fighter 6/Avenger 7/Cleric 3/Rogue 3: CR 19; Medium-size humanoid (dwarf); HD 13d10+3d8+3d6+76; hp 185; Init +1, Spd 20 ft.; AC 26 (touch 15, flat-footed 25); Atk +25/+20/+15/+10 melee (1d8+7/x3, battleaxe +4) or +19/+14/+9/+4 ranged (hand axe +1); SA spells; SQ dwarf abilities, cleric abilities, rogue abilities, Avenger abilities; Al LE; SV Fort +15, Ref +9, Will +13; Str 16, Dex 12, Con 18, Int 10, Wis 14, Cha 12.

Skills and Feats: Climb +12, Concentration +7, Craft (gem-cutting) +1, Diplomacy +10, Gather Information +6, Handle Animal +3, Knowledge (arcana) +1, Knowledge (history) +2, Move Silently +5, Open Lock +5, Pickpocket +7, Ride + 2, Search +4, Spot +5, Use Magic Device +2; Cleave, Combat Casting, Endurance, Great Cleave, Improved Critical (battleaxe), Iron Will, Leadership, Power Attack, Sunder, Weapon Focus (battleaxe), Weapon Specialization (battleaxe).

Special Qualities: Avenger abilities — Avenge Wrong, Damage Reduction (3), Determination, Overcome Odds, Tenacity, Vengeful Focus, Willpower. Dwarf abilities.

Cleric Spells (4/4+1/3+1); God of Death; Domains Death, Evil. 0 — *detect magic, light, resistance, virtue;* 1st — *bane, cause fear, command, doom, protection from good;* 2nd — *death knell, hold person, silence, sound burst.*

Possessions: *battleaxe +4, small steel shield +3, hand axe +1, dwarven plate +3.*

Colonel Cromarty is a wizened, battle-hardened dwarf. He is about as wide as he is tall (4'1") and has a barrel chest that would win him first place in most contests of strength if he had the time or inclination to enter such things.

As a former Sword, Cromarty understands the mind of the warrior and knows how best to use it. He has little time for arcane magic (though he respects its power) and believes battles are won by the spilling of blood. He's not overly concerned if the blood of his troops is mixed with the blood of the enemy, as long as the job gets done. Cromarty wants the job of Brigadier, and if the current Brigadier were to leave or die, Cromarty is clearly the right choice for the job. No matter how much he wants the job, however, he is fiercely loyal to the ideals of the Avengers and would never consider plotting Silvier's demise. After all, humans live but a heartbeat, dwarves for much longer. Cromarty can afford to wait.

Despite his evil nature, Cromarty is a potent ally in battle and a fast friend to those few who become his friend. Most who get close to him end up dead when he sends them on missions with high casualty expectations. This is not deliberate on his part; he simply sends those he trusts the most on the missions with the most danger in order to maximize the chance of success.

Wizard (Arcane) Colonel Weelow Sumguid - Female human Wizard 18/Fighter 2: CR 20; Medium-size humanoid (human); HD 18d4+2d10+20; hp 90; Init +3, Spd 30

ft.; AC 26 (touch 18, flat-footed 23); Atk +15/+10/+5 melee (1d8+4/19-20/x2, long sword +3) or +16/+11/+6 (1d4+5/19-20 x2 dagger +4) or +14/+9/+4 ranged (no preferred weapon); SA spells; SQ wizard abilities; Al LN; SV Fort +9, Ref +12, Will +12; Str 13, Dex 16, Con 12, Int 16, Wis 12, Cha 12.

Skills and Feats: Alchemy +15, Concentration +11, Craft (calligraphy) +8, Diplomacy +9, Gather Information +6, Intimidate + 3, Knowledge (arcana) +12, Knowledge (nature) +8, Knowledge (religion) +7, Knowledge (the planes) +13, Ride [horse] + 12, Scry +11, Search +6, Sense Motive +6, Speak Language (Draconic), Speak Language (Gnoll), Speak Language (Infernal), Spellcraft +9, Spot +4, Swim +8; Blind-Fight, Combat Casting, Empower Spell, Enlarge Spell, Extend Spell, Great Fortitude, Heighten Spell, Improved Critical (longbow), Maximize Spell, Scribe Scroll, Silent Spell, Spell Focus (evocation), Spell Mastery (GM's choice), Spell Penetration.

Familiar: Hawk (golden), HD 18, AC 26, HP 35, Spd 10, Atk +16/+11/+6 (1d4−2 claws)

Wizard Spells (5/6/6/6/5/5/5): 0—*any*; 1st—*burning hands, enlarge, feather fall, magic missile, magic weapon, reduce, shocking grasp, Tenser's floating disk*; 2nd—*cat's grace, darkvision, flaming sphere, shatter*; 3rd—*fireball, gust of wind, invisibility sphere, lightning bolt, magic circle against chaos, tongues, wind wall*; 4th—*remove curse, wall of fire, wall of ice, shadow conjuration*; 5th—*cone of cold, hold monster, shadow evocation, teleport, transmute mud to rock, transmute rock to mud, wall of force*; 6th—*antimagic field, Bigby's forceful hand, chain lightning, control weather, disintegrate, flesh to stone, globe of invulnerability, greater shadow evocation, Otiluke's freezing sphere, stone to flesh.*

Possessions: *longsword +3, dagger +4, chain shirt +4, ring of protection +5.*

Weelow is a slight woman of indeterminate age with a hawkish nose and a shrill voice that is often compared (behind her back) to the cry of her hawk familiar. She is a wizard and leader through and through but has no time for the politics of the upper echelon. Weelow harbors no desire to take the Brigadier job, now or ever. She is first and foremost a wizard, and little else matters to her. Rising through the ranks of the Arcane she used her abilities to lay low multiple enemies with each spell, and to pick out the opposition leaders and surgically remove them with precisely targeted magic that harmed nobody else.

The life if an archmage is not an easy one, and few humans live long enough to learn how to wield the most powerful of spells. Weelow is one of those few, but it has taken a toll on her. She is more than 60 years old but seems much younger due to the magic she has used to keep herself fit and able-bodied. The use of these powers is not something she can continue indefinitely, and she is aware that her time is running short. There are no regrets in her mind, though. She has accomplished what so few do in their lives—leaving her mark on the world, making a difference to the lives of people she never met.

The only thing Weelow wants to see resolved is the succession to the position of commander. She is aware of Cromarty's coveting the job and is also aware that Silvier wants to retire but does not want Cromarty to take the reins. She is firmly committed to following Silvier's wishes in this matter as in all others. He is the leader and his word is law as far as she is concerned. What she does not have is a solution, as Colonel Notarbuth would not be an acceptable leader from the perspective of most outsiders. While the opin-

ions of outsiders do not generally concern the Avengers, the way the Brigadier is viewed translates directly into contracts. Weelow will gladly take any person under her personal patronage if she believes that person would be a suitable candidate for the position of Brigadier.

Apart from her nose and voice, Weelow is almost boringly average in appearance—about five and a half feet tall, 120 pounds, with tight blonde curls tinged with gray and emerald-green eyes. She is living proof that in at least some cases size does not matter.

Priest (Angels) Colonel Quincy Notarbuth – Male half-orc Cleric 16/Avenger 4: CR 20; Medium-size humanoid (half-orc); HD 16d8+4d10+20; hp 128; Init +2, Spd 30 ft.; AC 22 (touch 15, flat-footed 20); Atk +22/+17/+12/+7 melee (1d8+6/x2, morning star +5) or +18/+13/+8/+3 ranged (no preferred weapon); SA spells; SQ cleric abilities, Avenger abilities, half-orc abilities; Al LN; SV Fort +12, Ref +8, Will +21; Str 12, Dex 14, Con 12, Int 15, Wis 20, Cha 10.

Skills and Feats: Climb +4, Concentration +9, Diplomacy +12, Gather Information +1, Heal +18, Knowledge (arcana) +10, Knowledge (religion) +13, Listen +9, Profession (apothecary) +13, Profession (herbalist) +13, Ride [horse] +7, Search +7, Speak Language (Draconic), Speak Language (Giant), Spellcraft +5, Spot +9, Swim +6, Use Rope +5, Wilderness Lore +9; Combat Casting, Endurance, Iron Will, Leadership, Maximize Spell, Skill Focus (diplomacy), Spell Penetration, Track.

Special Qualities: Avenger abilities—Avenge Wrong, Damage Reduction (1), Determination, Tenacity, Willpower.

Cleric Spells; half-orc abilities—Darkvision, Orc Blood. (6/7+1/6+1/6+1/5+1/5+1/3+1/2+1/2+1); Deity Wisdom/Truth; Domains Law, Strength: 0—*create water, detect magic, detect poison, guidance, light, read magic, resistance*; 1st—*bless, command, detect undead, divine favor, entropic shield, obscuring mist, protection from chaos, remove fear, sanctuary*; 2nd—*bull's strength (x2), calm emotions, hold person, lesser restoration, silence, spiritual weapon*; 3rd—*daylight, dispel magic (x2), magic vestment, negative energy protection, prayer, searing light*; 4th—*freedom of movement, neutralize poison, order's wrath, restoration, status, tongues*; 5th—*break enchantment, dispel chaos, flame strike, greater command, insect plague, raise dead*; 6th—*blade barrier, heal, stoneskin, word of recall*; 7th—*dictum, grasping hand, repulsion, summon monster VII*; 8th—*clenched fist, mass heal, shield of law.*

Possessions: *Morningstar +5, chain shirt +3, ring of protection +3, ring of counterspells, rod of lordly might, rod of thunder.*

Colonel Quincy, as he prefers to be known, has a penchant for showy clothes. His detractors, and there are many outside the ranks of the Avengers, believe this is an attempt to divert attention from his origins, but this is simply not true. The tall, heavily built half-orc has the symbol of his god carved into his tusks, making his smile a most frightening thing for the armies of undead he frequently faces.

Like most half-orcs, Quincy is a bit rough around the edges. He has learned many of the ways of civilization and can practice them when it suits him, but other than formal gatherings with outsiders it almost never suits him to affect the airs and graces he sees as a waste of time. This makes him both uninterested and unsuitable when it comes to deciding who will be the next Brigadier.

His strength lies in his faith, and when the mission involves the armies of the afterlife Quincy is the one who leads the Avengers into battle, blasting those who stand before him to dust with the power of his divine aura. This habit has led to the Avengers sometimes taking heavier casualties than they might expect under his command because the divine power lasts for only so long, and only against those opponents who are not alive yet not quite dead either. A few years ago, when Quincy was a lieutenant colonel, there was a rival mercenary band who dressed many of their number in grotesque masks so as to resemble zombies, knowing Quincy would be sent to deal with them and knowing his power would be useless against living opponents. Fortunately for both Quincy and the Avengers, the rival band neglected to take into account that Quincy's mace was just as effective against live targets as against undead. Since that incident, Quincy has been careful to use his abilities to determine that the enemies really are undead before he attempts to destroy them.

As he is unable to conceal his origins, Quincy has decided to take pride in them and remove the chance for others to be hurtful by remarking on his appearance. Apart from the holy symbol on his tusks, he also keeps his jet-black hair as unkempt as is possible while sticking to regulation length. His eyes are the normal orcish pink, but his mother's genes are strong in him and he does not suffer any ill effects from the daylight. He is a little uncomfortable in very bright light and has a set of smoked glass lenses he can put over his eyes on especially bright days to cut down the glare. Quincy is the reigning champion at arm wrestling in the Avengers.

Ranger (Blitz) Captain Ilana Liveoak – Female half-elf Ranger 9/Druid 5: CR 14; Medium-size humanoid (half-elf); HD 9d10+5d8+14; hp 97; Init +2, Spd 30 ft.; AC 17 (touch 15, flat-footed 15); Atk +15(+16)/+9(+10)/+5 (+6) melee (1d6+4/18-20/x2, scimitar +2(1d4+4/19-20/x2 dagger +3) or +14/+9/+4 ranged (no preferred weapon); SA spells; SQ druid abilities, ranger abilities, half-elf abilities; Al LN; SV Fort +11, Ref +6, Will +9; Str 14, Dex 15, Con 12, Int 12, Wis 14, Cha 14.

Skills and Feats: Animal Empathy +5, Climb +8, Craft (bowyer) +3, Diplomacy +8, Handle Animal +9, Heal +5, Hide +8, Intuit Direction +6, Knowledge (nature) +6, Listen +9, Move Silently +8, Ride [horse] +6, Search +9, Speak Language (Celestial), Spellcraft +2, Spot + 10, Swim +8, Wilderness Lore +8; Improved Two-Weapon Fighting, Leadership, Mounted Combat, Track, Weapon Focus (scimitar), Weapon Focus (dagger).

Special Qualities: Half-elf abilities—Immunity to *sleep* spells and similar magical effects; +2 saving throw bonus against Enchantment spells or effects; Low-light Vision; +1 bonus to Listen, Search, and Spot checks; Elven Blood.

Druid Spells (5/4/3/1): 0—*detect magic, detect poison, flare, light, read magic*; 1st—*calm animals, detect snares and pits, entangle, pass without trace*; 2nd—*barkskin, chill metal, speak with animals*; 3rd—*call lightning*.

Ranger Spells (2/1): 1st—*delay poison, resist elements*; 2nd—*sleep*.

Possessions: *Scimitar +2, dagger +3*, masterwork leather, *ring of protection +3, ring of animal friendship, ring of sustenance, potion of fire breath*, multiple *cure light* and *cure serious* potions.

Though only half elven, Ilana Liveoak is more like a typically beautiful elven woman in that surreal way that elves are beautiful to nonelves. Her mother's genes are clearly apparent in the looks department. She is also a thoroughly competent scout and tracker who is totally in touch with her surroundings.

Like most rangers and druids, Ilana is most comfortable above ground, under the trees. She is also able to follow a band of marauders through catacombs or even a crowded city market. The animals and plants are her friends, wherever she may be.

As Captain (and second in command) of the Blitz, Ilana is a shock trooper, a leader in the special forces. She is strong and brave, and sets a high standard for her troops to follow. While many of her section are not in touch with nature, they all know that Ilana is, just as she is aware of the strengths and weaknesses of the 68 members nominally under her command. Missions involving Ilana's personal touch usually involve no more than four or five of the Blitz, and they have a reputation for getting the job done.

Ilana wears leather armor. As a former Barb she prefers the longbow over other weapons, but her druid oath now prevents her using it. She is skilled in the Florentine style of fighting and can wield a blade in each hand with deadly precision should the need arise. The nature of Blitz missions is such that the need often arises.

Ilana's flashing blades, her unearthly beauty, and the lightning bolt on her tabard inspire those around her to lift themselves to a new level of fighting spirit. It doesn't matter if it's her own Blitz troops or soldiers of the line, she inspires all to achieve the impossible.

Captain Liveoak has brown hair and eyes, stands 5'7", and weighs in at 129 pounds. Her one vice is a determination to not reach 130 pounds, so she sticks to a tight training regimen. This striking woman is a scant 28 years old. A staunch ally and fearsome foe, Ilana Liveoak could well be Brigadier someday, if she can be convinced to move on from her beloved Blitz.

Platoon (Barb) Lieutenant Quillin Amenia – Male elf Fighter 8/Cleric 2: CR 10; Medium-size humanoid (elf); HD 8d10+2d8+10; hp 72; Init +4 (Dex), Spd 30 ft.; AC 18 (touch 14, flat-footed 14); Atk +11/+6 melee (1d8+4/19-20/x2, long sword +2) or +13/+8 ranged (1d8+2/x2 longbow +2); SA spells; SQ cleric abilities, fighter abilities, elf abilities; Al LG; SV Fort +10, Ref +6, Will +5; Str 14, Dex 18, Con 12, Int 11, Wis 11, Cha 12.

Skills and Feats: Climb +9, Craft (bowyer) +4, Diplomacy +5, Ride [horse] +10, Swim +7; Dodge, Far Shot, Leadership, Mounted Archery, Mounted Combat, Point Blank Shot, Precise Shot, Rapid Shot, Weapon Focus (longbow), Weapon Focus (longsword), Weapon Specialization (longbow).

Special Qualities: Elven abilities—Immunity to *sleep* spells and similar magical effects; +2 saving throw bonus against Enchantment spells or effects; Low-light Vision; +1 bonus to Listen, Search, and Spot checks; Elven Blood.

Cleric Spells (4/2+1); Deity God of Chivalry/Honor; Domains Law, Good: 0—*detect magic, guidance, light, resistance*;1st—*bless, command, protection from evil*.

Possessions: *Longsword +2, longbow +2*, masterwork chain shirt.

Amenia is the archetypical elven archer. He can fire arrows faster than the eye can follow his hand movements, or at least that's how it seems to most people. Of course, this is not really true, but it's a myth Quillin is willing to let alone. In his mind, anything that brings him to the notice of senior Avengers, and one senior Avenger in particular, is a good thing. Quillin is totally smitten with the half-elven Blitz Captain Ilana Liveoak and will do anything within the rules to be noticed by her. Currently, she's barely aware of his existence, since he's not a Blitz himself. Should anything ever come of it, Quillin could never join the Blitz while Ilana is still in it, as Avenger standing orders prohibit fraternization with others in the same chain of command.

Affairs of the heart aside, Quillin is an accomplished archer and is the current Barb champion target shooter at all ranges over which the longbow is contested. He is tall and slender for an elf, 5'7" and 126 pounds. Like all elves, he seems ageless to nonelves, but is 124 years old. Quillin loves his work in the Avengers, and he cares deeply for the well-being of his platoon. Each and every one of his troopers is like a child to him; he feels their pain as his own, and the loss of one of his own hurts him deeply.

Quillin's divine abilities are almost totally directed toward the preservation of life, especially the lives of his platoon, innocent bystanders, and other Avengers. He does not have enough divinely granted powers yet to make much of a difference, but many Barbs and more than a few Avengers from other cadres are alive today because Quillin was able to save them from the reaper when they fell on the battlefield.

Your Campaign

Neric's Avengers have been designed to be the focal point of a campaign. All PCs should be members of the Avengers, and the GM can structure adventures around the missions undertaken by the various groups. The size of the Avengers allows for full-blown battles to be run if that's how your campaign works. For smaller campaigns, use only the cadres, or parts of cadres, you want or need. For even smaller campaigns, Neric's Blitz can be run as though it were the entire Avengers group, and the GM can set the missions accordingly. Adjusting the minimum level requirements is recommended if you choose this option, as there is no longer an elite group within the Avengers for PCs to aspire to. If your players are not interested in joining the Avengers, the group can be used as an adversary, or the party may even be able to hire the guild to do its own dirty work.

Adventure Hooks

- The party members are sent by their liege to travel to the Avengers' keep and hire the Avengers to come break a dire siege on their home town. The party must travel swiftly and evade a number of powerful pursuers.
- An evil tyrant has hired the Avengers to guarantee the oppression of his subjects. The PCs cannot counter the force, but they may try to somehow convince the Avengers to refuse the assignment.
- The Avengers have been hired by a small kingdom to rid it of marauding bands, and the PCs are part of the contingent sent to handle the job. The king and his advisers do not know the make-up of the marauders, only that they are raiding farmland, killing farmers, and stealing livestock. This is bad for the

economy and for the public image of the king. The marauders are not stupid and will not face a well armed band of mercenaries head-on if they can help it. They will try to ambush the PCs, concentrating missile fire (and magic if they have it) on one or two PCs. Once the numbers are more to their liking (six to one or better), the marauders will go for the head-on approach to wipe out the rest.

Variations

Neric's Avengers is a large organization, possibly too large for some purposes. There are enough NPC pro formas to allow you to choose any one of them as the commanding officer and to resize the cadres accordingly. If your campaign is appropriate for it, the Blitz can be the entire mercenary company.

Neric's Avengers can also be used as an adversary for your campaign players. As a mercenary outfit, they recruit to fill vacancies left by casualties and in that way are a foe who never runs low on numbers. If you choose to use the Avengers in this way, you should limit membership to Lawful Neutral and Lawful Evil NPCs unless your players have Evil characters.

Roshanta Trading Guild

The Roshanta Trading Guild has grown from an older, less formal merchant association. It was originally founded by the wealthy merchants of the Roshanta family. The family no longer exists, but the guild still keeps the name.

In the past 75 years, the members of the Roshanta Trading Guild have become increasingly wealthy and powerful. The guild covers the territory of several independent states that should be located adjacent to one another on your campaign map. These states are referred to by the guild as the Trade Union of Roshanta, or simply the Union, even though there is no official political connection between the territories. Members of the guild may trade freely within the Union, and any merchant from outside who wishes to sell his goods in the Union states may do so only through members of the Roshanta Trading Guild.

The guild has a strong influence over the politics and control of the various states in the Union. In some instances, the ruling families of the states are effectively powerless, and the real authority lies with the Board of Syndics that runs the guild.

Guild members are called "shareholders"; in order to become a member of the guild, a merchant must buy at least one guild share. Guild shares are bought and sold among members, and advancement within the guild is based on the number of guild shares a member has. For obvious reasons, this tends to be the member with the most influence and wealth within the guild. The person with the most guild shares becomes the Chairman of the Board of Syndics.

All merchant ventures undertaken by guild members are taxed by the guild. At the end of each year, the guild's proceeds for the year are divided equally by the number of existing guild shares and meted out to the shareholders. Therefore, a member with four guild shares will get four times as much return as someone with a single guild share.

Roshanta

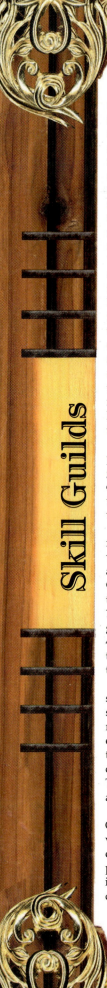

Purpose

Sharing: The primary reason the Roshanta Trading guild exists is to provide financial opportunities to its members. In the early years of the guild's existence, the members shared trade intelligence and helped fund trading ventures to far-off lands in search of exotic and expensive goods and lucrative markets. This continues today, only in a much more formalized way. Senior members remain a source of valuable information on the customs and cultures of other lands, what goods to buy and sell, where to buy and sell them, and how to deal with foreign powers and thieves of all sorts (official and unofficial). However, the funding of mercantile ventures has evolved into a much more complex arrangement than the mere lending or borrowing of money.

It is often the case that, because of his experience and contacts throughout the region, word of a trading opportunity reaches the ears of a senior guild member. This member (or consortium of senior members) determines the potential value of the venture and then offers shares in the venture to other guild members. These shares will be traded back and forth, rising or falling in value as the market sees fit. If there are any trade shares left after the first two days, the remainder are offered for sale to the general populace. Speculation on trade caravans has taken the place of most forms of gambling, and many vices, within the Union. Instead, the citizens risk their money on the trade caravans that leave and return.

Of course, the value of a trade share may rise, so that a person might pay 3 gp 5 sp for a share originally sold for 1 gp. The original selling price of the shares is used to purchase trade goods, hire labor, and finance the journey. Once the caravan returns and sells its goods, the venture is wound up and profits are distributed to all shareholders.

Every caravan must have a Roshanta Trading Guild member in charge. Junior members are most often the ones who actually accompany a venture, since they can rarely afford more than a few trade shares, and the position of Caravan Master provides a 10% share at no cost. The returns offered by ventures can be spectacular, as much as 10:1. That is, for each gold piece outlaid, the return is 10 gp. More often, the return is somewhere between 2:1 and 4:1. For a venture with an initial outlay of 10,000 gp, a return of 20,000 gp is considered marginally acceptable, although a return of 40,000 gp is naturally much better.

However, some ventures are failures, and the venture shareholders lose all of their money. There have even been several occasions when the cost of the venture has been more than the initial outlay, meaning the return was 1:2, or even 1:3. This normally happens when circumstances along the caravan's route change unexpectedly. The principal causes of failures are warfare and incursions by monsters. Thus ventures are insured, spreading the risk of failure across many more shareholders.

Protection: Another purpose of the Roshanta Trading Guild is the regulation of commerce in the Union to provide its craftsmen with the opportunity to sell the product of their labors for a reasonable profit without unfair competition from foreigners. It is also meant to provide its citizens with the opportunity to purchase quality merchandise at reasonable prices and allow each city-state to gather a just proportion of the wealth generated by trade as taxes.

Economic/Control: In reality, the Roshanta Trading Guild has become an oligopoly, preventing competition from foreigners and safeguarding the wealth and opportunities of its shareholders. With wealth comes political power and control of the means of generating yet more wealth.

Membership

Location: Membership in the guild is restricted to citizens of the Union area. In the past fifty years, shares have been passed down from parent to child. These days, it is very rare for anyone not born in the Union to be granted membership in the guild. Citizens of any class, race, and gender can become members.

Family: Only one member of a single family may be a shareholder in the guild. However, because of the ambiguous definition of the word "family", there are uncles, aunts, cousins, and even half-sibling shareholders.

Wealth: The cost of maintaining membership and of improving the character's position is quite considerable.

Joining the Guild

Obtaining membership in the Roshanta Trading Guild is not easy, and it is very expensive. Although there are no restrictions on race, gender, class, or alignment, the applicant must have a considerable sum of ready cash. Other means of obtaining support are also useful—and used. Blackmail, family connections, favors called in, and favors promised are all commonly employed to obtain membership.

Application: Those who want to join the Roshanta Trading Guild must apply to purchase shares in the guild. They must be supported in their bid by four members in good standing, and such support is often expensive to obtain. The approval of a majority of the Board of Syndics is required for the application to succeed. This usually entails a greater expense than that incurred in obtaining the support for the four supporting members because there are more of them. These financial inducements to the supporting members and Board of Syndics may run as high as 5,000 gp.

Citizenship: Applicants must be citizens of one of the city-states of the Union. If not born there, gaining membership in the guild is extremely difficult. The applicant will have to obtain (purchase) citizenship, and then convince (bribe) the officials to backdate the citizenship papers to some reasonable time in the past. This may cost the applicant as much as 3,000 gp.

Purchase: Once the application has been approved, the applicant must purchase one new share in the Roshanta Trading Guild, which has a reserve price of 1,000 gp. Only new members can purchase new guild shares; all other guild shares a character owns must be purchased from existing shareholders. There are currently 2,348 shares in the Roshanta Trading Guild. Each applicant must also pay a one-time subscription fee of 500 gp—to cover "administrative" costs of processing the application—and the requisite quarterly fee (as mentioned above) in advance.

Alignment: Although there are no alignment restrictions to membership, the prevailing attitudes of the membership are mostly Neutral to Neutral Evil (the selfish kind). The aim of every member of the Roshanta Trading Guild is to become as wealthy as possible, as quickly as possible.

Size and Scope

The Roshanta Trading Guild is limited to the member states of the Union. There are currently 258 members, but this can vary quite widely depending upon economic conditions both within and outside the Union. Apart from the harvest, the guild has the greatest economic impact upon the Union. Outside the Union it is not as influential, but it is still a force to be reckoned with.

Within the Union, guild members play an active role in governing the population. They regulate trade and restrict the flow of products coming from foreign lands. Most of the time this doesn't really affect the majority of people, who enjoy a good standard of living compared to some realms in that part of the world. The Union has a favorable climate, fertile soils, valuable natural resources adequate for the needs of the nation, and clever and industrious people. However, sometimes the restrictive practices of the guild cause some harm to the general population, especially when the practice prevents the adoption of new ideas or technology.

Trading ventures make use of ships, caravans of wagons, carts, and even pack animals. These caravans extend the influence of the guild far from the borders of the Union.

Guild Structure & Advancement

Graded (Shareholding): The Roshanta Trading Guild has several grades of membership. The grade of a member is based on the number of shares he owns.

In addition to the requirements listed in Table 2.3, certain grades have other restrictions for advancement. Candidates for the following positions must also meet these requirements:

Broker: Must have participated in at least five mercantile ventures and must have been Caravan Master of at least two of those ventures.

Banker: Must have 50,000 gp in investments, caravan shares, and ready cash. Must also purchase a banking license from the Trading Guild for 10,000 gp.

Chairman: The Chairman of the Board of Syndics is not a separate grade; he receives no additional benefits or disadvantages. The Chairman is simply the Syndic with the most Roshanta Trading Guild shares. The Chairman has the deciding vote should the Board be deadlocked in any decision.

Benefits

The overwhelming benefit of the Roshanta Trading Guild is that it can make a character very wealthy…if he can afford to keep up the pace until he reaches a position where he can afford to sit back and watch the money roll in. Prior to that time, the guild gives the character easy access to information and contacts that will help him throughout the region.

Access to Funds: The character has potential access to an almost unlimited amount of funds. To acquire these funds he must initiate a trading venture and issue trade shares for sale to guild members. An adventure into a dragon's lair or dungeon is not considered a trading venture and will not be financed.

Access to Information: Within the Union, a member can present himself at any Guild Hall (usually the most elaborate building in the center of every major town) and request information about the local area. The information will be given freely to members, whereas a nonmember would have to pay a steep price and would not receive a complete account. Members may find factors and Union merchants in other lands who will also assist with information, although this may cost a small amount.

Access to Skills: Upon joining the guild, the character counts the Diplomacy and Knowledge (business & finance) skills as class skills, regardless of his class.

Bonus Skills: At each grade above Shareholder, the character gains one free rank in Gather Information and in Profession (merchant).

Expanded Knowledge: When a character becomes a Syndic, he may purchase any one Knowledge skill as a class skill regardless of his actual class. Syndics receive one free rank in this skill.

Good Reputation: Within the Union, the member enjoys a good reputation. All reactions to the character receive an automatic shift of one place in his favor. Union factors and merchants met in other lands will also react more favorably to the character. Bankers and Syndics are met with considerable awe and respect within the Union. Even foreign merchants will treat a Banker with politeness, even if it is a little icy at times. The guild reinforces this by

Table 2.3 – Roshanta Trading Guild Advancement

Grade	Min. Shares	Prerequisites	XP Cost	Benefits Gained
Shareholder (1)	1	Appraise 1 rank, Diplomacy 1 rank, Knowledge (business & finance) 1 rank, Profession (merchant) 2 ranks; meet entry requirements	100	Access to funds, access to information, access to skills, Good Reputation, Income
Broker (2)	5	Appraise 3 ranks, Diplomacy 4 ranks, Gather Information 3 ranks; see advancement	200	Bonus skills
Banker (3)	50	Bluff 2 ranks, Diplomacy 6 ranks, Gather Information 5 ranks, Knowledge (business & finance) 3 ranks, Sense Motive 2 ranks; see advancement text	300	Bonus skills
Syndic (4)	150	Bluff 6 ranks, Diplomacy 10 ranks, Knowledge (business & finance) 3 ranks, Sense Motive 2 ranks	400	Bonus skills, expanded Knowledge
Chairman	151	As for Syndic; also see below	n/a	n/a

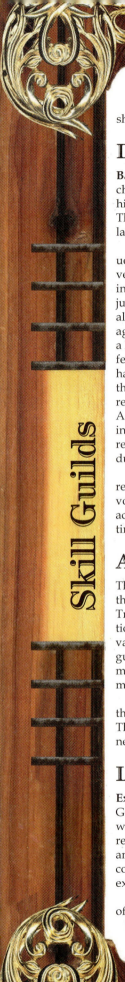

punitive economic punishment of realms that allow Bankers and Syndics to come to any harm.

Income: At the end of each year, each shareholder receives an amount of money equal to his percentage in the guild's profits, based on the number of guild shares he owns.

Disadvantages

Bad Reputation: In places other than within the Union, the character receives a penalty of one attitude shift against him from those who have heard of the guild's merchants. This becomes a two-shift penalty from merchants of such lands who have heard of the guild.

Fees: Shareholders must pay a steep price for continued membership: 35% of the net profit of every trading venture undertaken, including caravans, share deals, and interest on loans. Considerable jockeying occurs among junior shareholders to reduce their net profit, and they claim all sorts of things as expenses. In addition to this percentage of net, the guild also requires each shareholder to pay a levy of 100 gp per share to the guild each quarter. If these fees are not paid (and the shareholder's account books handed over) to the guild by the second tenday following the end of each quarter, membership is suspended until restitution is made and a suspension fine (500 gp) is paid. A suspended shareholder may not participate in any trading activities whatsoever. Shareholders who are away with registered caravans have special dispensation from this fee during the period of their journey.

Time-consuming: The time taken to oversee one's career in the guild is quite extensive. The character must devote at least one week out of every three months to guild activities, just to maintain the guild contacts he has. More time must be devoted if he wishes to advance.

Affiliations

The animal handlers, teamsters, and wagoneers who drive the animals of the caravan do not belong to the Roshanta Trading Guild, but they have formed their own association that is allied with the guild. The Teamsters and Caravaneers Union tries to exert the same kind of control the guild does, setting pay rates, bargaining with individual merchants, and trying to limit the participation of nonunion members. To date, it has met with little success.

The guild is also closely, if not intimately, involved with the ruling houses and councils of the states of the Union. This provides characters with the slim opportunity to garner political influence, if not outright power, in the Union.

Leaving the Guild

Expulsion: The only way to leave the Roshanta Trading Guild, short of dying, is to be expelled. The most common way to be expelled is to fail to pay the quarterly fee. Other reasons for expulsion are taking citizenship in other lands and being convicted of a crime within the Union. Being convicted of a crime outside the Union is not grounds for expulsion.

The best way to leave the guild voluntarily is to sell all of one's guild shares, which means automatic expulsion. Without the necessary one share, the person is unable to participate in any guild activities, although he can still buy and sell trade shares on the open market.

Chairman

Reeva Hoffnin: Human female Expert 8: CR 4; Medium-size humanoid (human); HD 8d6–8; hp 20; Init –1, Spd 30 ft.; AC 11 (touch 11, flat-footed 12); Atk +6/+1 melee (1d6/19–20/x2, shortsword); SA none; SQ none; Al NE; SV Fort +1, Ref +1, Will +11; Str 11, Dex 8, Con 9, Int 20, Wis 17, Cha 17.

Skills and Feats: Appraise +16, Bluff +16, Diplomacy +14, Forgery +16, Gather Information +7, Innuendo +14, Intimidation +14, Knowledge (dirty tricks) +10, Knowledge (financial) +16, Listen +5, Profession (merchant) +16, Read Lips +16, Sense Motive +14, Speak Language (Dwarven), Speak Language (Elven), Speak Language (Gnome), Speak Language (Orcish); Iron Will, Leadership, Skill Focus (bluff), Skill Focus (profession).

Possessions: goggles of minute seeing (used for Forgery), ring of protection +2.

Reeva Hoffnin is the Chairman of the Roshanta Trading Guild and the President-for-Life of one of the states within the Union. With 287 shares, she is by far the most significant shareholder of the guild and deserves her post as Chairman.

Always elegantly dressed, Hoffnin is a shrewd manipulator of people and rules the guild and her state in much the same manner: playing one faction off against another, always to her own advantage, although it is not always obvious to anyone else. She is fabulously wealthy and has a bevy of sycophants and bodyguards that surrounds her day and night. She is arrogant, overbearing, and condescending to everyone she meets but never makes the mistake of thinking that this makes her vulnerable.

Hoffnin can instantly, accurately, and intuitively analyze a situation, and she has the necessary means and contacts, both legitimate and shady, to ruthlessly "correct" any condition unfavorable to her. She is not crossed lightly. Hoffnin is a thin, wiry 53-year-old with pale skin.

Your Campaign

The location of the guild has been intentionally left vague to allow you to place it in your campaign. You may either add the guild into an existing area on the map, defining the boundaries of the so-called Union, or you may expand the map entirely to show the Union area.

If cannot find a match on your map for the Union and wish to add it to the edge, the following information can help you flesh the area out. The Roshanta Trading Guild encompasses the six northern city-states of the Pashtun region: Pashanta, Oshim, Nashtol, Pishok, Teshfol, and Feshunta. Every city except Oshim now has a ruling family which rose to power through the guild and which maintains close ties to, if not outright membership in, the guild.

The Roshanta Trading Guild can be an intimate part of a campaign, where all characters in a party are associated with a merchant caravan in some capacity, or it can be the "enemy" of your homeland, taking unfair advantage of its powerful influence over the trade of an entire region. A few examples of a campaign involving the Roshanta Trading Guild are:

- Defeating the guild.
- Defending the guild from attack.
- Protection of a guild caravan.
- Attempting to reduce the influence of the guild over trade in the region.

· Removing the guild oligopoly within the Union and restoring power to the proper authorities.

Adventure Hooks

- A merchant caravan backed by an influential guild member disappears in a thick forest, and the PCs are hired to find and rescue the caravan.

- Bandits are attacking a caravan and the PCs come to the rescue. In return, the Caravan Master provides a reward and tells them about the Union and the Roshanta Trading Guild.

- The opportunity arises to purchase some trade shares in a mercantile venture that "…just can't miss!" A friend/patron of the PCs asks that they accompany the caravan to ensure that it succeeds, promising them a share of the profits.

- The guild is exerting its power and influence over a bordering territory and attempting to force it, through economic strangulation, to join the Union. The PCs must break the embargo and stop the guild.

- A Syndic from one state wishes to protect himself from the machinations of a Syndic from another state and asks the PCs to protect his businesses, deals, and ventures.

Variations

There are many possible variations of a trading guild:

- The guild may spread across many lands, lobbying all governments for the right of legitimate and authorized caravans to cross state boundaries, the right to license and hold markets, and so forth, in return for a set fee or tax given to the local governments.

- The guild could consist of only a few men, as did the Roshanta Trading Guild in its early days.

- The guild could include other related professions, such as animal handlers, caravan guards, cooks, laborers, and even camp followers.

- The purpose of the guild could be altruistic, and it really could protect the country's craftsmen from unfair foreign competition.

Roshanta

Shondak Weaponsmiths' Guild

The Shondak Weaponsmiths' Guild is based in the city of Shondak. This city either can be added to your campaign, or you may rename the guild to fit into an existing city on your map.

The large city of Shondak is famous for the quality of the metallic items produced in its smithies. Considerable wealth is derived from the sale of these goods to visitors and merchants from near and far. Of especial note is the powerful Weaponsmiths' Guild. Shondak weapons, especially bladed weapons like swords, axes, and polearms, are much sought-after items across the known world. It is said that deep below the nearby mountains, even the dwarves are jealous of the skills of the Shondak weaponsmiths.

The Weaponsmiths' Guild began 232 years ago when the famous Blotak Mine began to play out, and the high-quality ore necessary for the construction of fine master-work weapons became scarce. Marxfeldt Krytofor, who became known as the Hammer of Shondak, called a meeting of all master weaponsmiths in the city to organize the guild for the purpose of forming an association of all weaponsmiths. Once united, the association would have far greater bargaining power to gain access to the ore its members needed. After weeks of intense negotiation, the guild charter was ratified by almost unanimous consent, and Marxfeldt Krytofor convincingly won the first Guildmaster Assay by producing a stunning sun blade.

Purpose

Sharing: To share knowledge among only registered weaponsmiths. Knowledge of new forging techniques, new sources of quality ore, new alloys, and even new spells is shared among masters through visits and gatherings of all kinds.

Protection: Protect the livelihood of existing and future weaponsmiths. By banding together, weaponsmiths protect their craft and present a united front to those who would seek to gain access to their knowledge or block their access to supplies.

Control: Control the spread of dangerous information about the crafting of weapons. The information and skills required to craft masterworks and magical weapons could be construed as dangerous. The spread of information is limited to weaponsmiths only, and most would die before divulging any craft knowledge.

Membership

Profession: Guild membership is available to professional weaponsmiths only. Journeymen and apprentices are classified as associate members and cannot vote. However, they are afforded the protection of the guild if persecuted. Weaponsmiths with the qualifying skills but who are retired or do not practice the craft full-time have full rights, except that they cannot vote or nominate for the position of Guildmaster.

Joining the Guild

Qualification (Apprentice): An apprentice applicant must be 8+ years old (or the nonhuman equivalent) and must demonstrate knowledge of tools, metals, ores, and smelting process (examination) to a Master's satisfaction.

Qualification (anyone else): Anyone joining the guild must do so as an apprentice, no matter how old. Before he can seek to become a journeyman, he must complete one full year of labor as an apprentice, no matter how promising he may be.

Size and Scope

The Shondak Weaponsmiths' Guild currently has 38 members and 124 nonvoting associate members. Every weaponsmith establishment in Shondak is run by a Master member, from the smallest establishment, which has but a single Master and a single apprentice, to the biggest establishment, that belonging to the Krytofor family, which has nine Masters, 11 journeymen, and 15 apprentices.

Guild Structure & Advancement

Graded (Merit): The guild has a very formal graded structure with eight different levels. Members must begin at 0 grade, where they must remain for at least a week and until they have acquired enough experience points to advance. Guild members progress though the grades by demonstrating their skills in weaponsmithing.

Grade 0 – Novice: In order to become a novice, the candidate must be at least 8 years old. He must demonstrate a knowledge of the purpose of the forge to a Master's satisfaction. This is usually an oral examination and is more to show the child's knowledge of the forge and the common tools used. As one might expect, the children of smiths have an overwhelming advantage in this examination, as they probably spend time as young children playing near the forge and hearing talk about the profession. In more remote areas, the forgemaster will often give a child who has expressed interest in becoming a smith a much more lenient examination. During this time, the novice is taught the basics of the craft, such as what the tools are called and what they are used for, what minerals and ores are used, how the smelting process works, and how to forge simple implements, beginning with his own hammer.

Grade 1 – Apprentice: The novice must show an aptitude for the craft and undertake an examination, both oral and practical. Both parts of the examination must be passed to the satisfaction of the Master before the novice can be advanced to the rank of apprentice. The practical examination is the crafting of a simple fork. The usual criterion for passing is that the fork does not break when the master smith puts his full weight on it. Along with his menial chores, the apprentice begins to learn the mysteries of the art: folding, adding foreign materials, hammering techniques, judging temperatures, determining quenching times, etc.

Grade 2 – Journeyman: After a minimum of one year, and usually after much longer, the apprentice must construct a usable, saleable weapon (usually a dagger) under the supervision of a Master. A Master will promote an apprentice to the rank of journeyman after he judges that this and two other conditions are met. The apprentice must be mature enough to begin his journey, including the ability

Skill Guilds

to protect himself. He also must be committed to the cause of the guild and will not willingly divulge what he has learned. A journeyman weaponsmith is expected to travel, to seek employment with other Masters, to learn different techniques, and to bring new techniques to other places. In most cases, journeymen will usually accept employment from a Master in return for food and lodging. If they are very fortunate, they may receive a small allowance.

Grade 3 – Venturer: Before a journeyman is promoted, he must craft a quality weapon (usually a sword). A Venturer is expected to take charge of all journeymen and apprentices within a forge, which usually means only one or two people, although in large forges it can be as many as ten. There is usually only one Venturer per forge, but some of the larger forges may have two. If so, one of the Venturers will be appointed the senior by the forgemaster.

Grade 4 – Bonded Master: To be promoted to Master grade, a character must pass the harshest examination yet — he must construct a masterwork weapon. The weapon may be of any type but must be capable of withstanding extreme punishment and being sold at no less than twice the normal cost. Once a Venturer has proven himself, he may seek more advanced study under a forgemaster. He must dedicate himself to his studies and must work exclusively for that forgemaster for a period of three years. This normally means the traveling days of the character are over.

Grade 5 – Forgemaster: Becoming a forgemaster is the goal of every apprentice. Only when the character is capable of forging a superior masterwork weapon will a weaponcrafter promote a bonded master. Once that happens, the new forgemaster can seek to establish his own business wherever he may. But there is much to learn yet. Although forgemasters have the ability to create magical weapons, they still must learn the secret ways and rituals required by the process. Usually, this will entail some questing, and so the weaponcrafter may take to the road once more, albeit usually for only a short while.

Grade 6 – Weaponcrafter: Only the guild can bestow the honor of Weaponcrafter on a forgemaster, and the honor goes only to those with the greatest skill at the forge and in the craftsmanship required for creating magical weapons of unsurpassed power.

Grade 7 – Guildmaster: When the previous Guildmaster dies, all weaponcrafters who meet the qualifications are invited to compete for the position. The test is to see who can create the best masterwork. This makes the selection process quite lengthy (some masterworks take many months to complete) and explains why a Guildmaster is selected for life. The new Guildmaster appoints four Masters to assist him. The candidates for these positions, usually eight or ten, are selected by all the membership. A unanimous vote of all four assistants can overrule the Guildmaster and can even force him to step down. In such a case, he is then not eligible to stand again.

Benefits

Access to Items: Working in a weaponsmith means having access to the items constructed in that workshop. These can be ordinary weapons, masterworks, or magical weapons of great power.

Access to Skills: The Craft (weaponsmith) skill can be learned only by becoming an apprentice weaponsmith. Knowledge (ores and metals) and Knowledge (smithing) can be learned in other places, but the most readily accessible place is at a smith's forge. Guild members receive all three of these as class skills.

Bonus Feats: The intensive training process of being a weaponsmith allows guild members to pick up additional feats for free. At grade 1, proficiency is gained in any one single weapon; at grade 2, the feat Skill Focus (craft [weaponsmithing]) is gained; at grade 3, Weapon Finesse; and at grade 4, Weapon Focus. The Craft Magic Weapon feat is gained at 5th grade, and the Craft Wondrous Item feat at 6th. A weaponsmith may gain the feats in this manner without being a spellcaster of 5th or greater level. Note that this feat allows the creation of magic weapons only, and not armor.

Good Reputation: Weaponsmiths are accorded respect wherever they go and are held in considerable awe by ordinary folk as magicians who work stubborn metals into wondrous and dangerous weapons. Such a reputation provides a +2 circumstance bonus to weaponsmiths in any Charisma-based or social encounters with ordinary people.

Table 2.3 – Shondak Weaponsmiths' Guild Advancement

Grade	XP Cost	Prerequisites	Benefits Gained
Novice (0)	n/a	Demonstrate some knowledge of the craft	Knowledge (smithing) +1
Apprentice (1)	100	Craft (weaponsmith) 2 ranks; Craft Weapon (DC 8): military fork	Craft (weaponsmith) +1, Weapon Proficiency (choose one), access to items
Journeyman (2)	250	At least 1 year as an apprentice; Knowledge (smithing) 2 ranks; Craft Weapon (DC 12): dagger	Knowledge (smithing) +1, Skill Focus (craft [weaponsmith]), Income
Venturer (3)	500	Craft (weaponsmith) 4 ranks; Craft Weapon (DC 15): sword	Craft (Weaponsmith) +1, Weapon Finesse (choose one), Good Reputation
Bonded Master (4)	750	Craft (weaponsmith) 6 ranks; Knowledge (smithing) 4 ranks; Craft Masterwork Weapon (DC 20): any	Knowledge (smithing) +1, Weapon Focus (choose one), Henchmen
Forgemaster (5)	1,000	Craft (weaponsmith) 8 ranks; Knowledge (smithing) 6 ranks; Craft Superior Masterwork Weapon (DC 25): any	Craft (weaponsmith) +1, Craft Magic Weapon
Weaponcrafter (6)	1,250	Craft (weaponsmith) 10 ranks; Knowledge (smithing) 8 ranks; Craft Magic Weapon (DC 30): any	Craft (weaponsmith) +1, Knowledge (smithing) +1, Craft Wondrous Item
Guildmaster (7)	0	Craft (weaponsmith) 12 ranks; Knowledge (smithing) 10 ranks; Craft Wondrous Magic Weapon (DC 35): any	n/a

Henchmen: Master weaponsmiths usually have a journeyman and one or two apprentices working in their forge. These underlings will staunchly defend their master.

Income: Weaponsmiths can practically name their own price for masterwork-quality weapons, and even more for magical ones.

Skill Bonuses: As a weaponsmith advances through the guild, he gains a number of insight bonuses to a number of applicable skills. These bonuses are shown in the chart above and are cumulative.

Special Abilities: Working at a hot forge day in and day out inures a character to heat, flame, and noxious gases. An apprentice gains a +1 bonus to Fortitude saving throws versus heat and flame damage. Journeymen gain a +2 bonus to Fortitude saving throws versus heat and flame damage and a +1 bonus to hit points. When a journeyman becomes a Master, he gains an ability increase of +1 to Constitution, regardless of level or class.

Disadvantages

Apprenticeship: Apprenticeship usually lasts for several years. During that time, the character will be subjected to extremely hard, hot work.

Cost: The cost of creating weapons is quite high. Some magical weapons can cost more than just money. Time and rare or unusual materials used in the making add to the cost of the finished product.

Deterioration: Working in a hot, smoky forge can cause serious health problems. Every year, each weaponsmith must make a Fortitude saving throw against DC 17 or permanently lose 1d2 points of Dexterity due to an industrial accident. All bonuses, including the ones gained by the Weaponsmith grades, count.

Experience Cost: There is an experience point cost to becoming a journeyman (1,000 XP) and becoming a master (3,000 XP). There is also the experience point cost of constructing magical items. The cost for these is given in the *Dungeon Master's Guide*, Chapter 8, "Magical Items."

Exclusions: Apprentices are forbidden to fraternize with people outside the guild. They have too much to learn to allow for social activity. Journeymen and higher have no such restriction.

Time: Crafting a masterwork, and especially a magical, weapon takes time.

Affiliations

The Weaponsmiths' Guild is associated with the Guild of Miners and other smiths' guilds (blacksmiths, goldsmiths, armorers). A city-based guild would probably have strong ties to similar guilds in other cities and other lands. If nothing else, journeymen and traveling masters may prove their worth at the forge and increase their own knowledge, or pass on techniques peculiar to their own lands.

Leaving the Guild

With Permission: Weaponsmiths can choose the leave the guild at any time. If a Master leaves the guild, he may not make weapons for purposes of sale. He can sell weapons as a merchant but cannot make them himself or directly employ others to make them for him. He may not take an apprentice or journeyman. He may never rejoin the guild.

Guildmaster

Odonchak Fahgroth-Hybu: Human male Adept 10/Warrior 4: CR 7; Medium-size humanoid (human); HD 10d4+4d8+14; hp 50; Init +1, Spd 30 ft.; AC 17 (touch 11, flat-footed 16); Atk +16 melee (1d10+6/x3, glaive); SA none; SQ none; Al LN; SV Fort +11, Ref +5, Will +11; Str 17, Dex 13, Con 14, Int 19, Wis 16, Cha 11.

Skills and Feats: Alchemy +14, Climb +5, Concentration +12, Craft (armorer) +9, Craft (jewelsmith) +9, Craft (weaponsmith) +22, Craft (woodcraft) +9, Diplomacy +8, Intimidate +4, Jump +5, Knowledge (artifacts) +9, Knowledge (gemstones) +9, Knowledge (metals) +14, Knowledge (weaponsmithing) +17, Profession (etcher) +9, Sense Motive +12, Spellcraft +9; Combat Casting, Craft Magic Arms and Armor, Craft Wondrous Item, Great Fortitude, Skill Focus (craft [weaponsmith]), Weapon Focus (glaive).

Adept Spells (6/6/5/4): 0—*detect magic* x2, *light*, *mending* x2, *read magic*; 1st—*comprehend languages*, *endure elements*, *magic stone*, *magic weapon* x3; 2nd—*lesser restoration* x2, *make whole* x2, *resist elements*; 3rd—*blindness/deafness*, *continual flame*, *locate object*, *protection from elements*.

Possessions: *glaive of thundering +3*, *studded leather armor of fire resistance +3*.

Odonchak Fahgroth-Hybu is a large man, standing 6'2", with dark brown eyes and hair, a strikingly sculpted beard, and a thick, furrowed brow. His swarthy skin is blackened and pitted from his time at the forge. He also has a racking cough, a legacy of breathing poisonous fumes and hot air for so many years. Despite these ailments and his age, he is still a highly capable smith, and no small warrior.

He has been Guildmaster of the Shondak Weaponsmiths' Guild for eighteen years and is feeling the weight of those years. He has let it be known that he will retire on his 70th birthday, should he live that long (he is now 68), so he can return to the foothills of his beloved mountains.

Odonchak is a well respected man and has a quiet competence about him that engenders trust. He has a subtle influence over local politics, always to the benefit of the Weaponsmiths' Guild and the protection of their "sacred knowledge."

Your Campaign

The Weaponsmiths' Guild can be situated in a city, kingdom, or region, or it could be a global organization. One way to integrate the guild into your campaign is to have one of the PCs be a journeyman weaponsmith. A journeyman has completed his apprenticeship under a Master and is required to journey the land to work under different masters. This broadens his outlook, increases his skills, and brings new ideas to the farther reaches of the guild's area of influence.

If there is one guild on an entire continent, the characters could travel quite extensively, learning as they go, always certain of a welcome by the smith's forge. Given the affiliation of the Weaponsmiths' Guild with other smiths' guilds, even the smallest hamlet might have a blacksmith who might welcome a journeyman to his forge, to fix weapons he doesn't have the skill for or for the chance to learn a little of the weaponsmith's secret knowledge.

The quickest way to bring the Weaponsmiths' Guild into your campaign is to mention the fame of the weapons they produce. If used in glowing enough terms, characters will be slavering to get their hands on a complete set.

The GM could introduce a journeyman weaponsmith NPC and have him accompany the party, fixing their blunted and damaged metal weapons, going on about the minerals and ores he sees in the dungeon walls, and so on.

Optionally, the GM can add the smoky, dirty, wealthy city of Shondak into the campaign. Perhaps the dwarves of the mountains have decided to do something about the upstart humans and their precious weaponsmiths. Perhaps it is an invading army of orcs who want to sack the city, find all its wealth, and especially its weapons, so the horde can travel to the mountains and slaughter all of the dwarves.

Adventure Hooks

- A master weaponsmith is searching for a tome of ancient metal lore that is rumored to be hidden in the tomb of a long-dead dwarven master smith. The tome is said to contain the secrets of the making of the metal *mithral* and would be incredibly valuable to human weaponsmiths. Of course, the dwarves don't want it found….

- A mysterious old man hires the PCs to accompany him to his home city. He has a cart loaded with very heavy sacks and requires that all the sacks be transported over a mountain pass when winter is about to set in. In the middle of a snow storm, the cart breaks an axle.

- One of the PCs finds a broken weapon, perhaps a sword with the tip broken off, in a deep dungeon. Since the weapon is very pretty once it's cleaned up, the PC decides to see if a weaponsmith can reshape the blade into something slightly shorter, or maybe replace the blade altogether. When the weaponsmith sees the sword, he becomes very excited, offering to pay the party handsomely if only they find the tip and return with it so he might reforge the blade to be whole. The weapon doesn't have to be a sword. It can be either mundane or magical. If mundane, it has great historic value. If magical, it can be of very minor enchantment or a singular weapon of great power, GM's choice.

Variations

The Shondak Weaponsmiths' Guild is an example of a craft guild where the members of the guild all belong to a single craft or trade. There are probably hundreds of different crafts, and groups of allied crafts might form a single guild. Some examples include:

Alchemists, Animal Handlers, Apothecaries, Armorers, Astrologers, Augurs, Baconers, Bakers, Bards, Blacksmiths, Bronzesmiths, Builders, Butchers, Butlers, Cabinetmakers, Carpenters, Carvers, Chandlers, Charcoalers, Clerks, Clothiers, Cooks, Courtesans, Drapers, Dyers, Entertainers, Farriers, Fishermen, Footmen, Fortunetellers, Fullers, Gardeners, Glovers, Goldsmiths, Harpers, Innkeepers, Jewelers, Joiners, Jongleurs, Leatherworkers, Lexigraphers, Lobstermen, Lumberjacks, Maids, Masons, Merchants, Millers, Milliners, Miners, Minstrels, Mystics, Orators, Ostlers, Oysterers, Pages, Palmists, Pantlers, Pastry Cooks, Physicians, Pilots, Poets, Rope Makers, Rune Masters, Sailmakers, Sailors, Sausage Makers, Scribes, Sealers, Seamen, Seers, Servants, Shearers, Silversmiths, Skalds, Smiths, Spinners, Storytellers, Tailors/Seamstresses, Tanners, Tarot Readers, Tent Makers, Thespians, Timbercutters, Tinkers, Tinsmiths, Traders, Usurers, Valets, Vintners, Weavers, Whalers, Wine Stewards, Woodworkers.

Relational

In contrast to guilds centered around a particular profession or skill set, a few organizations exist simply to help form or strengthen relationships between people. This group of guilds includes family guilds formed to advance the bond and prestige of a particular family, social guilds created purely for the enjoyment of the members, and town guilds founded typically to provide for the benefit of all residents of a particular town. This chapter provides a model of one of each of these three types of guilds, each with its own unique benefits and points of interest.

Clover Union

Some one hundred fifty years ago, the Ravanera family held high standing in its homeland. A noble family of ancient lineage, it had been ably served for generations by the common folk of the Calda clan. The ties between the families were strong; on occasion lesser members of the Ravaneras had even married Caldas, binding the family links even further. At that time a Ravanera was the constable of the land, the chief enforcer of law and justice.

This Ravanera was forced to administer rather unfair laws regarding the transport of goods, laws that had resulted in a large increase in smuggling. The Grisi family at that time had made smuggling its chief business in order to survive. Eventually the activities came to the attention of the Ravanera constable. Rather than punish the Grisis, though, he turned a blind eye to their lawlessness, recognizing they were merely trying to survive the way they knew best. The constable's motives weren't entirely altruistic, for he used the Grisi smuggling network to move goods for his own family's benefit.

In time, the relationship between the three families flourished. Eventually the Ravaneras' fortunes and influence dwindled, while those of the Caldas rose. The Grisis remained on the edge of lawlessness. Despite their different stations, the families recognized the benefits of joining together in an informal alliance that covered almost all levels of society. Eventually the association took the cloverleaf as an obvious symbol and took to calling the clan alliance the Clover Union.

This association has proven to be quite successful and has become a strong tradition for the three families. Nowadays the Ravaneras maintain their aristocratic standing, though their wealth has dwindled somewhat. The Caldas continue to provide service to their Ravanera patrons, but wise investments have also seen them become prosperous middle-class merchants. The Grisis remain a family of scoundrels for the most part, taking part in activities of dubious legality.

At the head of the union sits a committee of elders, the chiefs of each family. These worthies oversee the operations of all three families and ensure the union survives. They direct the actions of the union and guide their family members,

actively meddling as need be. No single family is favored, as the wisdom of combined efforts is always noted. The union maxim is that those who stand alone fall alone, while those who band together share their strengths and protect against individual weaknesses.

Purpose

Protection: The union families have been quick to recognize threats to their existence and do not intend to be destroyed or swallowed up by other clans. Rather than work separately they have seen the merit of an alliance and are determined to hold true to themselves and each other.

Economic: Money may not be everything, but it can certainly buy security and influence. The union families recognize the necessity of building and maintaining a healthy degree of wealth. All family members are taught to keep an eye open for economic opportunities.

Membership

Family: All members are related by blood or marriage to one or more of the three union families, the Ravaneras, Caldas, and Grisis. Apart from this one link, the members are varied in vocation and outlook, allowing for a wide range of members to be used by the GM. By this method, a GM might bind an otherwise disparate group of PCs together and give them a common purpose despite differing professions, alignments, and goals.

Joining the Guild

Application: Those not born to one of the union families may join only through marriage. However, to do so one must seek and receive the approval of the spouse-to-be's elders. Generally, the elders will attempt to ensure that the prospective spouse will be of stable character and at the very least provide no threat to the union. The GM should use his discretion as to whether a PC might marry into the union, based upon past exploits. Additionally, a new PC could start his career having recently married into the union.

Edict: Those born into the Calda, Grisi, and Ravanera families are immediately afforded membership in the Clover Union. Blood is thicker than water, as they say, and you can't choose your family. This rule allows PCs to claim membership upon character creation, should they so wish, with the GM's approval. Of course, a particular character

Table 3.1 – Clover Union Advancement			
Grade	Min. Level	XP Cost	Benefits Gained
Minor (1)	0	500	Experience bonus, Fraternity, Patronage, Shelter
Sentinel (2)	3	1,000	Access to items, Henchmen (1st level)
Savant (3)	6	1,500	Henchmen (2nd level), Income
Elder (4)	8*	2,000	Henchmen (4th level)
Dignitary (5)	10	2,500	Henchmen (5th level)
Patriarch/Matriarch (6)	12	3,000	Henchmen (6th level)
*Must also be middle-aged.			

Table 3.2 – Encountering Clover Members

Settlement Size	Chance to Find Member	Number of Members	Max Level*
Thorp	1%	1d8	2d4–1
Hamlet	2%	1d12	2d4
Village	5%	1d20	2d4+1
Small Town	10%	2d12	2d4+2
Large Town	20%	2d20	2d4+3
Small City	50%	1d100	2d4+4
Large City	75%	2d100	2d4+5
Metropolis	100%	5d100	2d4+6

*Level and age (for Elders) determines member's grade.

may reject his heritage and decide to have no part of the union.

Invitation: The Clover Union elders keep a close watch for potential partners for their children and seek good marriages for their scions. A PC who has won renown might be approached with an offer of marriage. Likewise, a union member may pursue a romantic interest in a PC independently of the elders. A GM who has a player romantically involved with an NPC might introduce the Clover Union in this manner, with all the benefits and complications it brings.

Size and Scope

Each family, truly a clan, numbers in the high hundreds to low thousands. They are predominantly found in their homeland, of course, spread throughout various settlements, from large cities to tiny hamlets. Family interests have seen other kinfolk travel farther afield, and clan members can be found in lesser numbers in far-flung places across the world.

Guild Structure & Advancement

Graded (Merit/Criteria): For all grades lower than Elder, advancement within the union is based primarily on class level, as this is seen as a suitable indication of experience. To become an Elder, a member must also have reached at least middle age.

Minor: Anyone entering the guild must be a family member by blood or marriage. Minors are ordinary family members and form the bulk of the union.

Sentinel: Sentinels are experienced family members who have displayed some degree of ambition and drive, and are thus accorded higher respect.

Savant: Savants are members who have made considerable achievements and proven themselves to be skilled and experienced to a high degree.

Elder: Elders not only are skilled in their chosen professions but also have the addition of further wisdom from age.

Dignitary: Dignitaries are close advisors to the patriarchs and conduct much of the important high-end business of the guild.

Patriarch/Matriarch: The three patriarchs are equivalent to guildmasters and have final say over the operations of the three families. Guildwide actions must be agreed upon by all three leaders.

Benefits

Access to Items: Upon reaching Savant grade, family ties mean that such members will be afforded discounts on the purchase of all items up to masterwork in quality wherever there is a family presence. The member receives a 10% discount on such items.

Experience Bonus: The families promote excellence in their offspring and ensure that the best training in chosen professions is available. Usually this involves training from older, more experienced kin. Because of this, members receive a 5% experience bonus for their initial class, and only that one class.

Fraternity: Union members look out for each other, pure and simple. A member can count upon kin for assistance in various forms—small loans of money, an extra blade in a fight, provision of testimony as a character witness, and so on. Fraternity works both ways, and there is a chance that a PC will be called upon for help by a fellow union member. More detail can be found in the Disadvantages section.

The chance of there being fellow Clover Union members in any given settlement depends upon its size, as detailed in Table 3.2.

Henchmen: At Sentinel grade, union members are entitled to call upon the services of junior family members to serve as henchmen. The maximum level of an individual henchman is listed in the advancement table, and a member may have a number of henchmen whose total levels do not exceed the member's own level.

Although these henchmen will be relatively self-sufficient, the member is still expected to contribute to their equipment and upkeep. Usually this involves a share in profits from endeavors that the henchmen have assisted in. If henchmen are continually mistreated or otherwise abused they may depart the member's service.

A Loyal Henchman

Cousin Harkin: Male human Fighter 2: CR 2; Medium-size humanoid (human); HD 2d10+7; hp 17; Init +2, Spd 30 ft.; AC 19 (touch 14, flat-footed 17); Atk +6 melee (1d8+2/19-20/x2, longsword) or +4 ranged (1d6/x3, shortbow); SA none; SQ none; Al N; SV Fort +5, Ref +2, Will +1; Str 15, Dex 15, Con 16, Int 10, Wis 12, Cha 10.

Skills and Feats: Diplomacy +2, Intimidate +2, Ride [horse] +5, Spot +2; Feint, Power Attack, Toughness, Weapon Focus (longsword).

Possessions: chainmail, dagger, large wooden shield, masterwork longsword, shortbow (20 arrows).

Cousin Harkin is a large reliable fellow who has been fortunate enough to be accepted as a member of the Golden Blades. Though no genius, Harkin is dependable and sensible. He makes a fine bodyguard, and his presence adds some muscle to any group.

Income: From Savant grade on, family members share in the profits of union endeavors. They receive an income equal to their level times 5 gp per month.

Patronage: The Clover Union cares for its kinfolk, doing all it can to help them in their working and private lives. The difference between Fraternity and Patronage is that a patron is of a higher level or more influential than the PC. The assistance a patron can provide is accordingly better—vouch for a member, find employment, and so on. To determine the chance of finding a higher-level or more influential member in a settlement, the GM should use the encounter table for Fraternity and consult the maximum level column. A member of at least 8th level (or four levels higher than the PC) should be able to serve as a patron.

Patronage works both ways, and a PC is expected to look after the interests of other members whenever possible. More detail can be found in the Disadvantages section.

Shelter: As long as there is a Clover Union member in a settlement, a visiting member may call upon that associate to house him, within the bounds of courtesy. The GM should determine the wealth of the household and the relative comfort, using the encounter table and NPC level as a rough guide.

Shelter works both ways, and a PC is expected to house Union members whenever asked. More detail can be found in the Disadvantages section.

Disadvantages

Fraternity: As noted previously, the tradition of fraternity can act as a disadvantage to the character. Fellow members of the Clover Union may call upon the character for assistance. Such assistance might take the form of a request for help with a problem, a loan of money, or a character reference. The GM should consult the encounter table and halve the chance of an encounter occurring to determine if a fellow member makes a call for help. In such a case, the member calling upon the character should usually be no more than 1d4 levels different from the character.

Henchmen: There is a chance that a PC might be called upon to act as a henchman for a time, providing service to a senior union member. The possibility of such happening is equal to one tenth of the encounter chance listed for a particular settlement. This will not happen if the maximum level for the settlement does not exceed that of the PC. The GM should determine what form of service is required, but usually it should be for a short time only and for a specific purpose.

Patronage: As with fraternity, a character may be called upon to help a junior member of the union. The same chance of such a situation occurring exists as listed directly above, but the junior member will be 1d6 levels lower than the character. Such requests for patronage might entail a character reference, a loan of money, assistance in finding employment, and so on.

Regulations/Traditions: Family tradition dictates that union members must make themselves known to the senior union member in a given settlement. This may not seem like a particular disadvantage, and often it isn't, but it means the PC member can then be called upon for requests due to the other disadvantages. A character who constantly avoids identifying himself to seniors might be punished or even expelled from the family.

XP Cost: As detailed in the Structure & Advancement section, there are XP costs associated with advancing through the grades.

Affiliations

Apart from the individual families within the Clover Union, this guild has no formal ties to any single group, whether as an ally or an enemy.

Optionally, though, the GM may decide that the Ravaneras have close ties with the Golden Blades, the Caldas deal with the trading guild, and the Grisis are known to the thieves guild. The GM might also wish to create a family feud, pitting union members against a rival clan or collection of families.

Leaving

As with most families, once a person is a member he is so for life. That said, characters might leave their family or become estranged.

With Permission: A member may voluntarily eschew his family ties at any time and become an independent agent in his own right. This might raise some questions if the PC is a member by birth, for it is unusual to forsake one's family. A member by marriage might decide to divorce his spouse, though if he is in good standing this does not necessitate departure from the union. However, a member who leaves voluntarily for whatever reason will suffer no penalties other than a few questions regarding motives.

Expulsion: A member might be ejected from the union for continually acting in an unacceptable or disreputable manner, or if his actions seriously endanger the Clover Union. Characters who have been ejected from the family will find their reputations will suffer with anyone who knows of their former family ties. Apply a –1 modifier to Charisma-based skill tests when dealing with people who know of the character's ejection—if his own family can't trust him, then who can? This modifier is –2 when dealing with Clover Union members who are aware of the former member's history.

Should a blood relation (not one who married into the union) have been ejected from the family there is further trouble ahead. The stigma attached to being abandoned by one's family is quite traumatic and affects the character considerably. Each time the character receives an XP award, he must make a Will save (DC 20) or reduce the XP by 5%. This represents time wasted dealing with the concerns of family rejection. A GM may wish to make this optional and remove the restriction if he feels a PC is not affected by the trauma. Likewise, the penalty could be applied to a married member who has been thrown out, if appropriate.

When a member leaves the Clover Union, he immediately loses all benefits and disadvantages. Henchmen may decide to remain in the character's service. Should the character desire this, have the player make a Diplomacy test for each henchman against a DC equal to 15 plus the henchman's level.

Assuming that any issues resulting in a character's ejection are resolved, a character can rejoin the Clover Union whenever the GM feels reconciliation has been properly reached. In such a situation raise the level required for each grade advancement by 2 and restore benefits and disadvantages as appropriate.

Ravanera Matriarch

Setrilla Ravanera: Female half-elf Aristocrat 16: CR 8; Medium-size humanoid (half-elf); HD 16d8; hp 72; Init +1, Spd 30 ft.; AC 15 (touch 15, flat-footed 14); Atk +15/+10/+5 melee (1d4+3/19-20/x2, +3 dagger) or +13/+8/+3 ranged (1d4/19-20/x2, throwing dagger); SA none; SQ half-elf abilities; Al N; SV Fort +5, Ref +6, Will +14; Str 10, Dex 12, Con 11, Int 17, Wis 17, Cha 22.

Skills and Feats: Appraise +8, Bluff +23, Diplomacy +27, Gather Information +21, Innuendo +22, Intimidate +16, Knowledge (politics) +13, Knowledge (trading) +13, Listen +9, Perform +7, Read Lips +8, Sense Motive +24, Spot +8; Alertness, Iron Will, Leadership, Skill Focus (bluff), Skill Focus (diplomacy), Skill Focus (sense motive).

Special Qualities: Half-elf abilities—Immunity to *sleep* spells and similar magical effects; +2 saving throw bonus against Enchantment spells or effects; Low-light Vision; +1 bonus to Listen, Search, and Spot checks; Elven Blood.

Possessions: *cloak of charisma +4, greater spell reflecting dagger +3, medallion of thoughts, ring of protection +4.*

An astoundingly lovely and elegant woman in her ninth decade, Setrilla is now the Matriarch of the Ravaneras and thus the most influential member of the Clover Union. A tiny raven-haired woman who stands barely five feet in height, the sheer power of her personality more than makes up for her lack of stature. Setrilla dresses in clothes of plain and simple appearance, but of the finest quality materials.

The lady cultivates a friendly and inoffensive manner, hiding a keen mind and a frightening ruthlessness. Though her preference is to lead her life in a fair and honorable manner, Setrilla will do whatever is needed to ensure the survival of herself, her family, and the Caldas and Grisis. She is willing to sacrifice whomever and whatever are necessary to meet her ends.

Over her many years Setrilla has gathered influential friends and servants about her, and has gained sensitive information regarding allies and enemies alike. She uses these associations and knowledge carefully, always with a deft touch, but is not above the use of force when it is needed. She prefers to use the carrot rather than the stick but knows when and how to go on the offensive.

Setrilla is aware of the power of loyalty and has done much to ensure that she has a devoted following of union members. In return she looks out for the interests of her kin and other associates. She makes a marvelous ally and a formidable enemy.

Your Campaign

A GM should determine where in his own campaign the homeland for the Clover Union is located. The three family names may be changed to suit the campaign, as long as the family roles remain the same: aristocracy, middle class, and slightly criminal. Player characters can marry into the union, or a GM can use the old chestnut of the hitherto-secret family heritage. It is suggested that a blood tie to the Union is best used for a brand-new character.

Adventure Hooks

- A PC is called upon by a junior family member to assist him in eloping. The family member's elders have previously barred the marriage.
- The character must escort a family elder on a business or diplomatic trip. Unfortunately, the elder is suffering from hallucinations and dementia due to a recent illness.
- A family member has been involved in some taboo actions. Sadly, he has been masquerading as one of the PCs when doing this.
- Someone has been making threats against the family. The PC and his associates are asked to get to the bottom of the matter.
- The Ravanera Matriarch has disappeared on a visit to a major city. She was engaged in some secret diplomacy. Has she been kidnapped, or has she gone to ground for some reason?

Other Family Guilds

- **Noble Blood:** A royal or aristocratic family could have deeply entrenched traditions and ages-old alliances and enmities.
- **Rightful Heritage:** In grand Shakespearean tradition, a family has been betrayed and its rights denied or stolen. The family conspires to regain what has been lost.
- **Family Feud:** A tight-knit family lives for one purpose, winning the feud with them thar varmints across the way. Plenty of scope for loyal family members and intolerant enemies.
- **Scattered to the Winds:** At some time in the past, a family was broken up and sent to various places. Now they seek to reunite, but who knows who is a relation and who isn't? Can they all be located? Family members have since become exceptional trackers of missing people.

The Feasters
(Social Guild)

Adventurers often find themselves in all sorts of sticky situations and need to resort to actions quite out of the ordinary to survive. Such a situation once occurred to a fellow called Bócrin Dail, the adventurous son of a rich merchant. Master Dail, an accomplished rogue, found himself trapped in some caverns for several weeks as a result of a careless mishap. In order to survive he was forced to resort to eating whichever strange creatures he could get his hands on. Eventually he was rescued from his plight, but in that time he discovered that he had developed, quite literally, a taste for danger.

Nothing more would have come from this had Dail not made the acquaintance of an associate of his father's, a boastful fellow named Trigget Firefist. Firefist was a well traveled fellow who liked to regale his acquaintances with wild and lurid tales from his journeys. While dining with the Dails, Firefist recounted some interesting dining experiences, hoping to impress and shock his audience. Rising to the challenge, Bócrin Dail told his own tale,

Feasters

inadvertently belittling Firefist's so-called achievements. Before long a friendly argument was taking place and a challenge was set down—a feast of unusual meats would be prepared for the two, and the winner would be the one with the ability to consume the most of the foods provided.

This dining duel caught the fancy of local society and attracted quite an audience. The result was finally declared a draw, with both competitors carried from the venue, but the flame of inspiration had been lit. Soon another feast was planned, this time merely to allow the participants to taste obscure foods. Adventurers were hired to hunt for the ingredients. So successful was this gathering that it was agreed that such meals should become a regular feature. With the agreement of all in attendance, including Masters Dail and Firefist, a club was formed, The Feasters.

Now, some fifty years later, The Feasters are still a going concern. Despite the strange premise of the club, membership has grown. Members are either daredevils looking for bragging rights or gastronomes with a taste for rare and strange dishes. Members come from all walks of society, though all are moneyed in one form or another. The raw ingredients are expensive due to their rarity. Some scoff at the stupidity of the Feasters' antics, but there is no doubt that for those who have a finely developed taste for danger, there are few more interesting or pleasurable pursuits.

Purpose

Sharing: The purpose of The Feasters is to provide a means by which folk with obscure tastes and the money to indulge them can gather together and do so. In addition, members might swap lurid stories and mingle with like-minded folk in a convivial atmosphere.

Membership

Miscellaneous: The members of The Feasters share one trait—they have dined on strange meals, whether the meats of strange creatures or rare magical fruits and other plants. All have found that their tastes go beyond the norm and seek to indulge their passion for different meals.

Joining the Guild

Application: Joining The Feasters simply involves a prospective member asking if he may enter the club. Assuming the initiation is performed and the entry fee is paid (see below), membership is gained.

Test/Examination: In order to join The Feasters, a character must take part in an initiation feast and last until the end. Prospective members must partake of a large meal consisting of a variety of rather strange dishes. As long as the character "goes the distance" to The Feasters' satisfaction, he has passed the test. This requires that the character succeed in two saves, first a Will save (DC 12) and then a Fort save (DC 15). Unless either save is exceeded by 10 or more, the character will be rather sick afterward, as expected by The Feasters.

Purchase: Once the initiation has been performed, the new member can purchase membership for a fee of 250 gp. The character is now a member of The Feasters.

Size and Scope

The Feasters are based in one large city, with approximately one hundred members. Members of the feasters are generally adventuring types and travel extensively. It is possible to find guild members in all corners of the world.

Guild Structure & Advancement

Graded (Merit): Advancement within The Feasters is based on the character's ability to consume increasingly rich meals, as well as provision of meals for fellow members. The requirements for advancement through the grades are:

Sampler: Those members who have met the initial entry requirements are known as Samplers.

Taster: To reach the grade of Taster, a member must have provided a total of 5 CR worth of monstrous ingredients over a number of club feasts, as well as passed the test of another huge feast, requiring success in Will (DC 12) and Fort (DC 17) saves.

Feaster: To reach the grade of Feaster, a member must have provided a further total of 20 CR worth of monstrous ingredients over more club feasts, as well as passed the test of another huge feast, requiring success in Will (DC 15) and Fort (DC 20) saves.

Connoisseur: To reach this grade, a member must have provided a further total of 50 CR worth of monstrous ingredients over more club feasts, as well as passed the test of another huge feast, requiring success in Will (DC 17) and Fort (DC 25) saves.

Gourmand: To reach this grade, a member must have provided a further total of 100 CR worth of monstrous ingredients over more club feasts, as well as passed the test of another huge feast, requiring success in Will (DC 20) and Fort (DC 30) saves.

Table 3.3 – Feaster's Guild Advancement

Grade	Minimum Total CR Provided	Feast Will/Fort Save	XP Cost	Benefits Gained
Sampler (1)	0	12/15	0	Fraternity, Shelter
Taster (2)	5	12/17	500	1st save bonus, access to skills
Feaster (3)	20	15/20	1,000	2nd save bonus, bonus feat
Connoisseur (4)	50	17/25	1,500	3rd save bonus
Gourmand (5)	100	20/30	2,000	4th save bonus, Poison Immunity

Benefits

Access to skills: Upon reaching Taster grade, the member is experienced in identifying the habits of various creatures and plants, having heard many tales from fellow members. Knowledge (nature) and Wilderness Lore become class skills for the member.

Bonus Feat: At Feaster grade, the member gains either the Great Fortitude or Iron Will feat for free.

Fraternity: Members of The Feasters are social folk and look out for one another. A member can count upon other members for assistance in various forms—small loans of money, a bed for the night, provision of testimony as a character witness, and so on. Fraternity works both ways, and there is a chance that a PC will be called upon for help by a fellow Feasters member. More detail can be found in the Disadvantages section. The chance of there being fellow Feasters members in a specific settlement depends upon its size and how many and what levels they are, as detailed in Table 3.4.

Poison Immunity: At Gourmand grade the member gains the special ability of total Immunity to Poison.

Save Bonus: Starting at Taster grade, members gain a +1 competence bonus to all Fortitude saves. This bonus is gained at each subsequent grade and is cumulative.

Shelter: The Feasters maintain a headquarters in their home city, where members in need of accommodation can find a bed for a night or two. Needless to say, meals are also provided.

Disadvantages

Deterioration: The regular consumption of often-rich foods in copious amounts is not conducive to good health. Members of The Feasters do not maintain a healthy diet. As such, after each full year of membership a character should make a Fort (DC 15) save. Failure results in the loss of 1 permanent point of Constitution.

Fees: In order to provide its members with their expected meals and to furnish the headquarters and pay the staff, there is an annual membership fee of 250 gp. The joining fee covers the first year.

Fraternity: As noted previously, the tradition of fraternity can act as a disadvantage to the character. Fellow members of The Feasters may call upon the character for assistance. Such assistance might take the form of a request for help with a problem, a loan of money, a character reference, and such. The GM should consult the encounter table and halve the chance of an encounter occurring to determine if a fellow member makes a call for help. In such a case, the member calling upon the character should usually be no more than 1d4 levels different from the character.

Regulations/Traditions: Feasts are held on the middle day of every month. Members are expected to attend at least one feast a year. In addition, each member is expected to contribute to the club's kitchen, providing at least 1 CR worth of "ingredients" per year. This provision can be included in that needed for grade advancement.

XP Cost: As detailed in the Structure & Advancement section, there are XP costs associated with advancing through the grades.

Affiliations

The Feasters maintain close ties with the Adventurer's Guild (the Sojourners; see chapter 4), which provides them with much of the raw ingredients needed for their meals. Likewise, they keep in touch with gladiatorial organizations that use monsters in their lethal arena bouts. The bodies can often be put to use in a nice goulash or as a roast.

Various druidic groups have declared their enmity toward The Feasters, decrying the unnecessary killing of living things for mere entertainment.

Leaving

Not being a particularly conspiratorial group, departure from The Feasters carries few consequences. Any accrued bonuses are kept, but all other benefits and disadvantages are lost.

Unless the GM decrees that a character's departure from The Feasters has been particularly acrimonious, a former member may rejoin at any time. However, he must start again as a Sampler—including performing the entry process—and advance through the grades as before. Benefits and disadvantages are restored, though the member does not gain any bonuses the second time around until he reaches a grade he has not ever previously attained.

With Permission: A member may voluntarily leave The Feasters at any time.

Expulsion: Generally a member is ejected from The Feasters for continually failing to show at club gatherings without good reason, or for failing to pay membership fees.

Head Chef

Finkle "Chops" Jeladinle, Head Chef of the Feasters: Male gnome Expert 8: CR 4; Small-size humanoid (gnome); HD 8d6+16; hp 40; Init +2; Spd 20 ft.; AC 13 (touch 13, flat-footed 11); Atk +6/+1 melee (1d6/19–20/x3, +1 cleaver) or +8/+3 ranged (1d4-1/19-20/x2, throwing knife); SA spells; SQ gnome abilities; Al LN; SV Fort +9, Ref +4, Will +12; Str 8, Dex 14, Con 17, Int 13, Wis 18, Cha 13.

Skills and Feats: Alchemy +10, Appraise +6, Craft (kitchen goods) +8, Diplomacy +6, Handle Animal +7, Knowledge (nature) +8,

Table 3.4 – Encountering Feaster Members

Settlement Size	Chance to Find Member	Number of Members	Max Level*
Thorp	1%	1	2d4–1
Hamlet	1%	1d4	2d4
Village	2%	1d6	2d4+1
Small Town	5%	1d8	2d4+2
Large Town	10%	1d10	2d4+3
Small City	25%	1d12	2d4+4
Large City	50%	1d20	2d4+5
Metropolis	75%	2d20	2d4+6

*Average Sampler is 1st-2nd level, average Taster is 3rd-4th level, average Feaster is 5th-7th level, average Connoisseur is 8th-10th level, and average Gourmand is 11th level and higher.

THE FEASTERS' CLUBHOUSE

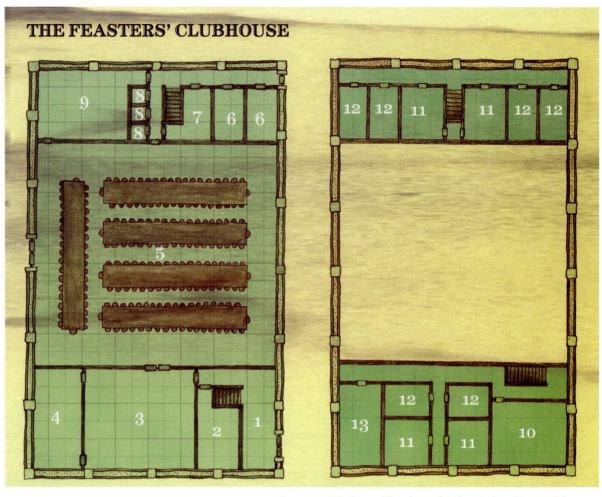

Knowledge (recipes) +11, Listen +8, Profession (chef) +11, Search +5, Speak Language (Dwarven), Speak Language (Elven); Iron Will, Leadership, Skill Focus (profession).

Special Qualities: Spells & spell-like abilities — may cast *dancing lights*, *ghost sound*, *prestidigitation*, and *speak with animals (burrowing mammals)* each once per day; Feasters abilities — +2 bonus to Fort saves, Great Fortitude feat; gnome abilities — Low-light vision, +2 save vs. illusions, +1 attack vs. kobolds and goblinoids, +4 dodge vs. giants, +2 Alchemy, +2 Listen,

Possessions: +1 keen cleaver, masterwork kitchen tools.

Chops is a cheery soul who runs The Feasters' kitchen with verve and style. A portly little gnome with the constitution of an ox, he channels his race's imagination into amazing feats of culinary skill. He also partakes in the feasting on occasion and holds the grade of Feaster.

The Feasters' House

As noted, the Feasters maintain a plush headquarters where they gather for meetings. This building also has quarters to house members and staff. The details of the clubhouse are:

1. **Front entry and public office:** A well appointed front entry where details of The Feasters can be found and outsiders can leave messages.

2. **Staff office and records:** The administration of the affairs of the club occurs in this room. The well secured and guarded treasury is here also.

3. **Kitchens:** This large kitchen is bustling and busy on feast nights.

4. **Larder:** The well stocked larder contains all manner of strange ingredients, many magically preserved.

5. **Dining hall:** The large hall can fit up to 100 diners at a time. Double doors at the back lead to a courtyard where feasters may take a breath and get some fresh air.

6. **Duty staff bedrooms:** Two bedrooms near a staff entrance are kept for those staff who see to the needs of members in residence.

7. **Vomitarium:** Sometimes members at a feast just have to be sick. This is where they go.

8. **Privy:** When nature calls, members come here.

9. **Members' room:** A comfortable room where members can sit and chat, day or night.

10. **Servant and staff dormitory:** This upstairs room has bunks for approximately 20 staff and servants of resident members.

11. **Superior member bedroom:** Maintained for senior and wealthier members, these rooms are very comfortable indeed. Two on the right side of the top floor are linked to form a suite of sorts.

12. **Common member bedroom:** These more spartan rooms house less wealthy members.

13. **Member dormitory:** Up to a dozen less discerning members may sleep here at a time.

Your Campaign

All that a GM should needs to do to insert The Feasters into his campaign is to choose an appropriate large city in which to locate the club. The GM may also decide that this guild maintains clubhouses in several locations.

Adventure Hooks

- ⚡ PCs are called upon by a Feasters member to provide him with a fresh monster carcass for the month's dinner.
- ⚡ A live beast has been brought to the headquarters ready for slaughter. Unfortunately it has escaped, alive and angry, into the city.
- ⚡ A group of druids has decided to start attacking members of The Feasters and must be stopped.
- ⚡ Recent feasts have seen some dishes poisoned and members sick or dead. Who is doing the poisoning, and why?
- ⚡ A competition has been sponsored by The Feasters for the person who can bring in the most spectacular creature for the next feast. The 2,500 gp prize money could be handy.

Other Social Guilds

The possibilities for social guilds are wide and varied. All that is needed are people with a common interest and a desire to share it with other people. Some other ideas are:

- ● **Did you hear the one about...?:** Adventurers get up to all sorts of exploits. Perhaps they might be interested in a club devoted to tales of the deeds of its members.
- ● **We is not all bad!:** Humanoids tend to have a bad reputation. Not all of them are bad, though. Half-orcs, orcs, hobgoblins, and so on with a good outlook on life might gather together in a charitable group to be accepted by society.
- ● **Too good to be true:** People of kind dispositions might gather together to form a social group that tends to the interests of the poor. What better way to while away spare time than working in the local soup kitchen?
- ● **Footloose and fancy-free:** Some people like to trip the light fantastic and gather for a cheery shindig. So why not join the local dance society? Some of those fancy steps could even be useful in combat.

Lochrinn Town Guild

The Lochrinn Town Guild is based in the town of Lochrinn, at the edge of a wilderness area. In order to make use of the guild the GM can either drop Lochrinn onto his map, or rename the guild and apply it to an existing town.

Lochrinn, a town of 1,734 inhabitants, is located on the edge of settled territory. Although there are smaller settlements further out, Lochrinn is the only population center of any size this close to the wilderness. Being so far from civilization and owing no allegiance to any realm or power, the town has to rely on its own resources for protection.

The townspeople have formed the Lochrinn Town Guild to ensure the cooperation of all in the protection of the town and its inhabitants. It is a very close-knit community, viewing strangers with some suspicion. All men and women above the age of 19 are able to vote and are required to practice with several weapons to help defend the town when it comes under attack.

One day in twenty is devoted to building and maintaining defenses, such as the town wall and central keep. This day is known as Hammerblow, reflecting the work that goes on and the purpose for which all the work is carried out. The day after Hammerblow is Resday, when the townspeople rest from their labors, pray to their deities, and celebrate the achievements of individual guild members over the past twenty days.

The town is protected by a deep ditch and a strong wooden palisade, covered by hardened clay and lime-washed for protection against fire. The ditch is filled with sharpened stakes set so closely together that only small children can work their way through to trim weed and grass. A walkway encircles the palisade, ending in high towers. Gaps in the walkway, normally covered with planks, provide a means of isolating sections of the wall should attackers gain entry.

In the center of the town, a squat, four-story stone keep has been built, encircled by an area free of houses and shops. The Citadel's walls are ten feet thick, and a single massive iron-bound door gives access. Otherwise, only narrow arrow slits pierce the walls. There are three sublevels and the bottom-most basement contains a deep well of fresh water. Half the ground level is a maze of corridors designed to slow down attackers and make them easier to dispatch. The other half is completely walled off and accessible only from either the second floor or the first subbasement, not the ground floor. The ceiling of the ground floor is twenty feet high, and access to the level above is by a wooden ramp which can be collapsed. Murder holes in the ceiling allow boiling oil and water to be poured onto attackers. The Citadel contains enough room to house all guild members, albeit with considerable crowding. Stores to last a lengthy siege are kept in the basements, along with hundreds of weapons.

In Lochrinn, the end of the summer marks the end of the year, and everyone is counted one year older. No one celebrates a personal birthdate; at each Somersend, everyone is one year older. Children from newly born to the age of 4 are counted the most precious members of the guild. Anyone older, even Cadets, will do almost anything to save a child. At the age of 4, all children are given a sling and taught how to use it. Competitions are held to encourage the youngsters to improve their skill with the sling. The children are loosely organized into bands, and a person may have a special place in his heart for those in the same Cub Band. Apart from the lessons their parents think they should learn, these children are allowed to play like normal children, albeit with slings always ready. On Hammerblow, Cub Bands are given the task of clearing away litter and detritus from the town's streets, and cutting weeds and saplings from the killing ground outside the palisade.

A Cub graduates to the Cadets on his tenth Somersend. The graduation present is a dagger, and it becomes his responsibility to learn how to use and care for this weapon properly. Cadets who allow their blades to be damaged in anything except combat suffer considerable shame. Older Cadets teach the younger ones how to sharpen their blades, how to use a dagger without nicking the edge, and how to throw it at targets, and start them on lessons in dagger fighting with special blunted blades of the same weight. As a Cadet gets older he may be given heavier blades to use or may seek training in different types of blades. On Hammerblow, Cadets carry food and drink, messages, and small loads to other workers. They even serve the Cub Bands.

At age 15, a Cadet graduates to the Reserves. These junior militiamen start training in earnest with real weapons. The Reserve will be tested for proficiency with all kinds of spears and polearms, short swords and long swords, flails, maces and hammers, and all kinds of bows. After this assessment, he will begin extensive training in one type of long weapon (spear or polearm), one type of sword, one type of bow, and one type of club (mace, flail, or hammer). He is also expected to maintain his proficiency with the sling and dagger. Every Lochrinn Town Guild member carries these two weapons all the time, no matter what he is doing.

While some latitude is afforded children and Cadets in their behavior, Reserves are subjected to almost adult discipline. In addition to the normal chores and work (like learning a trade) that such youngsters have to do, they are also required to attend lessons, drills, and training sessions every ten days. Their training is conducted by experienced Militiamen.

During their first year, Reserves are monitored and assessed by their teachers. There will be some Reserves who are not suited to fighting, and there is no shame in this. These become Auxiliaries and are given more extensive training in dagger fighting and sling, so they are able to defend themselves. Instead of weapons training, they learn to tend the wounded, to carry supplies to defenders, and the secret ways of the Citadel.

At age 19 Reserves become adults, are able to vote in the guild elections, and are called Militiamen, regardless of whether they are male or female. Females in charge are called "Sir." The new Militiamen join established groups, called Hammers; often, members of the same Cub Band will join the same Hammer. Over the next year, they are integrated into this tight-knit company of soldiers.

The number of Militiamen in a Hammer is approximately 100. Occasionally new Hammers are formed, with an even number of members from all existing Hammers. Each Hammer has a name, like Eagle, Hawk, Raven, Wolf, Bear, etc., and a battle standard. The battle standard is the rallying point for the Militiamen of that Hammer, and there is fierce competition for the honor of carrying the standard into battle.

Currently there are thirteen Hammers, so one day in thirteen, a Hammer has The Duty. The Duty is to guard the town gates, watch from the towers and walkways, and patrol the roads and byways of Lochrinn. Within the Militiaman Hammers is a rank structure. There are two nonofficer ranks and three officer ranks. A Hand of men numbers ten: eight ordinary Militiamen, a Second, and a First, both these latter nonofficers. A Minor leads a Fist, made up of Two Hands. A Major leads a Sword, made up of two Fists, and a Prime leads a Hammer, consisting of two Swords, a Hand of archers, a half Hand of Seekers (see Appendix B for information on the Seeker prestige class), and a half Hand of support staff (usually Auxiliaries).

Council of Speakers

Seven Speakers form the elected council of Lochrinn. Active Seekers are not eligible to run, as the need for their services in the field outweighs the work they could do on the council, but anyone else may choose to run for election.

Six of the seven are each responsible for a quadrant of the town, while the seventh represents the interests of the farmsteaders. Usually elderly folk who have served as officers in a long and distinguished career will run for election. Elections are held every Somersend, and three town Speaker positions become available each year. The Farmstead Speaker is also elected every second year, but only farmsteaders may vote for that position.

Speakers will hold court to hear criminal and civil cases. The Speaker for the quadrant where the crime took place will speak for the accuser, and the Speaker for the quadrant of the person accused will speak for him. If the quadrants are the same, the Speaker of a randomly chosen quadrant will speak for the accuser.

Purpose

Protection: The only goal of the Lochrinn Town Guild is to provide protection for the town, necessary because of its location. The town charter, which was developed when Lochrinn was a small village with a wooden palisade, provides for the conscription of labor to improve the defenses and to undertake any task assigned to them during an attack against the town.

Membership

Location: All permanent inhabitants of the town and nearby farmsteads over the age of 19 are full voting members of the guild.

Joining the Guild

Application: Anyone of any class can join the guild. Membership is not mandatory, but those who do not join the guild are not entitled to its protection and may not reside in the town.

Travelers who wish to stay at one of the three inns in the town are required to contribute to the town's defense to the best of their ability during an attack by outland barbarians and monsters, and pay a head tax which is used to finance the cost of defenses. If a traveler is present in town on Hammerblow, he is expected to work; if he elects to leave, he will not be welcome back any time soon, nor will he be afforded the protection of the town in any attack.

Table 3.5 – Lochrinn Town Guild Age Advancement

Category	Age	Benefits
Child	0–3	N/A
Cub	4–9	Fraternity
Cadet	10–14	Bonus feat
Reserve or Auxiliary	15–18	Bonus feat
Militiaman	19+	Access to prestige class, Shelter

Table 3.6 – Lochrinn Town Guild Advancement Table

Grade	Requirements	Benefits
Militiaman (1)	Age 19+	Access to prestige class, Shelter
Second (2)	Base attack bonus +3, Strength or Dexterity 13+, Balance 2, Climb 1, Jump 1, Wilderness Lore 2, Armor Proficiency (Light); Weapon Focus in any one of: [long sword, short sword, spear (any), polearm (any), bow (any), club (any), one-handed mace, flail, or hammer]	Combat bonus
First (3)	Base attack bonus +4, Strength or Dexterity 14+, Wilderness Lore 4, Dodge	Command (Hand)
Minor (4)	At least 2nd-level Seeker, Diplomacy 1, Knowledge (military tactics) 1, Leadership	Command (Fist)
Major (5)	Diplomacy 3, Knowledge (military tactics) 2, Sense Motive 1	Command (Sword)
Prime (6)	Diplomacy 5	Command (Hammer)
Speaker (7)	Diplomacy 4, Sense Motive 4, win election	Authority

Alignment: All outsiders who wish to join the Lochrinn Town Guild, and thus take up residence in the town, must be either Lawful Good or Lawful Neutral.

Size and Scope

Every inhabitant of the town is a member of the guild, even the newly born. There are 1,324 voting members, that is, people over the age of 19. The remainder of the population are children up to 18 years of age. There are several dozen farms surrounding the town, and the residents of these steads are also members of the Guild.

Guild Structure & Advancement

Age: Since everyone in Lochrinn belongs to the town guild, members' first advancements are based purely on age. All age advancements take place at Somersend.

Graded (Merit/Elective): Once the character is classed as a Militiaman, advancement is based on merit. The Militiaman ranks have the promotion structure shown in the table below. To become a Speaker, a character must be elected by the adult population and meet the grade requirements.

Benefits

The benefits of the Lochrinn Town Guild are most fully realized by a PC who has grown up in the town. Certain benefits can accrue to those who join later, however.

Lochrinn Natives Only

Bonus Feats: Because of their early training, Lochrinn natives receive Weapon Focus (sling) for free when they advance to Cadet and Weapon Focus (dagger) when they advance to Reserve.

Fraternity: A native has a special bond with the members of his Cub Band and his Hammer (which often overlap). These people will go out of their way to help the character.

All Members

Access to Prestige Class: Once a member of any class meets the requirements, he may choose to take levels in the Seeker prestige class.

Authority: Speakers form the government of the town of Lochrinn, have decision-making power, and are treated with great respect by citizens of the town.

Combat Bonus: Because of the intensive training with selected weapons and the expert assessment about which weapons would suit them, Seconds receive a +1 competence bonus to attacks with any one weapon of their choosing.

Command: Guild members that advance to the rank of First or higher receive command of a group of soldiers. The size of the group increases as the commander advances in grade.

Shelter: A Militiaman is welcome in any home or farmstead in or near Lochrinn. Wounds will be tended to, supplies will be offered, and any other possible assistance may be granted.

Disadvantages

Deterioration: If a Lochrinn native is ever without his sling and dagger, for whatever reason, he will become increasingly jittery, nervous, irritable, and eventually manic. Make a Will save vs. DC 20 to behave normally; otherwise a panic attack ensues and the character will be incapable of action until at least one of the weapons is restored.

Time: A PC who is a member of a Lochrinn Hammer is sworn to undertake The Duty every thirteen days and to help on Hammerblow every twenty. This can put a dent in any long-term adventuring.

Affiliations

The Lochrinn Town Guild has a strong affiliation with the Adventurer's Guild (the Sojourners; see chapter 4). The nearest chapter of the Sojourners, although several days' travel toward civilization from the wild lands around Lochrinn, has a deed of agreement with the Speakers' Council of Lochrinn that any information important to the well-being of the town will be shared with them as soon as possible. In addition, any adventurers in Lochrinn at the time of an attack will render all assistance they can to save the town and its people.

Leaving the Guild

Once a character is a member of this guild, he will never lose his membership. If he should ever come back to the town, he will be welcomed and sought out to relate his experiences in the outside world, especially in "civilization."

Expulsion: If a character breaks the law, the protection of the guild will be withdrawn. Depending on the severity of the crime, the punishment could be any-

thing from exile to being hurled from the wall onto the ditch stakes.

Your Campaign

Lochrinn can be integrated into an existing campaign in a number of ways:

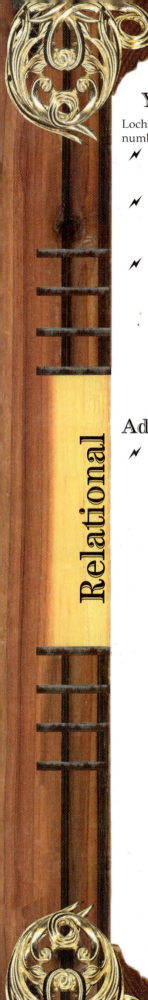

- Lochrinn could be used as a base of operations for a party of characters as they explore the wilderness outside the borders of the town.

- Coming back from a foray, the PCs find Lochrinn and decide to stay awhile. They learn the history and ways of the town and what is expected of them when an attack comes.

- Lochrinn could be the center of an entire campaign, with each PC being a member of a Militiaman Hammer. The campaign could center around the rise of a new evil in the wilderness which is marshaling hordes of monsters and other fell beasts to wipe the town, representing civilization, off the map. As the PCs begin, a number of the outlying settlements have been attacked, and Seekers are reporting the movement of many creatures toward a central but undefined point.

Adventure Hooks

- The PCs are resting from their latest foray when they are approached by the Speakers. A Seeker is missing, as is the party of five that went after him. A new party of five Seekers and ten experienced Militiamen is now overdue by two days, and the Speakers want the experienced adventurers to join forces with the town's most experienced Seeker to find out what has happened.

- While exploring an underground cavern, the characters stumble across the body of a Seeker. Knowing how the town honors its fallen, especially Seekers, they resolve to bring the body back to town. But something doesn't want that to happen.

- Thief PCs hear of fabulous wealth in the lowest level of the Citadel and decide that the town is being greedy, keeping all that nice gold for themselves.

- A young woman wants to escape the regimented life she leads in Lochrinn. Her Hammer thinks she is their good luck charm and desperately wants to keep her. Worse, her father is a Speaker and accuses the PCs of kidnapping her. Can they get away?

Variations

- Considerable variations exist in town guilds. One may represent every member of the town, or there may be a dozen different town guilds, from fraternity houses representing different hobbies or sports to rival criminal gangs that control certain areas of the town.

- **Protection**: The local ruler is a cruel tyrant, but he needs the revenue generated by the town. The association of the townsfolk matches the strength of the lord and his soldiers, and an uneasy relationship is established.

  - **Economic**: Some town guilds exist to provide for the regulation of markets in the town proper, with revenue going to the town to fix roads and other civil amenities.

  - **Control**: There are town guilds to which only craftsmen (carpenters, butchers, weavers, smiths, etc.) may belong. These are formed to control the entry of new craftsmen into the town's economy.

  - **Sharing**: Some town guilds exist for religious or social reasons, where the populace gathers together at certain times of the year to celebrate, worship, or just party.

  - **Goal**: Some towns form a guild to accomplish a specific goal, such as the granting of a town charter from the local ruler or the building of a splendid cathedral dedicated to a local saint.

Chapter 4 - The Collective

Marcus struggled wearily through the deep snowdrift, his two halfling companions following as best they could in the furrow he carved out. All three could hear the wolves baying, and the sounds were getting closer. It was only a matter of time, and a short time at that, before the pack closed in and the adventurers became a hot meal.

The snow thinned, and the travelers saw a copse of trees a little way ahead of them. If they could make it to the trees they could at least put up a fight and the pack would pay dearly for its supper. The pack apparently had the same thought, as the calls became louder and the humanoids could hear the sounds of the wolves closing in for the kill. With the last of their energy the three made it to the copse to find a wooden shack sitting empty. Without a second thought they opened the door, fell inside, and slammed the door behind them.

The wolf pack scrabbled at the door but could not knock it down, and the weary travelers were safe for now.

Marcus and the halflings took a few minutes to catch their breath, then began looking around the one room to see if anything of use had been left by the previous occupants. The fireplace had a good supply of chopped wood, and they soon had a cheery blaze going, which lifted their spirits enormously. In one corner was a chest whose top could be used as a seat, and inside the trio found some dried meat and nuts. In another chest/seat were a quiver of arrows and two sharp daggers. There were no bunks, but the rough-hewn table was large enough for the halflings to spread their bedrolls and be moderately comfortable. Marcus spread his bedroll on the floor and all three quickly fell asleep.

By morning the fire had gone out, the wolves had moved on, and the snow had stopped. As the travelers prepared to continue their journey, the door opened and a man dressed in leathers stood framed in the opening.

"Hail travelers and well met! I am Dorian, woodsman extraordinaire and keeper of this shelter on behalf of The Collective."

Marcus smiled at Dorian. "Ah, I had thought perhaps this was a Collective haven. Lucky we stumbled on it, or we'd have been wolfbait. What do we owe for our salvation?"

"Oh, just chop some wood to replace what you used, and leave what you feel is a suitable donation for any food or weapons you made use of. Unless one of you is a member?"

"I am Marcus Lerius, Silver of The Collective. But as this place saved our lives we will part with six gold as well as chopping the wood—a small price to ensure this haven is here for the next needy adventurer."

With that, Marcus and the halflings chopped firewood until they broke a sweat, handed their six gold to Dorian, and continued their interrupted journey.

Purpose

Protection/Sharing: The Collective Assembly of Sojourners and Miscellaneous Adventurers exists to provide assistance, accommodation, food, and potential employment to its members. It also provides emergency food and shelter to nonmembers for a nominal fee.

Membership

Profession: The Collective accepts any and all adventurers who choose to join, as long as they pay their dues. An adventurer is anyone who has at least one level of an adventuring class as described in whatever d20 rulebooks your campaign allows.

Wealth or Payment: Regular membership in The Collective costs 10 gp per month for up to 6th-level characters. For 7th-level characters and beyond, it costs 5 gp per level per month. For this money, a member can claim shelter in any Collective-run establishment, can expect one meal per day from that establishment, and has access to discounted equipment and repair services. In exchange for two hours of labor a member can have a second meal, and four hours of work earns a third meal. Members above 6th level can gain access to other benefits for additional payments, as described in Benefits.

Joining the Guild

Application: Anyone who wishes to join The Collective need only apply at any major Collective establishment and pay the first two months' membership. Members receive a simple magical device which can be recharged for any number of months at any Collective house the character visits. This device shows the character's membership is current. DMs running low-magic campaigns may choose to substitute a coin that is minted with the character's name, membership level, and an expiration date.

Size and Scope

The Collective is spread far and wide across the known (and some say the unknown) world. Wherever adventurers may be found, there too you will find The Collective in some form or another. In large cities, the presence is almost always low-key. Perhaps a Collective member runs an inn and provides basic needs to members who are passing through. In small cities and large towns, The Collective has a more noticeable presence, owning at least a partial share of most inns and stables and having notice boards in the common rooms where prospective employers can put up notices about what kind of adventurers they are looking for. Adventurers between jobs can also post notices stating their qualifications and experience and allow employers to seek them out. In smaller towns, chances are the only inn is owned (at least in part) by a Collective member. The notice board might be inside or on the verandah out front, but it will be there to assist adventurers and adventures in finding each other.

On the frontier, The Collective's presence may be a friendly farmer who can provide shelter in the barn overnight and a hot breakfast in the morning. Further out, in the untamed wilds, sturdy shacks are located to provide basic shelter to stranded adventurers. These shacks are usually unattended, with a local druid or ranger checking them every few days to restock the firewood and rations if needed. The shacks are protection against wild animals but are not proof against marauding orcs or other humanoid monsters. They do at least provide some cover if a party is trapped by a raiding party.

Apart from the notice boards on display, The Collective is usually among the first to get wind of legendary dragon hoards or lost cities rediscovered. These are not posted where all and sundry can see them, but the innkeeper or other Collective member will reveal this information to silver or gold members who know what questions to ask.

Structure & Advancement

The Collective has a mostly flat structure. By far the majority of members are simply dues-paying members. Characters with at least seven levels who enjoy the comforts a little extra money can buy are able to enjoy silver membership. For characters of at least 13th level, gold membership is available and additional benefits can be obtained.

The Collective is run by a council of twelve. Members of the council are at least 15th-level adventurers who have been gold members for at least two years. They serve three-year terms on the council, which equates to spending at least one quarter of the time during those three years at the library. They do duty as librarians, provide assistance to members, and resolve disputes. Four council positions come up each year, and any qualified member may nominate someone. All current members with at least six months' standing are able to participate in any vote which may be required. Most often, members will nominate themselves out of a sense of duty or a desire to pull back from adventuring for a while, rather than because they want the job. Votes are therefore rare.

Benefits

Access to Items: Collective members receive a 5% discount on all common adventuring equipment including spell components, but not on enchanted items. Silver members receive a 10% discount on all items, again excluding enchanted items. Gold members receive a 10% discount on mundane items and a 5% discount on magical items.

Adventurers for Hire: Though The Collective, members can locate other members who are willing to sell their services to a short-handed expedition. See the "Adventurers for Hire" section later in this chapter for full details.

Bank: Collective members may deposit their wealth with The Collective bank rather than carry it around with them. There is a small fee for this service. See the "Banking Service" section later in this chapter for full details.

Current Information: The Collective maintains lists of local goings-on that may be of interest to members. These lists are freely available in all Collective establishments.

Historical Information: Silver and gold members have privileged access to The Collective's library. Silver members may access adventuring reports up to ten years old, and if they choose to pursue an adventure which is apparently unfinished The Collective will provide as much assistance as is feasible in obtaining information, equipment, and fellow adventurers. Silver members gain a +1 circumstance bonus to all Charisma-based rolls while on such an adventure due to their fame. This bonus becomes permanent if the adventure is concluded successfully but is lost if there is no successful outcome. Gold members may access the entire collection, which includes some tomes more than a thousand years old. These tend to contain references to dragon hoards, civilizations long forgotten, and other legendary adventures. Gold members who choose to pursue a legendary adventure will receive as much assistance as The Collective can provide. For the duration of any such adventure, the member gains a +2 circumstance bonus to all Charisma-based rolls because of his fame in undertaking the quest. On successful completion this bonus becomes permanent, but it is lost if the quest is not successfully concluded. These fame bonuses do not stack with one another.

Knowledge: Members of The Collective gain the benefit of the shared knowledge of other members. Silver members gain a +2 insight bonus to any one Knowledge skill check. Gold members gain an additional +1 insight bonus to all Knowledge skill checks.

Lifeline: Any Collective-sanctioned expedition can leave a sealed plan of its journey with an expected return date written on the outside. If an expedition is more than one week late in returning, the plan will be opened and The Collective will attempt to mount a search and rescue mission. See the "Lifeline Service" section later in this chapter for details.

Local Experts: The Collective provides access to useful NPCs. See the "Local Experts" section later in this chapter for full details.

Shelter: Any Collective member may claim shelter from any Collective establishment. Shelter includes a place to sleep and at least one meal. The standard of accommodation and meals will vary greatly depending on whether it's a large city, a farmhouse in the country, a shack on the edge of the wilds, or anything in between. Silver and gold members may obtain a higher quality of shelter where it is available. In a few places, such as major cities, gold members are provided with luxurious accommodations. In the wild, though, a shack is a shack and there is nothing better.

Trading Post: The Collective operates a number of trading posts on the fringes of civilization. After an expedition

Table 4.1 – The Collective Advancement

Current Grade	Prerequisites	XP Cost	Benefits Gained
Basic Member	At least one level of any adventuring class	500	Access to items, Adventurers for Hire, Bank, Current Information, Local Experts, Shelter, Trading Post
Silver	7th level; 5 gp per month per level	1,000	Historical Information, Knowledge, Shelter
Gold	13th level; 10 gp per month per level	1,500	Knowledge, Shelter

into the wilds, members may sell goods they have acquired and receive a better price than other establishments might pay them. See the "Trading Service" section later in this chapter for more details.

Disadvantages

Distrust: The average commoner doesn't much care for adventurers; they attract trouble. In large population centers this manifests by increasing the chances of members being singled out by street gangs for "special" treatment. In less populated areas, folk will likely shut their doors and ignore any approaches.

Reporting: All members are required to provide The Collective with a detailed written report of each and every adventure they undertake. These reports are stored in The Collective's library and may be accessed by other members. Some reports are available only to silver and/or gold members.

Adventurers for Hire

From time to time a party will be down a member or two due to illness, recovering from wounds, family commitments, or sometimes incarceration. Or perhaps the upcoming expedition is a little tougher than the team feels comfortable with and some extra help would be useful.

This is where adventurers for hire come into play. Some adventurers just don't fit in with a regular group and prefer to sell their services on an expedition-by-expedition basis. These adventurers can often be found in the halls of The Collective, carousing, practicing their skills, or actively seeking to join a group that takes their fancy. Their rates vary, as do their abilities and personalities. It is up to each group to decide who to hire and whether to negotiate for a better deal.

Agron Mindbane

Male dwarf Fighter 10/Cleric 3: CR 13; Medium-size humanoid (dwarf); HD 10d10+3d8+26; hp 105; Init +1, Spd 15 ft.; AC 20 (touch 12, flat-footed 19); Atk +20/+15/+10 melee (1d8 +9/19-20/x3, battleaxe +3) or +13/+8/+3 ranged (no preferred weapon); SA spells; SQ cleric abilities, fighter abilities, dwarf abilities; Al NG; SV Fort +12, Ref +5, Will +8; Str 18, Dex 12, Con 14, Int 11, Wis 14, Cha 10.

Skills and Feats: Climb +7, Concentration +4, Craft (gemcutting) +3, Diplomacy +2, Handle Animal +3, Heal +3, Jump +7, Knowledge (religion) +2, Ride [horse] +4, Search +1, Spot +3, Swim +7, Wilderness Lore +4; Blind-Fight, Cleave, Combat Casting, Combat Reflexes, Enlarge Spell, Great Cleave, Improved Critical (battleaxe), Leadership, Power Attack, Weapon Focus (battleaxe), Weapon Specialization (battleaxe).

Special Qualities: dwarf abilities

Cleric Spells (4/3+1/2+1): Deity: Any dwarven good; Domains Earth, Protection: 0—*detect magic, guidance, light, read magic;* 1st—*bless, divine favor, invisibility to undead, magic stone;* 2nd—*bull's strength, hold person, shield other.*

Possessions: dwarven plate, *battleaxe +3, wand of cure moderate wounds.*

Agron is a gruff dwarf, about as wide as he is tall. He loves a good battle and also a good ale, although he claims finding a good ale outside of dwarven keeps is an impossible task. His lifelong quest is to locate a stash of ancient dwarven spirits in some long-disused dwarven keep under some long-abandoned mine in some mountain range which used to have a name but has since been humanized by the dominant species. Most folk doubt such a place exists, but Agron is willing to go on any adventure into any mountainous region if he thinks there's a slight chance of finding the keep, or even evidence of its existence.

He loves gems, as does any dwarf, and is happy to accept his share of any booty in that form, or in any other form as he'll convert it to gems via The Collective's trading and banking services. He asks for an equal share in any venture into the mountains, one and a half shares for other ventures, if he can be convinced to go at all (DC 25 Diplomacy check). Agron can usually be found at the guildhall bar, drinking with anyone he can see.

Baye Karin

Female half-elf Cleric 6/Sorcerer 6: CR 12; Medium-size humanoid (half-elf); HD 6d8+6d6+12; hp 69; Init +0, Spd 30 ft.; AC 16 (touch 13, flat-footed 16); Atk +9/+4 melee (1d8+1/x2, masterwork morningstar) or +7/+2 ranged (no preferred weapon); SA spells; SQ cleric abilities, sorcerer abilities, half-elf abilities; Al CG; SV Fort +8, Ref +4, Will +13; Str 12, Dex 10, Con 12, Int 14, Wis 16, Cha 16.

Skills and Feats: Alchemy +8, Concentration +5, Diplomacy +7, Heal +9, Knowledge (arcana) +6, Knowledge (religion) +6, Profession (herbalist) +9, Scry +6, Search +7, Speak Language (Draconic), Speak Language (Infernal), Spot +8, Swim +5; Brew Potion, Extend Spell, Skill Focus (heal), Spell Focus (conjuration), Track.

Special Qualities: Half-elf abilities—Immunity to *sleep* spells and similar magical effects; +2 saving throw bonus against Enchantment spells or effects; Low-light Vision; +1 bonus to Listen, Search, and Spot checks; Elven Blood.

Cleric Spells (5/4+1/4+1/3+1): Deity: Any chaotic non-Evil elven; Domains Chaos, Protection: 0—*detect magic, guidance, mending, resistance, virtue;* 1st—*command, detect undead, entropic shield, sanctuary, shield of faith;* 2nd—*hold person (x2), lesser restoration, shatter, silence;* 3rd—*dispel magic, prayer, protection from elements, searing light.*

Sorcerer Spells (6/7/6/4): 0—*detect poison, flare, ghost sound, light, mending, ray of frost, read magic;* 1—*comprehend languages, grease, mage armor, true strike;* 2—*acid arrow, summon swarm;* 3—*flame arrow.*

Familiar: Fluffy (owl); HD 6, HP 25, AC 20, Atk +12/+7 (1d4-2/x2, claws(2)), speed 10.

Possessions: Masterwork morningstar, *leather armor +1, ring of wizardry (II), rod of thunder, wand of color spray, wand of cure moderate wounds, ring of protection +3.*

Baye is a striking half-elf female who just radiates magical power. The source of her power isn't immediately obvious but her magical nature is. She dresses like a wizard but doesn't go so far as a pointy hat with stars on it. Her personality is politely described as bubbly, but some have less flattering words for it. Whatever her social skills, or lack thereof, Baye is a competent companion and an asset to any group. She likes to adventure because she can, and as long as her expenses are covered she isn't too particular about what rewards may be offered.

Baye doesn't spend much time in the guildhall, preferring to pray in the temple, either to her elven deity or to the pantheon in general when she seeks to understand her sorceress side.

Bob

Male human Fighter 8/Cleric 7: CR 15; Medium-size humanoid (human); HD 8d10+7d8+15; hp 102; Init +1, Spd 20 ft.; AC 16 (touch 11, flat-footed 15); Atk +15/+10/+5 melee (1d8+2/17-20/x2, masterwork longsword) or +14/+9/+4 ranged (1d6/x3, shortbow); SA spells; SQ cleric abilities, fighter abilities; Al LG; SV Fort +12, Ref +5, Will +14; Str 14, Dex 13, Con 12, Int 14, Wis 16, Cha 12.

Skills and Feats: Bluff +4, Climb +6, Concentration +5, Craft (carpentry) +4, Diplomacy +7, Gather Information +5, Handle Animal +3, Jump +5, Knowledge (arcana) +7, Knowledge (engineering) +8, Knowledge (geography) +7, Knowledge (religion) +7, Listen +6, Ride [horse] +5, Scry +3, Search +4, Sense Motive +4, Speak Language (Celestial), Speak Language (Draconic), Spot +7, Swim +4; Alertness, Cleave, Combat Reflexes, Expertise, Great Cleave, Improved Critical (longsword), Power Attack, Run, Skill Focus (knowledge [engineering]), Skill Focus (knowledge [geography]), Weapon Focus (longsword).

Cleric Spells (6/5+1/4+1/3+1/1/1+1): Deity: none, domains Knowledge, Protection: 0—*detect magic (x2), detect poison, guidance, light, read magic*; 1st—*bless, command, detect undead, entropic shield, remove fear, sanctuary*; 2nd—*delay poison, endurance, hold person, lesser restoration, shield other*; 3rd—*daylight, dispel magic, negative energy protection, protection from elements*; 4th—*divination, neutralize poison*.

Possessions: Masterwork longsword, masterwork chain shirt.

Bob is an older chap (64 years, stats modified to reflect this) who spends much of his time hanging around the guildhall in the hope of being offered work. His adventuring days are mostly in the past and his prime asset now is as a source of knowledge or entertainment. He has many stories about "when I was a lad...," and his age belies his ability to be a useful addition to any adventuring party.

Grnugh (pronounced Grunge)

Male half-orc Druid 2/Sorcerer 2: CR 4; Medium-size humanoid (half-orc); HD 2d8+2d4+8; hp 27; Init +1, Spd 30 ft.; AC 13 (touch 11, flat-footed 12); Atk +3 melee (1d4+1/x2, sickle or quarterstaff) or +3 ranged (no preferred weapon); SA spells; SQ druid abilities, sorcerer abilities, half-orc abilities; Al N; SV Fort +7, Ref +1, Will +8; Str 12, Dex 12, Con 14, Int 10, Wis 14, Cha 14.

Skills and Feats: Alchemy +1, Animal Empathy +3, Concentration +4, Diplomacy +4, Handle Animal +4, Heal +3, Knowledge (arcana) +1, Knowledge (nature) +2, Search +1, Spot +3, Wilderness Lore +3; Spell Focus (Evocation), Track.

Special Qualities: Half-orc abilities—Darkvision, Orc Blood.

Druid Spells (4/3): 0—*detect poison, guidance, purify food and drink, resistance*; 1st—*entangle, faerie fire, pass without trace*.

Sorcerer Spells (6/5): 0—*dancing lights, detect magic, disrupt undead, light, mending*; 1st—*burning hands, magic missile*.

Familiar: Harold (rat), HD 2, HP 8, AC 15, Atk +6 (1, bite), speed 15

Possessions: quarterstaff, sickle, leather, several *potions of cure light wounds, potion of neutralize poison.*

Grnugh is not your typical half-orc. For a start, he's quite good-looking and has a pleasant personality to boot. He is quite the ladies' man, tossing off magic to highlight the hair of his female companions or simply flattering them with his smooth-as-silk tongue. Men often take a dislike to Grnugh if he pays too much attention to their female companions, but he is hard to dislike on a long-term basis.

Apart from the looks and charm, Grnugh does not share his fellows' phobia of things magical. While he neither understands nor cares for the ways of the wizard (he lacks the attention span to dedicate himself to the rigorous study), he has a natural talent for spells that makes him a valuable companion in the wilds.

Grnugh likes the shine of gold and he is willing to work with any group that gives him the same share basis as they use for themselves, be that per person, level, or any other means. As long as he is treated fairly, he is happy just to get out and do something interesting.

Grnugh is ashamed of his heritage. His human mother had a miserable life both before and after his birth. No human man wanted her or her illegitimate offspring, and as Grnugh was the result of an orcish raid where his father left his mother for dead, there was no way they could go to the orcs for shelter. Because of this, Grnugh despises all male orcs and has no time for bullies of any ilk. Despite his build, Grnugh prefers to use magic in combat and only use close combat if there is some advantage to doing so.

Hieral Topitt

Male human Ranger 6/Assassin 8: CR 14; Medium-size humanoid (human); HD 6d10+8d6+14; hp 90; Init +3, Spd 30 ft.; AC 18 (touch 16, flat-footed 18); Atk +15(+15)/+10(+5)/+5 melee (1d8+4/19-20/x2, longsword, 1d4+3/19-20/x2, dagger) or +17/+12/+7 ranged (1d8/x3, longbow); SA spells, sneak attack, death attack; SQ assassin abilities, ranger abilities; Al LN; SV Fort +9 (+12 vs. poison), Ref +11, Will +6; Str 15, Dex 18, Con 12, Int 10, Wis 14, Cha 10.

Skills and Feats: Climb +6, Decipher Script +3, Diplomacy +2, Disable Device +2, Disguise +4, Gather Information +3, Hide +12, Intuit Direction +6, Listen +10, Move Silently +12, Ride +7, Search +4, Spot +9, Swim +8, Tumble +7, Use Magical Device +3, Use Rope +7, Wilderness Lore +6; Alertness, Cleave, Improved Two-Weapon Fighting, Power Attack, Track, Weapon Focus (dagger), Weapon Focus (longsword).

Special Qualities: Ranger abilities—favored enemy (dragons), favored enemy (orcs), two-weapon fighting at –2/–2 (already factored into attack bonuses); assassin abilities—poison use, uncanny dodge (AC bonus), uncanny dodge (can't be flanked), sneak attack +3d6, death attack.

Ranger spells (2/1): 1st—*delay poison, resist elements*; 2nd—*sleep.*

Assassin spells (1, 10% chance of failure): *spider climb.*

Possessions: *Ring of protection +2, longsword +2, dagger +1*, masterwork longbow.

Hieral is an enigma. He is not obviously of any particular class and does not brag about his talents at every opportunity. His resume says he's a troubleshooter, and his reputation is very good to excellent. He rarely adventures with the same group more than once. He spends about half his time around the guildhall, the rest of it in places nobody knows nor cares to ask.

Hieral has a simple system for charging for his services. Hieral gets one and a half shares in all treasure. He does not care how the party divides up what's left after he has his share. His preferences are for small magic weapons, gemstones, and cash, in that order. He is willing to negotiate about the magic weapons if a party member desperately wants one.

GM information: Hieral is an assassin, and a good one. He is Lawful Neutral in alignment, as all true assassins should be. He is paid to kill things in defense of his current group, and that's what he does. Once he accepts a contract with a group, he will work with that group and pull his weight. He truly is a "troubleshooter", using his skills to save the skins of more than one adventurer in dire straits. Hieral does not detect as evil and it should not be possible for characters to discern his class. Hieral is not one to deliver the *coup de grâce* to a downed opponent, but he will not seek to prevent others from doing so if they choose. A vanquished foe is no longer a threat and therefore killing him is a waste of effort.

Markeet Greenaxe

Female elf Barbarian 5/Sorcerer 5: CR 10; Medium-size humanoid (elf); HD 5d12+5d4+10; hp 65; Init +4, Spd 30 ft.; AC 19 (touch 16, flat-footed 15); Atk +8/+8 melee (1d8 +1/19-20/x2, longsword) or +13/+8 ranged (1d8/x3, masterwork composite longbow); SA spells; SQ barbarian abilities, sorcerer abilities, elf abilities; Al CG; SV Fort +6, Ref +8, Will +6; Str 12, Dex 18, Con 12, Int 12, Wis 12, Cha 14.

Skills and Feats: Alchemy +4, Climb +4, Concentration +5, Craft (bowmaking) +3, Handle Animal +6, Intuit Direction +4, Jump +4, Knowledge (arcana) +3, Knowledge (history) +4, Knowledge (nature) +3, Ride [horse] +8, Search +5, Speak Language (Orc), Spot +5, Tumble +6, Wilderness Lore +6; Point Blank Shot, Precise Shot, Track, Weapon Focus (composite longbow).

Special Qualities: Elf abilities—Immunity to *sleep* spells and similar magical effects; +2 saving throw bonus against Enchantment spells or effects; Low-light Vision; +1 bonus to Listen, Search, and Spot checks; Elven Blood.

Sorcerer Spells (6/7/5): 0—*dancing lights, detect magic, flare, light, mending, read magic*; 1st—*magic armor, magic weapon, shield, shocking grasp*; 2nd—*cat's grace, flaming sphere.*

Familiar: Slippery (weasel), HD 5, HP 27, AC 17, Atk +11/+6 (1, bite), speed 20.

Possessions: masterwork composite longbow, *leather +1, ring of animal friendship, ring of protection +2, wand of invisibility, staff of swarm insects.*

Markeet is a strange elf, perhaps explaining why she's an adventuress for hire rather than being a regular party or tribe member. She commonly wears leather armor, well worn and with little nicks all over it. Nonetheless, the armor is still quite capable of performing its assigned role. Unlike many elves who follow the demanding path of the wizard, Markeet is a sorcerer, gaining her magic from the natural forces of the forest and the plains where she grew up. She is often mistaken for a wizard by those who do not know her but who choose to judge her by appearance when she is not in armor. When in armor, she is often mistaken for a ranger; while she has many things in common with that class, her growing up near the plains drew her to the ways of the nomadic tribes. When she was 60 years old she was kidnapped by a nomad chieftain and raised as his daughter, so she learned the skills of the barbarian.

Markeet's kidnapper is long dead, and while she harbors no grudge (he treated her well), it is her dream to someday return to her people, perhaps even finding her real parents. The longevity of elves suggests they are still alive, but the forest where Markeet was born has been felled for timber to build dwellings for humans and the land is now used to graze cattle. Markeet does not know where her family is but she will gladly accompany any party that is heading into unexplored woodlands or even low-lying mountains. She doesn't care for the upper mountain regions, although her love of the outdoors and the joy of simply bounding around over rocks that her more clumsy companions must toil to climb sometimes piques her interest.

Markeet carries most of her possession with her wherever she goes. She doesn't care much for material goods other than what she needs to survive and to feed her horse, Dayglow.

Her sense of what's right demands she not work for free, so she expects a reasonable share of any

profits from an adventure, but she can be persuaded to take payment in kind by way of information leading to any elven group she is not aware of already. Silver or gold members may be able to find such information in the library. Directly useful information is unlikely to be in the restricted collection as it dates back only ten years, and Markeet's kidnapping was more than a century ago. The gold collection may well have references to the migration of Markeet's family; if a gold were to offer such information, Markeet would quickly turn from employee to employer in her eagerness to follow any lead. Markeet is a beautiful woman, but her introspective nature makes her seem aloof to those who don't take the time to find out what drives her.

Paddy Paddyson

Male gnome Wizard 8: CR 8; Small-size humanoid (gnome); HD 8d4; hp 36, Init +2, Spd 20 ft.; AC 21 (touch 21, flat-footed 19); Atk +7 melee (1d4-1/19-20/x2, *dagger of wounding*) or +4 ranged (no preferred weapon); SA spells; SQ wizard abilities, gnome abilities; Al LE; SV Fort +3, Ref +4, Will +7; Str 8, Dex 14, Con 13, Int 18, Wis 12, Cha 12.

Skills and Feats: Appraise +6, Bluff +3, Concentration +5, Craft (calligraphy) +7, Diplomacy +6, Gather Information +4, Knowledge (arcana) +9, Knowledge (history) +7, Knowledge (the planes) +8, Ride [horse] +3, Scry +7, Speak Language (Abyssal), Speak Language (Draconic), Speak Language (Elven), Speak Language (Goblin), Speak Language (Infernal), Speak Language (Orc), Speak Language (Undercommon), Spellcraft +10, Swim +3; Extend Spell, Maximize Spell, Scribe Scroll, Still Spell, Toughness.

Special Qualities: Gnome abilities—Low-light vision, +2 save vs. illusions, +1 attack vs. kobolds and goblinoids, +4 dodge vs. giants, +2 Listen, +2 Alchemy.

Wizard Spells (4+1/5+1/4+1/4+1/3+1): Specialty Evocation; Prohibited Transmutation; 0—any; 1st—*color spray, grease, hold portal, identify, mage armor, magic missile, obscuring mist, ray of enfeeblement, shield*; 2nd—*darkness, flaming sphere, invisibility, shatter*; 3rd—*fireball, flame arrow, lightning bolt, wind wall*; 4th—*fire shield, ice storm, wall of fire, wall of ice.*

Familiar: Beak (raven), HD 8, HP 12, AC 18, Atk +8(1, claw (x2)), speed 10.

Possessions: *bracers of armor +5, dagger of wounding, ring of protection +3, wand of lightning bolt, wand of web.*

First off, that's not his real name. Being a gnome, Paddy's real name takes about half an hour to say, so Paddy is what he goes by outside of gnome enclaves. A wizard through and through, that's Paddy—lots of combat spells and the willingness to use them. He cares little for the lives of others, but he sticks to any agreement he makes with a party. Like all adventurers for hire, he is aware that a double-cross will ruin his reputation and make further jobs difficult to gain at best, and most likely he would be a marked gnome.

Paddy's services do not come cheaply. He requires two full shares of any booty from the adventure, plus replacement of used spell components, but he does cover his own costs apart from the components.

Paddy has an outwardly jovial nature, but inside he is always looking to work the angles to improve his lot in life, as long as he can do so without violating his principles. Paddy will not engage in melee combat unless there is no other choice. His strengths are elsewhere. He can be found in the guildhall most days, especially around meal times.

Tusslehat Seedhand

Male halfling Rogue 6: CR 6; Small-size humanoid (halfling); HD 6d6; hp 26; Init +5, Spd 20 ft.; AC 19 (touch 17, flat-footed 14); Atk +6 melee (1d4/19-20/x2, masterwork dagger) or +11 ranged (1d6/x3, masterwork composite shortbow); SA sneak attack +3d6; SQ thief abilities, halfling abilities; Al CG; SV Fort +3, Ref +11, Will +4; Str 10, Dex 20, Con 10, Int 10, Wis 12, Cha 13.

Skills and Feats: Balance +9, Bluff +5, Climb +7, Craft (locksmith) +6, Decipher Script +4, Diplomacy +4, Gather Information +5, Hide +13, Knowledge (history) +1, Knowledge (nobility) +1, Listen +7, Move Silently +11, Open Lock +13, Pick Pocket +8, Search +3, Sense Motive +4, Spot +4, Tumble +6, Use Magic Device +3, Use Rope +6, Wilderness Lore +2; Dodge, Skill Focus (open lock), Track.

Special Qualities: Halfling abilities—+4 Hide; +2 Climb, Jump, Listen, and Move Silently; +1 to all saving throws; low-light vision; +2 bonus to fear saving throws; +1 attack modifier to thrown attacks; Small creature attack modifiers.

Possessions: masterwork dagger, masterwork composite shortbow, *ring of protection +1.*

Tusslehat is a halfling and people therefore assume he is a rogue. In this case they are correct, but he doesn't like people jumping to conclusions and gets quite indignant if he's approached in what he considers an improper manner ("We're looking for a thief, do you want the job" would be improper).

Apart from the chip on his shoulder about being typecast, Tuss is a typical halfling. Food and comfort are his two main drives. He doesn't like dungeon delving because "caves are cold, damp, and hard to sleep on." He does like his creature comforts, and as they do not come cheaply, he will go on almost any adventure if the price is right. For urban jaunts, he'll take an equal share with everyone else of whatever profits there are. For wilderness expeditions, he asks for a 5% cut plus an equal share of the remaining 95%.

If the adventure looks like it's going underground for more than a few hours, he demands a 10% cut plus an equal share of the remainder. He will try for "first pick" and will accept that in lieu of the 10% if he can be convinced (Diplomacy, DC 20) that magical treasure is likely to be found.

Tuss puts the sanctity of life (especially his own) above all else and will not kill wantonly. He will attempt to stop any party member who is fond of the *coup de grâce* on helpless opponents but he won't risk his own neck to save a bad guy from this fate. He will risk himself to save a companion if the need arises. Despite his reverence for life, Tuss is not above sneaking behind an opponent and stabbing him in the back.

Banking Service

The Collective provides its members with a banking service. Adventurers often acquire encumbering amounts of money in their explorations and, if they survive, usually end up very wealthy. However, money is usually in the form of precious metals and is worth its own weight, whether gold or silver coins or platinum bars. Transporting large amounts of coinage long arduous distances or through dangerous territories is unwieldy and an undesirable risk for fear of robbery, extortion, or unforeseen accident. With its network of guildhalls, remote trading posts, and associated trusted merchants, Collective members are able to deposit money at a guildhall or other fortified Collective center and receive a coded chit as a form of receipt and as a means of exchange—a "promissory note." This note is recognized at any guildhall, guild trading post, and associated merchant and may be used to purchase goods or services or to exchange for money in the amount shown.

Service

In every guildhall or fortified guild outpost is a special room where a member can present his money for conversion to a promissory note. After the member and the local banker agree on the amount, the money is taken away to a secure room and the member is issued the note. This transaction carries a fee dependent on the level of membership. The fee may be paid at the point of deposit or as a reduction from the amount deposited.

- *Basic*. Basic members pay 6% of the deposited amount as the transaction fee.
- *Silver*. Silver members pay 4% of the deposited amount as the transaction fee.
- *Gold*. Gold members pay 2% of the deposited amount as the transaction fee.

The guild's promissory notes are signed and sealed with The Collective's arms. Notes for large amounts are often protected with various spells, sigils, or glyphs, and, of course, the bearer of a note will take added precautions against theft or accident. Perhaps the greatest defense against theft is the guild's reputation for sending teams of members to hunt down all note thieves, irrespective of the amount on the note, and make examples of the perpetrators.

Promissory notes come in many forms, depending on the race and culture within which they are issued. Usually they are slips or scrolls of paper, parchment, or vellum. Sometimes they are ornately carved sticks of wood or bone, sometimes small pressed bars of steel or other metal. Whatever the shape or nature of the note, they all visibly bear the guild's arms and are recognized at all guild centers. Particularly ornate or complex notes do require an additional charge for their production.

The guild's banking service also provides a currency conversion service for its members. As long as sufficient funds of the right currency are available at a location, the guild will convert a member's coins between different currencies free of charge.

A promissory note may be upgraded at any time by taking the note and more currency to a guildhall or other guild banking center, depositing the additional money (for the usual fee) and the note, and receiving a new note in exchange. Further, it is not unusual for some members to choose not to fully redeem a note but rather to exchange only part of its value in coins and receive a new note for the balance.

It is not unusual for some guild members to always carry a note for funds held within the guild. On setting out on a long trip through territory covered by the guild network, some members take very little hard cash but instead deposit most of their money reserved for the journey at the local guildhall and receive a note. At each overnight stop, a member can stay in guild lodgings and hand his note to the local guild bank representative, who pays for the cost of the lodgings and any meals by deducting the cost from the note and issuing a new note for the balance. When the trip is over and the weary member returns home, he presents the final note to the local guildhall treasurer. Any credit balance is returned in cash.

Carrying a promissory note is also a risk in its own right since these notes guarantee payment to the bearer, no matter who the bearer is or how he looks. Stolen notes may be exchanged for hard cash by a thief or fence and are just as light and easy for the thieves to carry as they are for the owner. In some situations, stolen Collective notes are treated as a means of exchange between various criminals. Attempts at forgery of promissory notes also occasionally occur. Forged or stolen promissory notes guarantee a ruthless response from the guild.

When a member dies with unredeemed promissory notes, the guild pays the balance to the member's immediate family or to the beneficiaries in the member's will. If no will was made and the member has no immediate family, the notes are absorbed into the guild's treasury for the benefit of all members.

Areas Covered/Not Covered

The Collective banking network covers an extensive area, but its branches are found only where the guild has influence and where secure storage and transport exists or can be established. All guildhalls provide a banking service branch, but these are usually found only in cities or large towns. Members returning from an exploration of remote realms are usually interested in divesting themselves of bulky and heavy recovered treasures and coins long before they reach a guildhall. For this reason, the guild also runs several remote trading outposts located at the fringes of civilization. These trading posts operate as a service for travelers and locals but also contain secure storerooms and are frequently visited by armed and armored couriers. These secure trading posts also provide the banking service for Collective members.

Many places exist where the guild's banking service does not reach. These locations include realms hostile to The Collective, too dangerous for an outpost or a regular courier service, too inaccessible for an outpost, too infrequently traveled by Collective members, and too strange for any sort of permanent presence.

The more remote wilderness areas served by trading posts are dangerous and all too frequently suffer attacks, vandalism, and burglary attempts. The guild keeps a steady eye on these remote trading posts and usually establishes some sort of agreement with local barbarian tribes and sometimes even monsters, if possible. If an agreement is not possible, the avenging of all attacks with ruthlessness and speed a few times is usually enough to cause potential attackers to think twice before proceeding with an assault.

Collective

Exceptions

Though carrying a promissory note guarantees payment in the amount recorded, irrespective of the bearer's identity, sometimes the payment will be refused. These circumstances include:

♦ The bearer is a known forger or an associate of a known forger.

♦ The bearer is a known enemy of the guild.

♦ The note was stolen.

♦ The branch does not have the hard cash needed to cover the note.

If a third party, such as a king or local warlord, seizes some of the guild's notes and demands they be redeemed by The Collective, the guild will usually refuse the order and declare the notes void. If this act will put members at risk, the guild will try diplomacy to resolve the issue. If in the end there is no other recourse, the guild will redeem the notes.

Game Consequences

The frequent use of these guild promissory notes may have a larger impact on the game than first realized. If a character does not have to carry a large weight of coins around, he may be able to carry additional weapons, *e.g.*, an extra sword or more arrows. Additionally, a guild member has no need to store his wealth in coins but rather may have just one promissory note for the value of all his worldly wealth; a single note is far easier to secure than a load of coins. However, if a character chooses to carry his funds as a guild note but finds himself in a city or land where the guild has no presence, the character is effectively a pauper.

Game Examples & Plot Hooks

There are many ways of using the guild's banking service in a game:

√ A guild member has died leaving a large deposit. The guild sends a party to locate the late member's heirs.

√ A promissory note for a significant amount is missing. The party must find the note and, if it was stolen, teach the thieves a lesson they won't forget.

√ Conversely, a note for a significant amount has been found but the bearer is unknown. The guild hires the party to find out to whom the note belongs and to deliver it to him.

√ A known group of powerful brigands, monsters, or barbarians is raiding a guild trading post (or other guild center) or has stolen a promissory note with a very high value. The party is hired to deal with these people/monsters to stop their actions from reoccurring and to make examples of them.

Lifeline Service

Adventurers face many dangers in their explorations and pursuits. All too often, these dangers are faced with only a few companions. If the party is not strong enough, death is certain even if it is not immediate, especially with no one willing or able to find and rescue the party members. With the formation of The Collective, this truism of adventuring life has been overturned. One of the first things the guild created for its membership was search and rescue expeditions for missing-in-action members. This proved to be a very costly service and quickly became a user-pays service where the guild provides free of charge only the administrative function.

Before departing on a potentially dangerous journey, guild members may leave a sealed plan (sealed to protect any special or private information) of their trip with the local guildhall seneschal. This plan contains the (known) details of where they will be going and the dangers they anticipate they will face. It also contains a figure for the maximum amount of money they guarantee will be paid to any rescuers. A small refundable percentage of that amount is left with the seneschal on submitting the lifeline plan. On the outside of the envelope is a date, set by the party. If the guild members have not returned or made contact by that date, the seneschal breaks open the sealed plan and, with the information provided inside, tries to raise a rescue expedition. Once the rescue mission has been launched, the money must be paid, even if the expedition is not in danger but merely a couple of days late in returning.

Service

When members have not made contact by the due date written on the sealed plan, the seneschal breaks open the plan and puts out a call for rescuers. The details of the missing members' planned expedition is included in a briefing as well as any other information the guild has about the planned destination that was not in the sealed plan (unlikely though this is). The cheapest, most trustworthy group that announces it is available for the mission is contracted for the rescue, as long as the cost is below the amount listed in the filed plan. Once this contract is issued, the missing members are committed to pay it, whether they need rescuing or not. If no group answers the first call, a new call is issued and, if there is still no response, a third call. If after the third call no one will attempt a rescue for the amount set out in the plan, the seneschal stores the rescue file and notes the members as missing in action.

The members must make this judgment call when filing their expedition lifeline plans—how much to offer for rescue and what should be the drop-dead date? If too little money is offered, only the cheapest and least-skilled teams will attempt the rescue, if any at all. If too much is promised and the rescue turns out to have been unnecessary, the members may be seriously out-of-pocket. If the drop-dead date is set too late, then all that may be rescued is a few old bones, but if the rescue date is set too soon and the members are delayed getting a message to the seneschal, they will have to pay for an unnecessary rescue mission.

The member's grade (only the highest grade among a party is considered) determines the quality of the lifeline service:

• **Nonmembers** may take advantage of the lifeline service but the full amount of the rescue fee must be deposited up front, refundable on return, and an additional 1% management fee must be paid.

• **Basic** members must deposit 15% of their promised rescue fee, refundable on return. The guild will check and make sure that the bidding rescuers have the requisite skills and abilities.

• **Silver** members must deposit of 10% of their promised rescue fee, refundable on return. The guild will

Collective

attempt to recruit a rescue party from among the best people available and will guarantee half of the promised rescue fee to the rescuers.

- **Gold** members must deposit 5% of their promised rescue fee, refundable on return. The guild will ensure the best are recruited and guarantees 75% of the promised rescue fee to the rescuers.

Part of the help the guild provides members, as they write their lifeline sealed mission plans, are recommended amounts that should be offered as rescue fees, based on destination and threats. This advice is based on the guild's previous experience with raising successful rescue missions.

The guild allows the friends and family of missing guild members to increase the offered rescue fee as set in the original sealed plan as long as they demonstrate they can cover this extra cost. This may happen if the amount specified is too small to raise a sufficiently skilled rescue party—sufficiently skilled according to friends and family, anyway.

An important incentive for the search and rescue team is the requirement that the missing members be returned alive in order for the team to be eligible for the rescue fee. If the team sets out in good faith but the rescue was impossible for reasons beyond its control, the guild will usually pay some small percentage of the rescue fee (typically the deposit amount) as compensation for the effort made.

Occasionally, a rescued guild member will not or cannot pay the rescue fee guaranteed. This should not occur, as the guild will lend the required amount to cover the cost of the rescue if necessary. If a member will not pay, he is expelled from the guild.

Areas Covered/Not Covered

The lifeline service does not limit areas covered. As long as sufficient fees are offered for rescue, someone should be found who is willing and able to go there, *e.g.*, the elemental planes.

Sometimes, even though the missing guild members have been found, a rescue can have unforeseen problems. The missing members may, for some reason, wish not to be rescued. This is a serious problem for the rescue team, since it can receive the fee only if the missing members are returned. At best, it could hope for some small reward from the guild for its effort.

Another problem may occur if the missing guild members also require some special or personal pieces of equipment, or other people (*e.g.*, freed slaves), to be rescued as well. In this situation, negotiation should be possible and a larger rescue fee agreed upon if the additional rescue requirements are at all physically possible.

Exceptions

As mentioned above, the lifeline service has few restrictions or limitations. However, two circumstances exist in which no rescue attempt will be mounted and a sealed plan may be trashed:

- There is evidence that the missing member situation is a set-up, perhaps to ambush a rescue party.
- The missing member has been expelled from the guild since lodging the sealed plan.

Game Consequences

The possibilities provided by a lifeline service may increase the risks that characters are prepared to take, but the main effects will be in the opportunities it provides GMs. The major consequence of the use of the lifeline service may well be characters with no equipment (the rescuers were interested only in the characters' lives) and no money (payment of the rescue fees took all the cash the characters had left). However, the characters are still alive and motivated to regain their wealth.

Adventure Hooks

- The character party accepts a guild lifeline contract for search and rescue of a missing party.
- Some guild associates are missing, but they did not guarantee enough of a fee for anyone to be willing to accept a rescue contract. The characters must decide whether to do the right thing and take the contract, or the safe thing and walk away.
- A famous old rescue contract worth a large fortune still exists. Every rescue party that has set out to attempt the rescue has never returned. Once the characters have achieved a few levels, they may wish to attempt the rescue and win fame as well as possibly fortune.

Local Experts

The Collective expends much effort in identifying and fostering close ties with local craftsmen and other experts. These worthies provide services of a known quality at fair and predictable prices to the guild. When members bide their time at a guildhouse they can be assured that they can be directed to skilled and trustworthy vendors whose services they require.

Individual guildhouses are expected to put some effort into nurturing these ties with skilled folk. Healers, herbalists, smiths, armorers, and even ordinary laborers are on the list of desired associates. While the benefits to the guild of having a regular collection of skilled vendors of known ability are obvious, it is equally of value to the vendors themselves to maintain a regular and reliable client base.

At times a guildhouse may sponsor a promising youth through apprenticeship and onward throughout his career. In this way the guild earns the gratitude of a tradesman and builds a firm sense of trust and rapport. In return the professional enjoys the patronage of the guild and the expectation of regular business. Both parties profit from the arrangement.

Guild members can often provide service to the professionals who serve them by providing rare materials and by passing on news from afar. Adventurers end up in the strangest of places and quite often have access to people, objects, and places beyond the reach of so-called ordinary folk. A guildhouse may take requests from its contract vendors for rare and obscure items. Once again this helps to strengthen ties.

Typical Benefits

The advantages of using the same vendors for their services should be readily apparent. Below are details on the more prominent benefits:

Collective

♦ Members need not search for reliable and skilled craftsmen. This is done by the local staff. Thus members need only inquire with the local seneschal, rather than doing the shopping around themselves. Some care is spent ensuring that said vendors are suitably skilled, meeting certain minimum standards—usually at least skill rank 6 in their chosen crafts and professions—and that they are trustworthy. This process of vetting involves questioning other customers as well as examining the work of the vendors regularly. Some of these tradesmen may even be retired members of the guild.

♦ Services may be contracted through the guildhouse while the member is absent. Time constraints may dictate that a member must suddenly absent himself before a particular service may be found or completed. The member can provide the local staff with details of his requirements—a search for rare herbs, forging a new sword—and the guildhouse will arrange for the service to be performed. Usually this requires an initial down payment of 10% of the cost of the service needed, as well as a 1% gratuity or administrative charge to the guildhouse staff.

♦ Members receive discounts on purchases from co-operative merchants ranging from 5% to 10% on various items, depending upon the member's status in the guild and the items being purchased. The seneschal of a guildhouse, or his delegate, is charged with maintaining the relationships with such vendors to ensure that discounting continues.

♦ Members will often be given first option on the purchase of rare and obscure items. Adventurers are known for their propensity for spending, and a canny trader knows that a happy customer will often return several times.

♦ On occasion a member can receive credit when his funds are low. More often than not this credit is established through the guildhouse, but some traders will enter into private arrangements with customers. The guild keeps a close eye on such bargains and makes sure that debts are paid off if the member cannot do so himself. Good relationships with vendors are important enough to warrant this.

♦ Guild members interested in crafts and professions might be able to receive training from trusted tradesmen. As long as no rules of the professional's guild or organization are broken, instruction may be arranged through the local guildhouse.

Sample Expert (Animal Trainer)

Booker Moog: Male gnome Expert 6: CR 3; Small humanoid (gnome); HD 6d6+6; hp 24; Init +1 (Dex); Spd 20; AC 11 (touch 11, flat-footed 10); Atk +5 ranged (1d2 subdual/x2, whip); SA spells; SQ gnome abilities; Al LN; SV Fort +3, Ref +3, Will +9; Str 7, Dex 12, Con 13, Int 14, Wis 18, Cha 16

Skills and Feats: Alchemy +8, Craft (leatherwork) +6, Heal +9, Innuendo +8, Gather Information +8, Handle Animal +14, Listen +11, Knowledge (nature) +11, Profession (animal keeper) +15, Sense Motive +9; Exotic Weapon Proficiency (whip), Skill Focus (handle animal), Skill Focus (profession).

Special Qualities: Spells & spell-like abilities—may cast *dancing lights*, *ghost sound*, *prestidigitation*, and *speak with animals* each once per day; gnome abilities—Low-light vision, +2 save vs. illusions, +1 attack vs. kobolds and goblinoids, +4 dodge vs. giants, +2 Listen, +2 Alchemy.

Possessions: a variety of animals, *Merloc's spoon*, whip.

Booker Moog is a tiny but energetic gnome whose chirpy personality more than makes up for his size. Talkative even by gnomish standards, Booker's beleaguered parents set the young lad to watching their flock of woodland goats in an effort to get some peace and quiet. This didn't stop the little gnome fellow from talking. If anything it made him even more loquacious. Booker discovered that while other gnomes could converse with burrowing mammals, he was even more charmed and could speak with any animal at all.

The step from herdsman to animal trainer came quite naturally, and Booker was able to apprentice himself to a traveling animal healer. Luckily this fellow, an aged human man, was hard of hearing, and Booker's incessant chatter failed to bother him. Booker traveled for some years with his master, eventually taking over the "business" upon the old man's retirement.

Over the years Booker's interest shifted from healing animals to training them. With his ability to speak with them, he had an edge in the field. In time Booker has come to be one of the best there is. Combining an honest love of animals with his experience and talent for animal speech, he is quite the expert.

Some years ago Booker got himself into a fix when a chase for a straying nanny goat, a particular favorite of his, saw him ambushed by a band of hobgoblins. That would have been the end for the little gnome, and his beloved goat, had it not been for a band of adventurers from The Collective. They rescued Booker and his goat and healed his injuries. The experience left Booker with a limp and a soft spot for adventurers.

Eventually deciding to settle down, Booker remembered his debt to The Collective, and as soon as he found there was a guildhouse in his chosen community he made his presence known to the seneschal. Over a little time Booker's abilities became well regarded and he developed a fine arrangement with The Collective. He would tend to their animals, training horses and dogs and so on for the adventurers, and heal their injuries. In return he had a wide range of people whom he could speak to—or at, as the case may be.

Booker's skill with animals is much admired. Druids seek him out to discuss matters pertaining to their animal companions; rangers swap stories on the behavior of creatures; even paladins ask his advice on choosing and caring for their mounts. He is a useful little fellow to know, and he is always happy to do a favor for adventurers he knows or who are recommended to him.

Trading Service

Adventurers often return from explorations, missions, and general adventuring with many objects and treasures they have acquired (*e.g.*, 13 rusty broadswords, two rolls of silk, a map to a lost castle, and a holy marble statue of Bess the Six-armed Goddess). Wherever they were found (taken from defeated opponents, discovered in hidden chambers, lost cities, etc.), the items tend to be bulky and demanding to transport and are visible signs to tempt bandits and thieves. Adventurers also need to convert their treasures to coins if they wish to buy food, drink, and lodging and wash off the dust of the road. For this purpose, the guild established a network of trading posts on the borders of civilization to aid the guild's membership.

On returning from an expedition into the wilds, members may sell the goods they acquired and receive a fair price at one of these trading posts. It is possible that better prices for some select items could be obtained in cities, but the members would have to transport these items to the cities, risking robbery and accident, and the additional risk that the items may not fetch a superior or even equal price to that offered at the trading post.

Service

These trading posts operate a thriving general business with travelers and locals but also provide special services to Collective members. As well as the banking service, these posts provide a trading service and will convert any item presented by guild members into cash. The amount of money offered for each item depends on its quality and upon the adventurer's guild membership grade:

♦ **Nonmembers:** 25% of book price, maximum.

♦ **Base:** 30% of book price, maximum.

♦ **Silver:** 35% of book price, maximum.

♦ **Gold:** 40% of book price, maximum.

In return for the traded items, the trading post provides hard cash, a promissory note, or a combination of the two. Hard cash is usually a mixture of coins of different denominations and currencies, whatever the trading post has at the time. For more information on promissory notes, see the section on the guild's banking service.

These trading posts also provide a free appraisal and valuation service to guild members. Even if a guild member does not wish to part with a discovered item, he can gain some idea of its monetary worth at a Collective trading post. Nonmembers must pay for the evaluation service.

Goods can also be bought from Collective establishments at half of book price (less any discount for being a member), but all such goods are used and no warranty is given for quality or fitness to purpose. Full plate cannot be obtained for half price, as this must be fitted to the individual. The Collective can arrange to have adjustments made to recovered plate, but the cost ends up being the same as for a custom-made set, less any member discount of course.

The trading posts dispose of the objects and treasures traded by adventurers in two ways. Many of the more mundane items (saddles and swords, pots and pipes) are sold to locals, travelers, or other passing Collective members (at only half the book price). The more valuable objects and treasures (masterwork objects, jewelry, magic items, holy artifacts) are usually sent to a guildhall with the armed and armored couriers of the banking service. At the guildhall, these items may be offered in a special sale, stored as a guild asset, or traded to other organizations for monetary or non-monetary benefits. Many mundane objects also find their way to the guildhalls.

The Collective's guildhalls also provide a trading service, though usually only for highly valuable or unique items which guild members do not want traced back to themselves. The guildhall disposes of such items through

its many contacts in the local professional and criminal guilds.

All too often, a guild member will disagree with the price offered for an object presented to a trading post. This is especially true if the member had been previously quoted an incorrect value or had invested a large amount of effort in its retrieval and transport. On these occasions, the trading post will advise the member of other trading posts or locations where he may trade the object, but the trading post never negotiates prices; it is always a take it or leave it proposition.

Additional services provided to guild members by the trading posts are storage and transport. Guild members may store their equipment and treasures at a trading post at the cost of one percent of appraised value per month of storage. This service is used by members who need to return to the locations from which they have just come and do not wish to carry all their bulky, extraneous equipment or treasures back with them. At a cost of an additional one percent of appraised value, the trading post will arrange to transport any item to the nearest guildhall, where the member may later retrieve it.

The trading posts located in wilderness areas on the edge of civilization are subject to raids from bandits, barbarians, and monsters and are constructed for both business and defense. They consist of one or more inner buildings surrounded by a palisade. A bastion rises above a corner of the palisade enclosure, usually 10 feet square, for defense against attacks. A secure underground chamber, accessible from the central trading building, is used for storing money and valuables. Some of the guild's most experienced rogues, fighters, and spellcasters have usually added additional special defenses to these trading posts.

Areas Covered/Not Covered

All Collective members know the locations of the guild trading posts. Wherever the guild has influence and membership, a trading post is set up at the locations where guild members will pass on their return to civilization. However, there are some areas where the guild has not successfully established trading posts. These areas include monster-infested regions where the expense of defending a trading post could not be justified, and regions whose rulers are hostile to the guild.

The districts on the edge of the wilderness usually welcome the establishment of a guild trading post. The trading post brings a boost to the local economy with its trading, it brings in luxury items that are not normally available in these remote districts, and a fortified inn is usually soon built next to a new trading post, bringing in even more wealth to the district.

Occasionally, someone claims his trading post is an official guild trading post and proceeds to offer false price estimates for returning guild members and other travelers in the hope of making a quick and substantial profit. As with attempts to disrupt or corrupt the guild's banking service, the guild sends parties of members or mercenaries to take care of such false trading posts and provide a lesson for any other would-be cheaters.

Exceptions

Rarely, a trading post will refuse to trade with a guild member. These occasions include:

- The guild member is suspected to be in collusion with hostile forces.
- The guild member wishes to trade an item which is too dangerous for the trading post to handle.
- The guild member wishes to trade an item of a value so great that the trading post does not have the hard cash to cover it and the member will not take a guild promissory note.

Game Consequences

The existence of these trading posts has consequences for a game. The easy disposal of treasure and other objects closer to their source of acquisition may encourage players to attempt to loot and carry more of their defeated enemy's equipment than was previously the case. Further, the ability to dispose of bulky objects and awkward treasures at the edge of civilization leaves characters far lighter on their feet when traveling through the so-called civilized realms. Lastly, the ability to use a trading post as a point of disposal of acquisitions also means more enthusiastic players do not have to return to cities or big towns after each adventure.

Game Examples/Hooks

√ Brigands, barbarians, or monsters have frequently attacked a guild trading post. The party is sent to protect the trading post and stop the raids.

√ A new trading post must be established in a wild and dangerous area. The party is sent to survey the location chosen, select the most advantageous point for construction, negotiate with the locals (if any), eliminate monsters, and build the new trading post.

√ A unique and special holy artifact was traded in at a trading post at great cost to the guild. The couriers transporting the item back to a guildhall were attacked in a well armed and coordinated ambush. The party is sent to discover the identity of the ambushers and to retrieve the artifact.

Sample Trading Post Master

Dogfish: Male half-orc Ranger 6: CR 6; Humanoid (half-orc); HD 3d6+3d10-6; hp 24; Init +1 (Dex); Spd 30; AC 15 (touch 13, flat-footed 14); Atk +6 melee (1d6/x3 handaxe & 1d4 19–20/x2 dagger), +5 ranged 1d10 19–20/x2 heavy crossbow; SQ half-orc abilities, ranger abilities; Al N; SV Fort +4, Ref +4, Will +2; Str 17, Dex 12, Con 9, Int 14, Wis 16, Cha 9.
Skills and Feats: Animal Empathy +5, Appraise +10, Climb +6, Decipher Script +5, Diplomacy +5, Gather Information +8, Handle Animal +4, Heal +6, Knowledge (nature) +6, Listen +5, Move Silently +4, Profession (trader) +9, Search +5, Sense Motive +9, Speak Language (Common), Speak Language (Draconic), Speak Language (Goblin), Speak Language (Orc), Spot +5, Use Rope +4, Wilderness Lore +9; Endurance, Skill Focus (profession), Track, Toughness.

Special Qualities: Half-orc abilities—Darkvision, Orc Blood; ranger abilities—Favored Enemy (beasts), Two-Weapon Fighting, Track.
Possessions: wolves, leather armor, buckler, heavy crossbow, handaxes, daggers, *ring of protection +2, bracelet of friends* (6 charms).

Dogfish is a large dark man with a somber air about him. Born to a human mother in a barbarian tribe, he was not slain at birth, as half-orcs usually are, because of his mother's high tribal status. However, he was not permitted to remain with the tribe and so was placed with a traveling peddler's family. On returning to civilization, the peddler left Dogfish at a city's orphanage. Always an outcast but easily defending himself with his superior strength and smarts, Dogfish grew up running the streets. At a young age, he was recruited by the thieves' guild as a thug and eventually moved on to join a smugglers' band.

Dogfish did not stay long with the smugglers. After meeting up with the peddler who had brought him to the city as a baby, he decided to leave and track down his biological parents. Traveling into the wilderness, Dogfish found a solitude and peace he had never known. He enjoyed his wanderings but had no luck in tracing his mother or father, or even identifying which was the orc and which was the human. After a year of unsuccessful searching he apprenticed himself to a ranger he had befriended.

A couple of years later, in the depth of winter, Dogfish helped an adventuring party fight off a hunger-maddened bear and then found them shelter and dry wood. Thereafter, while not searching for his parents, Dogfish traveled with the party, becoming an adventurer himself. On his fellow adventurers' recommendation, he joined The Collective.

Some years later, Dogfish finally located his mother's tribe. His mother was long dead, but her family accepted him—for a time. Dogfish decided to end his search there and then, giving up on his father, and left the tribe a short while later.

On returning to a Collective guildhall, Dogfish saw a notice recruiting a master of a new trading post on the edge of a hill region. Since he knew that wilderness well and felt it was time to settle down, Dogfish applied for and won the position.

Dogfish operates the trading post with two assistants, two guards, and their families. He raises partly tamed wolves in the compound and often travels into the wilderness to scout out the hills. Though a dour and formidable man in appearance, he is skillful and fair in his dealings with the locals and with traveling Collective members.

Affiliations

The Collective has affiliations with all the major class-based guilds and exchanges relevant information with them. Wizard and cleric organizations in particular have standing offers with The Collective to purchase any arcane or divine trinkets expeditions may acquire. Loose affiliations also exist with merchant groups, as these folk travel the lands and collect information. The Collective frequently requires skilled craftsmen and artisans and therefore has affiliations with their organizations as well.

The Collective's library has some very rare tomes in it, and for security there are copies of these stored securely a long way from the library. The council was able to think of no better place than a vault under the keep of Neric's Avengers, guarded by at least 150 mercenaries at all times. This is a purely business-related affiliation.

The only organizations with which The Collective does not have some kind of affiliation are groups which are secretive or closed by nature.

Other guilds value a relationship with the Collective for many reasons, including commercial, informational, social, and professional. Reasons may overlap—a traders' guild may interact with adventurers for both commercial and professional reasons; a thieves' guild may have commercial, informational, and professional reasons for associating with The Collective; an explorer's club might interact with adventurers on informational and social levels.

The majority of the examples given apply equally to Sojourner guildhalls within both large and small communities, but some cases are different, depending on the size of the local population or the relative importance of the guild in the local area. DMs will have to determine what kinds of interactions exist, or if they are even possible, in his local area.

Commercial Interactions

The primary motivation to associate with The Collective for most guilds is purely commercial. Adventurers often have a lot of money to spend and are quite happy to spend it; no shopkeeper or tavern owner in the known world is going to pass up the chance of having as much of that money as possible being spent on his business premises. In order to get the adventurers to come through their doors, they will usually offer inducements. They might throw in free lamp oil when a party buys two or more hooded lanterns, or fifty feet of rope for the price of forty-five. There may also be kickbacks to The Collective itself. Perhaps it receives a small percentage of every sale made to adventurers, or large discounts when the guild itself is the customer.

In smaller centers, villages, and hamlets, the single chandler's store may not be associated with a guild. In this case, the Sojourners could make sure members don't get ripped off but get a fair deal and pay a fair price. With its economic power, The Collective could threaten to finance a rival chandler if the existing one doesn't toe the line.

Professional guilds also have a vested interest in maintaining a good working relationship with the adventurers' guild. A tavern fight might see a party incarcerated in the local lock-up by the authorities. A litigant who knows the local laws would be invaluable in arguing their case. It's also in the interests of The Collective to associate with only the best, so there might be some minimum criteria that craftsmen and professionals have to meet.

For example, a weaponsmith may be required to attain a certain level of skill before The Collective would consider recommending him to its members. If all the weaponsmiths within a city were independent, they might compete fiercely with each other for the favor of the guild. However, a guild of weaponsmiths might interact at a higher level, lobbying the Sojourners to maintain a list of all eligible weaponsmiths, asking that recommendations be spread among all those on the list and promising it will maintain the standards of those on the list.

A thieves' guild may look upon the loot that adventurers bring back from their sojourns as rightfully theirs, with the minor inconvenience of lack of possession keeping them from enjoying that treasure. However, a thieves' guild that constantly targeted adventurers and their treasure would probably find itself on the wrong end of the guild's wrath. It would be much more profitable to approach the guild and ask for a share of the loot in return for protection from theft and other "accidents." An even smarter guild would look to interact on a much more professional basis, offering training to adventuring member thieves, fencing the loot, or at least moving the treasure through its own channels, which are probably much more extensive and more professionally run than any the guild could devise.

Fighters' schools could depend on adventurers looking to improve their skills. Local churches and monasteries may depend on sojourning priests and monks of the faith for substantial donations and bequests of both money and magical items. Their presence in the city or town might be advertised in the adventurers' guildhall in return for services, such as healing a member or performing an exorcism. The local magicians' guild may interact at a commercial level by selling spell components, spell scrolls, and magic items, or even teaching adventuring magicians new spells—for a hefty price, of course. In fact, the teaching of new skills and abilities covers all classes and all the different types of guild members.

Informational Interactions

The information that adventurers gather on their sojourns can be just as valuable as the treasure they haul away from the depths of the ancient cavern complex. Many guilds would be willing to pay highly for access, especially exclusive access, to this information.

Thieves' guilds want to know where the treasure came from and, more importantly, where it's going so they can get a piece of the action. Although a guild may have an agreement with the Sojourners not to try to steal from them, once the goods are sold to someone outside the organization, they become fair game. Knowing with whom and where the items are to be stored or sent would help the thieves *acquire* them more easily. An informal contact with The Collective could provide this information. A more formal informational interaction might be to invite rogue class members to the local den to discuss what they have seen and done, what traps were present and how they were disarmed, and maybe even a sort of thieves' workshop could be arranged.

Magicians of all sorts want to know where magic items came from, what they are, and whether there may be more, or more powerful, items. This may extend to learning about any strange writings a party comes across. Sages especially might be willing to exchange information with guild members. The local sages' guild interaction with the Sojourners may be information exchange only and involve no money at all. In return for carrying out tedious research on behalf of its members, the sages get to hear the adventures of all sojourners newly arrived and even question them. This works both for the guild and for the sage, for some time in the future, this may allow the sage to come to a conclusion about something that he otherwise would not, and this may benefit the guild as well.

Priestly and paladin orders want to know where areas of opposition exist so they can go forth and do good deeds (at least, according to their own doctrine the deeds would be good). The priests of the Church of Light would be very interested in knowing where the priests of the Church of Night hang out. They could then mount a raid and dispose of those blasphemers once and for all. Other information adventurers might have could lead to learning more about a deity, finding old holy artifacts, or even verification that an old legend is actually false.

Professional Interactions

There are many ways that other guilds could interact with The Collective on a professional basis. There is interaction with the Sojourners as an entity, or interaction with its members. First, The Collective has needs of its own. It has buildings which must be built and maintained, services that members need, and supplies used within the guildhall. A good example of this is food. Not only does raw produce have to be acquired, prepared, cooked, served, and consumed, many other things are necessary for this process to happen. You need utensils to prepare the food; pots, pans, skillets, cauldrons, etc. to cook the food; plates, bowls, cups, knives, forks, spoons, etc. to serve and eat the food; and preparation tables and dining tables, chairs, or trestles. Finally, there are the minor but equally important things, such as fuel for the fire to cook the food, water for washing and other preparations, soap to clean the floors, plates, and utensils, cupboards to store food and utensils, and barrels or sinks to wash things.

If the guild houses adventurers, they will need beds, sheets, and blankets, towels and bathing facilities, chamber pots, mops and brooms to keep the guildhall clean, desks and cupboards to store things, keys and locks to keep things safe, paper, parchment, ink, and quills for making lists and keeping track. Similarly, if the Sojourners maintain a stable, Ostlers, horse trainers, and animal handlers could provide the service on behalf of the guild itself. The million and one items that a guildhall needs to function are all products of other guilds, and so the guild must interact with them as just another customer, or as a very special customer, if that is what is required.

None of the discussion so far has touched on how other guilds interact with Collective members, the adventurers themselves. The Collective may go so far as to require other guilds to act through it to deal with the members, taking a cut of any financial agreement reached. Sages may be researching a particular problem and wish the adventurers to go to a specific place at a specific time and observe the behavior of a culture or race of beings, or of ants. The sage might require them to gather a certain flower or find evidence of some kind. Priestly orders, colleges of magicians, etc. might want the adventurers to go places and do specific things on their behalf. For whatever reason, it is common for other guilds to hire adventurers, and most often they will approach the guild either for permission to recruit themselves or to seek advice on a suitable party that might undertake the task.

Fighters' schools may ask The Collective for advice on the best person within the membership to teach a particular weapon or to provide some other form of instruction at the school, splitting the fee with the member and the guild, of course. Conversely, the local Sojourners guildhall may form an alliance with a specific fighters' school to teach all its members how to fight. This might be because the local sword master used to be a member of The Collective and knows a great deal about fighting the monsters within that area, or because it's part of the service the guildhall offers to members.

Social Interactions

A number of different social interactions occur between guilds. Some glamour is attached to an adventurer. These people are risk takers, bold and brave; more timid souls are often drawn to these kinds of people. To be seen with a brave adventurer is to have some of that quality rub off. Adventurers are also very confident people, and usually rich. These qualities also make others want to spend time with them.

More mundane social interactions may take place with members of The Collective, including invitations to explorers' clubs, naturalist societies, and maybe even retirement homes for aged adventurers. They would be provided a good meal and then asked to speak about their latest adventures, etc.

The guildhall itself may be the scene of parties of all kinds, where the beautiful and/or popular people of the city or town meet to have fun in the company of glamorous adventurers.

Leaving the Guild

With Permission: Any member may leave The Collective by simply not paying the monthly dues. No formal system exists for resigning. Members lose all member privileges, with the exception of knowledge bonuses, if they choose to leave. Members may rejoin at any time by paying their dues again but will be at the Basic Member grade. To regain their former grade they must spend the relevant XP again.

Expulsion: A member may be expelled from The Collective for failing to provide a report of his adventures or for acting in a manner the council believes is detrimental to The Collective. This can include things like damaging material in the library, damaging a Collective shelter, and failing to replace consumables (or at least report their use). A member may also be expelled for allowing anyone else to use his identification amulet. An expelled member loses all membership privileges and can never again be a member of The Collective.

Guild Seneschal

Each medium to large hall of the collective has its own seneschal. This one is typical of what you'll find. Some will be retired adventurers rather than active adventurers taking a sabbatical.

Grufald Umsber: Male human Fighter 10/Cleric 5/Sorcerer 3: CR 18; Medium-size humanoid (human); HD 10d10+5d8+3d4+18; hp 116; Init +1, Spd 30 ft.; AC 20 (touch 14, flat-footed 19); Atk +19/+14/+9 melee (1d8+6/19-20/x2, long sword +1) or +18/+13/+8 (1d8+4 x2 heavy mace +1) or +15/+10/+5 ranged (no preferred weapon); SA spells; SQ none; Al NG; SV Fort +13, Ref +6, Will +15; Str 16, Dex 12, Con 12, Int 10, Wis 16, Cha 14.

Skills and Feats: Alchemy +3, Climb +9, Concentration +5, Diplomacy +9, Gather Information +4, Handle Animal +7, Heal +5, Knowledge (arcana) +3, Knowledge (history) +3, Knowledge (religion) +4, Ride [horse] +7, Search +1, Spellcraft +3, Swim +9; Alertness, Cleave, Combat Casting, Enlarge Spell, Great Cleave, Iron Will, Maximize Spell, Power Attack, Skill Focus (diploma-cy), Skill Focus (ride), Track, Two-Weapon Fighting, Weapon Focus (longsword), Weapon Specialization (longsword).

Cleric Spells (5/5+1/4+1/3+1); Deity God of Magic/Foresight; Domains Magic, Knowledge: 0—*detect magic, guidance, read magic, resistance, virtue*; 1st—*bless, detect secret doors, divine favor, protection from evil, remove fear, shield of faith*; 2nd—*aid, consecrate, hold person, identify, lesser restoration*; 3rd—*daylight, dispel magic, invisibility purge, wind wall*.

Sorcerer Spells (6/6): 0—*arcane mark, detect magic, light, ray of frost, read magic*; 1st—*color spray, comprehend languages, magic missile*.

Possessions: *longsword +1, heavy mace +1, chain shirt +2, ring of protection +3*.

Grufald is a burly gent with a sparkling personality and charming wit. His outer appearance hides a man with no small abilities in combat and he is not to be trifled with. He commonly wears his chain shirt and has his longsword peace-knotted at his side. Only if he is adventuring does he carry his battleaxe. Grufald loves The Collective because it lets him enjoy the adventures of others now that he is past his prime (he's 34 years old) and doesn't get out much anymore. His duties as seneschal would keep him from too many expeditions even if his age did not. Nevertheless, Grufald is a source of knowledge for adventurers, and his negotiating skills are available to members free of charge if they are needed. He stands a smidge under six feet tall and weighs in at a healthy 200 pounds, little of it fat. He has a clean-shaven square jaw, black hair with flecks of gray at the temples, and deep brown eyes.

Typical Collective Guildhall

Below is a layout of a common guildhall that might be found in a city or important town. The normal layout consists of two main buildings: the guildhall proper and a detached auxiliary building usually holding the stables. The building described below could hold up to fifty residents and twenty mounts in relative comfort.

The Guildhall

The primary building is a long single-story one with two smaller wings on each side. It is sturdy and well constructed, usually of stone. Each entrance has an iron door, some of which are protected by *arcane lock* spells. The roof is slate tiles and difficult to break through; it is also well guttered. Adventurers in general tend to make a considerable amount of wealth, and this is shown in the general superior quality of the building.

1. **Entry Hall:** This spacious area is entered through a pair of impressive iron double doors, intricately carved and well secured (Good lock plus *arcane lock* spell; DC 40 for Open Lock tests). Inside the entry hall are displayed trophies from various exploits of members of the guild. Weapons, treasures, and stuffed remains of vanquished creatures may be found here. Though some may consider such displays barbaric, they are nevertheless impressive. Secret peepholes allow staff in the offices (#2) to keep a close watch on visitors.

2. **Offices:** The day-to-day running of the local guild takes place in these rooms. Details of proposed

and ongoing adventures are kept here, as well as details of numerous people of note in the vicinity, guild members or otherwise. Records and maps of many interesting locations are also safely archived, and members may pay for copies or for access to these documents. Keys to all rooms in the building are stored here as well. In each back wall are peepholes allowing staff to keep a close watch on visitors in the entry hall (#1). Each room is locked when unattended and breaking in is nigh impossible (Amazing lock plus *arcane lock* spell; DC 50 for Open Lock tests).

3.   Study Rooms: These plain rooms may be hired by members at a rate of 1 sp per day. Each is a plain room furnished with a study table and half a dozen chairs. Members often use these rooms for private study or for planning their next expeditions.

4.   Strongroom: This well secured strongroom (Amazing lock plus *arcane lock* spell; DC 50 for Open Lock tests) contains the guild's finances as well as various riches stored for members. In addition it also serves as the guildhall's armory. Any number of interesting weapons, armor, and items may be found here, and a staff member is always nearby to ensure the room remains secure. On special occasions a *glyph of warding* and/or *alarm* may be placed upon the door, though members are always warned if such is the case. A trapdoor (Good lock plus *arcane lock* spell; DC 40 for Open Lock tests) near the center of the back wall leads down to a lower storage room (not shown on the map) which is some 20 foot square and provides further storage space.

5.   Dining Hall: Though perhaps not quite as sumptuous as other dining halls owned by wealthier folk, this hall is well furnished and comfortable. It can usually seat up to sixty diners at once in comfort. Portraits and other images of renowned members of the guild, alive and dead, adorn the walls. Unlike the entry hall, this room honors various individuals, rather than the guild as a whole.

6.   Kitchen: Well stocked and tidy, the kitchen is nothing out of the ordinary. When members gather for a feast it becomes a hive of activity. Otherwise the kitchen varies depending upon the personality of the head cook at the time.

7.   Staff Rooms: These two rooms are set aside for staff members who are assigned to work in the guildhall. These servants tend to members' requests and arrange errands and the like if rewarded with appropriate gratuities. These staff members are very knowledgeable and are privy to many rumors — information that may also be purchased. Their rooms are small and neat, kept clean and well ordered. Like all private rooms they may be locked (Good lock; DC 30 for Open Lock tests). The external door in the corridor next to these rooms is almost as secure as the doors in the front hall (Good lock plus *arcane lock* spell;

DC 35 for Open Lock tests).

8.   Simple Private Rooms: Several rooms are reserved for the use of members who seek temporary lodgings. Unless special circumstances arise, a member may stay in a room for no longer than a month. Each spartan room is furnished with a simple bed (or perhaps two bunks), a small desk, and a sturdy chest (Above Average lock; DC 25 for Open Lock tests). Each room may locked (Good lock; DC 30 for Open Lock tests). A side entrance allows members access day and night, though it is locked similarly as other doors.

9.   Superior Private Rooms: A few bigger rooms are reserved for the use of more important or senior members. As with the simple rooms, a member may stay in a room for no longer than a month. These rooms are furnished with larger beds and better fittings, though each also has a small desk and a sturdy chest (Above Average lock; DC 25 for Open Lock tests). As ever, these rooms may locked (Good lock; DC 30 for Open Lock tests), and a side entrance allows day and night access.

10.   Baths: There is one bathing room in each of the residential wings of the guildhall. A large tub is provided in each and hot or cold water will be provided upon request, though a small charge (no more than a few cp) may be incurred for off-hours requests. Usually only basic bathing facilities are provided, though members who pay extra can receive better toiletries and the services of bath attendants.

11.   Storage Rooms: These unlocked rooms are merely extra storage space for items that members do not wish to, or cannot, store elsewhere.

12.   Privies: Two small rooms allow members to attend to calls of nature. These "thunder-boxes" are cleaned out regularly and it is not rare to find aromatic herbs kept in them to mask unpleasant odors.

The Guildhall
■ =5

Typical Guildhall Servants

Guildhall Servant: Human Commoner 1: CR 1/2; Medium humanoid (human); HD 1d4+5; hp 7; Init +1 (Dex); Spd 30; AC 13 (touch 11, flat-footed 12); Atk +1 melee (1d6+1/x2, club); SA none; SQ none; Al LN; SV Fort +2, Ref +1, Will +0; Str 12, Dex 12, Con 15, Int 10, Wis 10, Cha 10

Skills and Feats: Craft (varies) +4, Gather Information +2, Listen +4, Profession (servant) +4, Spot +2; Alertness, Toughness.

Possessions: guildhall keys, leather armor, club, dagger.

Usually a handful of ordinary servants is on hand in the guildhall at any given time. These are generally ordinary people employed by the guild and have no adventuring backgrounds themselves. They may be paid to fetch and carry and perform tasks usually assigned to servants. In a pinch they can grab a club and provide some extra muscle, though they are far from trained warriors.

Office Staffer: Human Expert 2: CR 1; Medium humanoid (human); HD 2d6+2; hp 7; Init +1 (Dex); Spd 30; AC 11 (touch 11, flat-footed 10); Atk +1 melee (1d4/x2, dagger); SA none; SQ none; Al LN; SV Fort +0, Ref +1, Will +4; Str 10, Dex 12, Con 12, Int 15, Wis 12, Cha 12

Skills and Feats: Bluff +5, Craft (scribe) +8, Gather Information +6, Innuendo +6, Knowledge (guild business) +8, Listen +5, Profession (secretary) +8, Sense Motive +6, Spot +4; Alertness, Toughness, Skill Focus (profession).

Possessions: guildhall keys, scribe's tools, dagger.

The office staff members are more intelligent and attentive than the ordinary servants. Little passes in the guildhall that they do not notice. These people become quite offended if asked to perform menial tasks but enjoy the challenge of more cerebral activities. Thus, they may be paid to gather rumors and provide local advice and information.

Your Campaign

The Collective is a mix of the old English Explorer's club, the YHA, and the National Geographic Society. It can provide a little color to your campaign or be the major focus of it. Characters can seek work with Collective expeditions with an NPC or two as expedition head, or a party may take on an expedition on behalf of The Collective with no NPC overseers. Perhaps, like Stanley, your group specializes in search and rescue of missing expeditions (Dr. Livingstone, I presume?). The amount of involvement is limited only by what your group wants to do.

Adventure Hooks

↗ An adventuring party has just returned from the mountains with tales of giants hurling boulders at them and a horde of filthy humanoids chasing them out of the mountains. The party is badly beaten up and won't be going back to the mountains any time soon. There's a chance for an opportunistic group to pick up where these folk left off.

↗ A local kingdom has declared adventurers a public nuisance and is trying to get at the Collective's membership records so as to issue arrest warrants for all official members.

↗ Sojourners are being ambushed and wiped out by an unknown group. Evidence suggests that the killers are getting their information from itineraries logged with The Collective. Perhaps a counterambush is in order.

↗ Someone is forging Collective bank notes and slowly leeching the guild dry of funds. Who is behind this and how can they be stopped?

↗ A stack of old files in the guild archive has disappeared, along with one of the historians. The guild's other historians do not know what the files contained. What is someone trying to hide?

Guild Design

Though care has been taken to provide as broad an assortment of guilds as possible, it may happen that none of the guilds presented in this book quite fits a certain specific purpose and that you'd like to design one of your own. The template that has been used to create all of the guilds in this book is presented here to assist you in doing just that, along with explanatory notes to help you decide what works best for your game.

Though guilds are wide and varied, and from the outside may look completely different, they all share certain similarities when viewed more closely. Certain identifiable elements may be deemed common for almost all guilds. These are the purpose of the guild, similarities its members share, criteria that make it unique, method by which entry is controlled, structure of the guild and rules for advancement, benefits of being in the guild, and restrictions and disadvantages of membership. To design a guild, take the following template and fill in all the necessary information.

Purpose

What is the reason for the guild's existence? Guilds generally do not form without good reason; they serve a particular aim or intention. Pick a reason for your guild and flesh it out. Guild purposes typically fall into one of several basic categories:

Control: At times a guild's existence may not be for the benefit of the members but to allow the guild or another agency to regulate and control certain activities. Members might be required to join the guild and abide by its rules whether they want to or not. Members' activities would usually be closely monitored and they would have limits on what they could or could not do. The classic example is that of a city thieves' guild; if you're not in the guild you don't steal things. Bad things happen to those who break this rule.

Economic: The whole purpose of an economic guild is to make money. The members intend to get rich by being part of the guild. Depending on the structure of the guild, individual members may or may not see immediate benefits, but as a whole the guild maximizes its profit-making potential. The perfect example of an economic guild is a trading conglomerate or merchant house, such as the Hudson Bay Company.

Goal: The primary reason for the guild is to achieve some goal or aim, usually a definable purpose that can be gained in a finite period. In certain cases the goal may be conspiratorial and quite secret. Generally the aim is something that might take a considerable length of time to achieve. Perhaps in one city the baker's guild is attempting to legalize a particular strain of wheat which makes bread making easier but which has been claimed by the local clergy as sacred to the region's patron god.

Protection: Safety in numbers is often the way to tread. By banding together, members of such a guild are in a better position to look after their interests more effectively and work together to protect and defend individual members' safety and rights. Such a group could also be intent on preserving traditional methods and techniques that might otherwise be lost. Consider a guild of sailors in a town that has recently been assimilated by a neighboring realm who wish to ensure that newcomers don't steal away their business and "corrupt" the local waters with their newfangled ideas of how sailing should be done.

Sharing: This type of guild has been established so that its members can exchange knowledge and skills. By grouping together, the people within the guild broaden the knowledge base and maximize their potential for learning new skills and ideas, as well as for helping each other improve. A guild of mercenaries may travel the world to learn many techniques of war and battle, which they subsequently share among themselves.

Membership

Beyond a guild's purpose, some distinct feature usually links its members together. This is some characteristic that can be easily identified by outside observers. Note that this is what existing members have in common, not what they have to do to join, which is detailed next. Decide what links the members of your guild. Membership features generally fall into one or more of the following categories:

Belief/Code: Members all share some form of belief or opinion. It may be religious, political, or social. A bard's guild might exist only so that the members can get together for a good laugh.

Family: Members of the guild are all related by blood or marriage to one or more founding families. Every member has some family tie to at least one, likely several, other guild members.

Location: Members all live in a particular settlement or region. A town guild might be created when pioneers found a new community, which allows them to decide who can live in the area.

Profession: All of the members share a common profession or character class.

Joining the Guild

Just because someone agrees with the purpose of a guild and meets its membership requirements does not mean that membership is automatic. Most guilds will control access to their ranks and have certain rules and traditions for joining. Define how nonmembers can join the guild. Entry to a guild is nearly always through one of the following methods:

Application: Prospective members ask to join the guild. Usually local or guild laws decree that an applying member who meets the selection rules must be accepted.

Edict: Members have no choice but to be in the guild. This may be local law or by decree of the guild itself. Either way, people who meet the criteria are told to join the guild or else.

Foundation: A new guild is being formed and the individual is one of its founding members.

Invitation: Members deemed as suitable are invited to join the guild. Without the invitation they may not join, even if they are otherwise suited to be a member.

Purchase: A member must buy his way into the guild, through money or through deeds and effort on the guild's behalf.

Membership Criteria

In addition to how one can become a part of a guild, it is also important to define the selection criteria that dictate what types of people are eligible for membership. Such criteria usually can be categorized by one or more of the following:

Alignment: Members must meet particular alignment criteria to join the guild. A conspiratorial guild might accept only Lawful Evil members.

Deed: All members of the guild have performed a particular deed, one that cannot be described merely as an examination.

Sex: Members must all be of one sex.

Level-based: Each member has achieved a certain level in his chosen class or classes, but what that class is does not matter, nor do the actual skills and abilities of the member. He is of sufficient experience to be considered desirable by the guild. Such a guild might value experience and wisdom, or it might just be elitist.

Miscellaneous: Members must meet some esoteric criterion to join the guild. For example, only left-handed people may join a certain guild of smiths.

Number Limit: The guild either has a minimum or maximum member limit. With a minimum limit new members are sought to keep the numbers up. With a maximum limit in place prospective members will have to wait until a position becomes available.

Qualification: Each member meets a set of skills, knowledge, and abilities desired by the guild. Class or profession doesn't matter, only that one's abilities are up to scratch. Members might need to have one or more skills at a number of ranks or a particular skill total, or they may need to know a particular feat.

Race: Only folk of a particular race may join the guild.

Social Class: Only people of a particular social class may join the guild. The neighborhood thieves' guild might accept only commoners, in contrast with the banking house that requires members to be at least of the minor nobility.

Test/Examination: Each member has passed a particular test or tests. Their actual skills and abilities may vary, and some members may be of a low standard, but whether by luck or talent they passed the tests to get in. The difference between this and the qualification criterion is that here each member need only have made a small number of tests successfully; the actual total of one's skill or ability is not important.

Wealth: Members must have a certain degree (minimum or maximum) of wealth to join. A charitable or beggar's guild might deem that when members have reached a certain higher level of funds it is time for them to move on.

Size and Scope

A guild may be small or large, depending on what its purpose is. Similarly, its influence may extend no further than the local village, or perhaps the city gates, or it may make its presence felt across the known world. Define the size of the guild, how many members it has, where it is located, and what the reach of its influence is.

Guild Structure & Advancement

How the guild organizes itself can have a bearing on how members advance within the guild, or indeed if there is any concept of rank and advancement. Choose from one of the following structures (graded guilds may have more than one type of gradation). Define titles for each rank within the guild, and the requirements to advance through these ranks.

Collective: All members of the guild are considered equals and there is no rank or advancement. Decisions are made by consensus, and guild activities can at times be rather disordered.

Dominated: The group is under the control of one or more powerful individuals. There are two levels within the guild—those who are in charge and those who are not. The control may be internal, with guild members directing what goes on, or external, where someone outside of the guild calls the shots.

Graded (Criteria): Membership is ranked and advancement is through meeting certain rules and criteria set down by the guild. Usually this has to with meeting requirements that have little to do with skill or ability. Length or service in the guild is a good example, or just plain age of the member.

Graded (Elective): Membership within the guild is ranked and advancement is by choice or decree of other members, often through election. Actual skill or ability may have nothing to do with the member's rise though the ranks.

Graded (Merit): The guild has a number of ranks and levels, and advancement is by deed and merit. Achieving certain skill levels or passing several tests determines how members climb the ranks.

Graded (Wealth/Purchase): A member's standing or rank in the guild is controlled by how much wealth he has, or it is purchased directly. This may take the form of open purchase, or secretive bribes and the buying of influence.

Benefits

More often than not the reason for joining a guild is due to the benefits that membership provides. Some of the benefits are tangible; others are less obvious. Most guilds will provide their members with several advantages, noticeable or not. Define what the benefits are for your guild, using the following options as a guide. It should be noted that some of the benefits received as guild members can also act as disadvantages, as members may have obligations resulting from some of the benefits detailed. Such benefits are marked with an asterisk (*).

Access to Items: The guild provides its members with access to rare or restricted items. Additionally, members may be able to purchase more common items at a reduced price.

Access to Prestige Classes: Guild members may take on a prestige class that they might not otherwise have access to.

Access to Skills, Feats, or Spells: Members of the guild gain improved access to skills, feats, or spells that would otherwise be restricted or even disallowed.

Bonuses: To reflect the improved knowledge and training available to members of the guild, a distinct bonus is applied to one or more of each member's abilities, skills, saves, spells, feats, attacks, AC, initiative, or

so on. Training at a fighter's school might give its members a +1 attack bonus.

Experience Bonus: Members gain a percentage increase in experience points allocated for advancement in a class or profession closely associated with the guild. Members of a thieves' guild might gain a 5% experience bonus for the Rogue class.

Fraternity*: The guild members provide a support structure for each other, and individual members can call upon the assistance of their fellows in times of need. Usually the assistance comes from guild members the character would view as peers. This could take many forms; loans, physical assistance, character statements. The fraternity could also extend to an alliance with people or groups outside of the guild.

Good Reputation: The guild is held in high regard or is otherwise respected or feared, and its members benefit from that reputation. They themselves are well reputed because of their membership, and this will beneficially affect encounters with those who know and respect the guild. This might take the form of a bonus to Charisma-based skill tests or a shift in a NPC's initial reactions to guild members.

Henchmen*: A member who has advanced in seniority might have subordinates from the guild assigned as henchmen, followers, or minions.

Income: Whether through an allowance, payment based on skill tests, or some other method, guild members enjoy a regular income in the form of coinage or goods.

Increased Limits: Due to the improved training or knowledge available to guild members, certain limits such as maximum skill ranks developed per level may be increased. A barbarian horde's members may be allowed to learn Wilderness Lore ranks up to their level plus 4, an increase of 1 over the normal limit. This benefit does not provide any bonuses to apply to the skill, it just increases the limit to which the skill may advance.

Patronage*: Akin to fraternity, guild members receive support and assistance from other members of the guild. In this instance, though, the folk assisting are superior in some way to the character, be it in authority, influence, wealth, or some other fashion.

Shelter*: The guild provides its members with some type of free housing or other form of accommodation. This may be an actual guildhouse, an inn with agreements to lodge members, or individual members who shelter their fellows in their own residences.

Social Rights: The guild has managed to reserve for its members certain social rights that would otherwise not be allowed. Perhaps only members of a fighter school are allowed to wear weapons publicly. Only members of the scribes' guild may be allowed to read certain texts. Or consider the club of gentlemen who are the only ones in town who may vote.

Special Abilities: The guild has access to special knowledge or skills that it teaches only to its members. Characters will be taught such special abilities or at least be permitted to gain them upon meeting certain conditions. These abilities would likely be akin to prestige class abilities—things that aren't otherwise detailed by skills and feats.

Table 5-1: Guild Purpose

1d20	Result
1–3	Control
4–7	Economic
8–10	Goal
11–14	Protection
15–18	Sharing

Table 5-2: Guild Membership*

d20	Result
1–3	Belief/Code
4–6	Family
7–9	Location
10–14	Other Criteria (see Table 3-4)
15–18	Profession
19–20	Roll twice

Table 5-3: Joining the Guild*

d20	Result
1–3	Application
4–6	Edict
7–9	Foundation
10–12	Invitation
12–15	Other Criteria (see Table 3-4)
16–18	Purchase
19–20	Roll twice

Table 5-4: Membership Criteria*

d20	Result
1	Alignment
2	Deed
3	Gender
4–6	Level-based
7–10	Miscellaneous
11	Number Limit
12–14	Qualification
15	Race
16	Social Class
17–19	Test/Examination
20	Wealth

Table 5-5: Guild Size

d20	Result
1	d4 x 5 members
2–3	d8 x 5 members
4–5	d10 x 10 members
6–7	d20 x 10 members
8–10	d10 x 20 members
11–13	d20 x 20 members
14–15	d10 x 50 members
16–17	d20 x 50 members
18–19	d10 x 100 members
20	d100 x 100 members

Table 5-6: Guild Scope

d20	Result
1–2	Single small settlement
3–4	Single large settlement
5–7	Single huge settlement
8–10	Several settlements (single region)
11–13	Several settlements (several regions)
14–16	Single country
17–18	Several countries
19–20	Global or beyond

Table 5–7: Guild Structure & Advancement

d20	Result
1-3	Collective
4-6	Dominated
7-9	Graded (Criteria)
10-12	Graded (Merit)
13-15	Graded (Elective)
16-18	Graded (Wealth/Purchase)
19-20	Roll twice

Table 5–8: Guild Benefits**

d20	Result
1-2	Access to Skills, Feats, or Spells
3	Access to Prestige Classes
4	Access to Items
5--6	Bonuses (see Table 3-8A)
7	Experience Bonus
8-9	Fraternity*
10	Good Reputation
11	Henchmen*
12	Income
13	Increased Limits
14-15	Patronage*
16	Shelter*
17	Social Rights
18-19	Special Ability
20	Roll twice

These benefits may also act as disadvantages at the same time that they are benefits.

Table 5–8A: Bonuses

d20	Result
1-2	Ability
3-4	Armor Class
5-6	Attack
7-8	Feat
9-10	Initiative
11-12	Hit Dice
13-14	Saving Throw
15-16	Skill
17-18	Spell
19-20	Other

Table 5–9: Disadvantages*

d20	Result
1-2	Apprenticeship
3-4	Bad Reputation
5-6	Deterioration
7-8	Enemies
9-10	Exclusions
11-12	Experience Cost
13-14	Experience Reduction
15-16	Fees
17-18	Regulations/Traditions
19-20	Time

* Roll 1d4 times. **Roll 1d6 times.

Guild Design Tables

You can either choose items from the tables or roll randomly for each aspect of a guild. Care should be taken when randomly generating guilds to avoid obvious contradictions.

Disadvantages

Regardless of a guild's particular nature, the odds are that there are some disadvantages to being a member. Most often these would be more than balanced by the benefits, but this may not always be the case. Some more restrictive guilds with less than voluntary membership might be rather detrimental to their members.

Apprenticeship: In order to become a guild member, a character must suffer through an apprenticeship period, during which time he is bonded to one or more masters. This can be effective slavery, where the master is completely in control of the apprentice's existence. At the very least the apprentice will suffer serious restrictions to his freedom of movement and activities, often for a period of several years.

Bad Reputation: The guild, and thus its members, is looked upon with ill feeling by society as a whole or by some significant group. This adversely affects social encounters for its members, be it through penalties to Charisma-based skill tests or unfavorable shifts in the reactions of NPCs.

Deterioration: Due in some way to activities performed in the guild's service, the members suffer some form of deterioration, usually in the form of health or skills. Look at the miners' guild whose members all must make a Fortitude save each year or lose a point of Constitution due to the hardship of their work. A fighter school might have its members suffer 5 hp damage every day due to the rough and tumble nature of their training techniques.

Enemies: Beyond even a bad reputation, the guild has one or more groups who harbor enmity toward it and its members. This will result in the chance of the members being abused or assaulted in some way by the enemy organization.

Exclusions: Members of the guild are barred from partaking in some activity or associating with a particular group of people. A town miller in a countrywide guild may be allowed to mill grain only for folk in his local region. A guild of rangers may be on bad terms with the local army that has a history of despoiling nature, and thus the rangers may not associate with those other warriors. Certain skills, feats, or spells may not be allowed for members of the guild. This can lead to restrictions in experiments by members ("We don't do things that way!").

Experience Cost: The guild expects members to put much effort into guild activities, to the extent that their personal time is reduced. Members must make one or more payments of XP to reflect this. Each member of a bardic college whose members teach local children must expend 200 XP per year for the guild. A fighter guild that puts prospective members through rigorous testing means a new member must pay a once-only 500 XP cost to join. Guild designers should take care to balance such a cost, along with other disadvantages, against the benefits received.

Experience Reduction: Similar to an experience cost, the reduction in XP is ongoing and constant. An adventurer's guild might require its members to help common folk in small ways whenever they can, resulting in a general 5% reduction of all XP awards.

Fees: The guild demands payment of some form from its members. This may be dues, bribes, gifts, or other forms of expenditure. The fee may be a one-time payment, such as an entry charge, or a regular tithe such as a general percentage reduction of each member's wealth.

Guild Design

Regulations/Traditions: Unlike exclusions, where members are restricted from doing something, some guilds may demand that its members do certain things. These may range from duties that make sense ("It's your turn to tend the ovens tomorrow.") to traditions that may seem foolish ("Lodge night tonight; don't forget your goose hat."). This might also take the form of obedience to the wishes and desires of superiors within the guild.

Time: Membership in the guild is time-consuming. Members may be expected to attend meetings, perform menial duties, assist other members, etc. Unlike other disadvantages listed, this will result in a reduction of time available to members. The time may be as little as a few days or as much as several months in a year. It might be one large period. A monastery of warrior monks may require that all members must at some stage spend a year as a hermit doing nothing but meditating.

Affiliations

Unless a good reason exists for remaining isolated, most guilds will form at least a loose affiliation with other guilds that complement their purpose or membership criteria. Thieves' guilds have affiliations with other thieves' guilds in neighboring regions to provide a place to hide members who've made the ten-most-wanted list and to fence loot that's too hot for the local area. Town guilds form alliances with neighboring towns to provide better protection against marauding bands of monsters. Generic adventuring guilds, such as The Collective, form associations with any other guild that can be of use to them (and vice versa). Groups of mercenaries, like Neric's Avengers, form no alliances, as these may bring undue influence to bear. Determine which guilds, if any, would have direct associations with yours.

Leaving the Guild

From time to time, characters will leave guilds, either because they choose to or because the guilds no longer accept them as members. There are almost always consequences of leaving, and their severity depends on the circumstances. Define how characters can leave the guild and what happens to them when they do. A character generally has three options for leaving, although some guilds do not allow members to leave at all.

With Permission: If a character wishes to leave a guild and requests (and obtains) the permission of the guildmaster(s), the consequences are generally limited to loss of membership rights. Accrued benefits are usually retained.

Without Permission: To leave a guild without the blessing of the leader(s) is generally a serious infraction of the rules. Whether permission to leave was denied or not sought, the penalties are usually loss of all guild-associated benefits.

Expulsion: This is the most serious way of leaving a guild. It is only for use when a character has committed a serious offense against the guild and will often result in punitive action, up to the death of the offender.

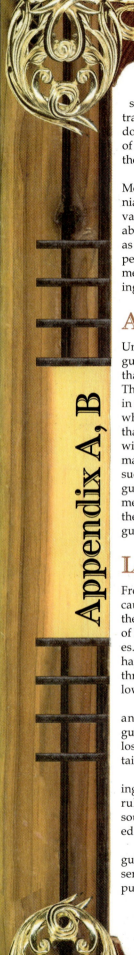

Appendix A, B

Appendix A - NPC Fast Name Chooser

When dealing with guilds and other large social organizations, you will find that you will have to invent a great deal of characters from all walks of life. While there are many NPC's in this book to choose from, and likely many already in your own campaign, it is inevitable that you will have to come up with a name for a character on the fly. Use these lists when you need a NPC name in a hurry.

Single Names

Male: Alon, Bazel, Bri-Ark, Denrik, Enzer, Frado, Goran, Hederic, Karrel, Lind, Mokar, Nebbin, Ogram, Perrin, Shtaal, Sodo, Tekrin, Tobin, Uther, Wort.

Female: Alhonna, Ateris, Betrula, Domino, Doria, Egned, Felina, Gertin, Hanniah, Ingrith, Juanita, Krislan, Marikka, Nerice, Persephone, Rekka, Sabine, Theodozia, Trineesh, Una, Zinna.

Double Names

Male: Aziz Bikam, Balthazar Hobbins, Bim Borrin, Harim Betts, Kres Marek, Liam Chroma, Minsin Tatiz, Nord Erth, Shar Fazir, Talavar Shalt, Voldar Mutombe, Xander Warlock.

Female: Baraan Quelt, Bolla Narcis, Cheranise Guden, Hella Ness, Karamee Prince, Lynelle Polan, Mara Sollinen, Penny Mallard, Scylla Sardis, Tala Falan, Vivienne Queen, Zoelle Pradon.

Appendix B - Feats, Skills, and Prestige Classes

This appendix contains a number of new character aids. These include a new feat, a new use for the Diplomacy skill, and two new prestige classes. All of these items are tied to the guilds in this book, but may be used independently if it is desired.

Feint [General]

You have been trained in deceiving an opponent in combat, making him easier to strike with a subsequent attack.

Prerequisites: Proficient with weapon, base attack bonus +1 or higher, Weapon Focus

Benefit: Instead of making a normal attack, you instead declare a Feint. Your opponent must make a Reflex save versus a DC of 10+ (attack bonus for that weapon using Weapon Focus). If the opponent fails he is flat-footed for your next melee attack.

New Uses for the Diplomacy Skill (Cha)

A character can use the Diplomacy to show the presence and experience to get troops to follow him into battle, even if the situation seems hopeless. Many officers of Neric's Avengers make use of the Diplomacy skill in this way.

Check: You can inspire the troops under your command to lift themselves above and beyond their normal abilities in battle. A successful check grants your companions a +1 bonus on all "to hit" rolls for the duration of the encounter. A failure means the troops are unsure. A failure of 5 or more means your companions (NPCs) may make a morale check and refuse to follow you into battle ("You want us to do WHAT!?").

Retry: Yes, but with a –2 penalty to the roll. Only one retry is permitted.

Special: A character with the Leadership feat gets a +4 bonus to the skill check when it is used in this manner.

Table B.1 – Diplomacy DCs

Enemy is	DC*
Obviously inferior in numbers/equipment	10
Inferior in numbers but well equipped (armor, good-quality weapons)	15
Equal, or larger numbers but poor equipment	15
Larger in number	18
More than double the party's numbers	21
More than three times the party's numbers	24
More than four times the party's numbers	27
Overwhelmingly superior	30

*When the opposition is accompanied by one or more spellcasters or has obvious magical devices, the DC is increased by 5 unless the party also has magical capability.

Avenger

Avengers are ferocious warriors driven more by force of will than by sheer strength. Avengers are strict in their routines of discipline and training, and constantly test themselves with painful acts of willpower. In addition to upholding the laws of his chosen homeland, an Avenger is avowed to enact revenge upon all who wrong him and his friends, and lives to take such action, preferably on the battlefield. Members of the mercenary company Neric's Avengers have developed and perfected the art of the Avenger, and many amongst their ranks take levels in this class.

Hit Die: d10

Requirements

To quality to become an Avenger, a character must fulfil all the following criteria:

Alignment: Any Lawful
Base attack bonus: +6
Wisdom: 12+
Feats: Endurance, Iron Will

Class Skills

The Avenger's class skills (and the key ability for each skill) are Balance (Dex), Climb (Str), Concentration (Con), Craft (Int), Handle Animal (Cha), Intimidate (Cha), Jump (Str), Listen (Wis), Ride (Dex), Search (Int), Sense Motive (Wis), Spot (Wis), Swim (Str), Tumble (Dex), and Use Rope (Dex).

Skill Points at Each Level: 2 + Int modifier

Class Features

Weapon and Armor Proficiency: Avengers are proficient with all simple and martial weapons, with all types of armor (heavy, medium, and light), and with shields.

Willpower: An Avenger is able to overpower his body with his sheer force of will. If an avenger ever fails a Fortitude save he may immediately attempt a Will save vs. the same DC. If this second save succeeds, the Avengers is considered to have made his Fortitude save. This ability may be used once per day per level of Avenger the character has acquired.

Determination: Similar to Willpower above, an Avenger that fails a Constitution based roll may reroll the check substituting his Wisdom for his Con. This applies, for example, to Concentration checks as well as to roll to avoid suffocation. This ability may be used once per day per level of Avenger the character has acquired.

Tenacity: An Avenger is not knocked unconscious if brought to 0 hit points or below. He is able to function normally until he reaches –10 hit points, at which point he dies. He also does not suffer damage from blood loss when at negative hit points.

Damage Reduction: Avengers have learned to ignore pain completely. Hence, physical blows have less of an effect on them. An avenger can ignore a certain amount of damage (shown in the table) from all attacks, regardless of their source.

Avenge Wrong: An Avenger is at his most powerful when taking revenge for a severe wrong committed against him or against one of his close companions. When in combat against a foe that has committed such an act, the Avenger may add his Wisdom bonus to all to hit and damage rolls. If the Avenger is avenging a murder, he may add an additional +1 to these rolls.

Vengeful Focus: When actively pursing an enemy upon whom the Avenger intends to exact his revenge, the character need not sleep until either he gives up the chase or his foe lies dead. Once he kills his foe, an Avenger must sleep for at least eight hours before he can use this ability again.

Overcome Odds: An Avenger lives to beat the odds, especially in battle, and whenever he faces a force obviously more powerful than his own he is able to push himself to his full limit, gaining an extra partial action each round, a +4 dodge bonus to his AC, and can jump one and a half times as far as normal, just as if a *haste* spell had been cast upon him. This ability can be turned on and off at will, but cannot be used longer, cumulatively, than 2 rounds per day per level in Avenger the character has attained.

Greater Avenge: At 8th level and beyond, when Avenging a wrong, an Avenger may also add his Wisdom Bonus to his Armor Class. This bonus applies regardless of armor worn, and regardless of whether the character is able to receive a Dexterity bonus or not.

Retribution: Once per day, an Avenger may turn an ordinary melee strike into a coup de grace, regardless of whether his opponent is helpless or not. The use of this ability must be declared before the attack is made, and if the attack roll misses, the ability is lost for the day. If the attack hits, the defender must make a Fort save (DC is 10 + damage dealt) or die. Unlike a normal coup de grace, the attack does not deal critical damage unless an actual critical hit is rolled. Creatures immune to critical hits, such as some constructs and undead, are immune to this ability.

Seeker

Members of the Seeker prestige class are employed as scouts by the Lochrinn Town Guild. The class is easily adaptable to other locations and situations, and characters who are interested in functioning primarily as scouts would do well to take a few levels in the class.

Seekers are much like rangers, but they are more specialized because their focus is on the preservation of Lochrinn. Where a ranger might never harm the forest, a Seeker may choose to start a wildfire if a large force of the enemy (whatever they may be) could be caught in the flames. However, their primary function is scouting and reporting.

Each Hammer (battalion) in Lochrinn employs five Seekers. These rugged individuals range the hills and forests surrounding Lochrinn, returning to report every ten days. Should a Seeker not return within twelve, Lochrinn goes on alert. The Seeker's route is checked by a group of five seekers from different Hammers, because it is possible he had an

Table B.2 – Avenger Class Progression

Class Level	Base Attack Bonus	Fort. Save	Ref. Save	Will Save	Special Abilities
1st	+1	+0	+0	+2	Willpower
2nd	+2	+0	+0	+3	Determination, Tenacity
3rd	+3	+1	+1	+3	Damage Reduction (1)
4th	+4	+1	+1	+4	Avenge Wrong
5th	+5	+1	+1	+4	Vengeful Focus
6th	+6	+2	+2	+5	Damage Reduction (3)
7th	+7	+2	+2	+5	Overcome Odds
8th	+8	+2	+2	+6	Greater Avenge
9th	+9	+3	+3	+6	Damage Reduction (5)
10th	+10	+3	+3	+7	Retribution

accident and is unable to travel well, if at all. If the missing Seeker has been captured by an advancing enemy, five Seekers should be enough to return with word.

A Militiaman can be a Seeker for only a short period of time; by the age of thirty-five, younger men will take his place. A Seeker can go back to being a Militiaman in his old Hammer. If there is a vacancy, he may become an officer. These men will often need additional training in order to lead others effectively.

Because of their past service, they may choose to retire honorably from the Militiamen. Many Seekers become increasingly uncomfortable in Lochrinn and choose to move or even start a farmstead.

Hit Die: d8

Requirements

To quality to become a Seeker, a character must fulfil all the following criteria:

Lochrinn Militiaman: Any rank for at least one game year

Alignment: Lawful Neutral

Base Attack Bonus: +6

Wilderness Lore: 5 ranks

Feats: Dodge, 3 Weapon Focuses: dagger, sling, and either sword (any one-handed), bow (any), spear (any), polearm (any), or club (any one-handed mace, flail, or hammer).

Note: GMs not using the town of Lochrinn in the campaign may choose to adjust the requirements, eliminating the militiaman requirement, and allowing substitution of other missile weapons for the sling.

Class Skills

The Seeker's class skills (and the key ability for each skill) are Balance (Dex), Climb (Str), Concentration (Con), Gather Information (Cha), Hide (Dex), Intuit Direction (Wis), Jump

Table B.3 – Seeker Class Progression

Class Level	Base Attack Bonus	Fort. Save	Ref. Save	Will Save	AC Bonus	Special Abilities	Spells 1st	2nd	Caster Level
1st	+1	+0	+2	+2	+1	Track, 1st favored enemy			
2nd	+2	+0	+3	+3	+1	Blend with foliage (1/day)			
3rd	+3	+1	+3	+3	+1	Creature sight (1/day)			
4th	+3	+1	+4	+4	+2	Preternatural hearing			
5th	+4	+1	+4	+4	+2	Blend with foliage (2/day), 2nd favored enemy			
6th	+5	+2	+5	+5	+2	Creature sight (2/day)			
7th	+6	+2	+5	+5	+3	Darkvision, Spell Use	—		+1
8th	+6	+2	+6	+6	+3	Blend with foliage (3/day)	1	—	+2
9th	+7	+3	+6	+6	+3	Creature sight (3/day)	2	0	+3
10th	+8	+3	+7	+7	+4	Chameleon (1/day), 3rd favored enemy	2	1	+4

(Str), Knowledge (nature) (Int), Listen (Wis), Move Silently (Dex), Ride (Dex), Search (Int), Sense Motive (Wis), Spot (Wis), Swim (Str), Use Rope (Dex), Wilderness Lore (Wis).

Skill Points at Each Level: 4 + Int modifier

Class Features

Weapon and Armor Proficiency: Seekers are proficient in all simple and martial weapons and light armor. They do not automatically gain proficiency in shields or armor heavier than leather but may have it as a consequence of another class. Seekers will not wear armor heavier than leather while in the field (and usually wear none) but may wear heavier armor if fighting on Lochrinn's walls.

AC Bonus: Seekers gain an additional dodge bonus to their ACs, much like a monk does. This bonus is only applied when the seeker is in light or no armor, and when he is able to apply his Dexterity bonus. This AC bonus increases as the seeker progresses in level.

Track: At 1st level, the Seeker gains the bonus feat Track.

Favored Enemy: Also at 1st level, the seeker gains this Ranger class feature (PHB).

Blend with Foliage: Beginning at 2nd level, a Seeker may blend into the surrounding foliage and become effectively invisible for 10 minutes. He may attempt to move while blending, but the invisibility effect is broken, this ability instead affording him a +10 bonus to his hide checks. This is a supernatural ability.

Creature Sight: Beginning at 3rd level, a Seeker may see through the eyes of an ordinary animal, reptile, or bird. The creature must be within 60 ft. of the seeker in order to initialize the link. The Seeker cannot control where the creature looks. There is no limit to the duration of this ability, although only one creature at a time may be sighted through, and there is a limit to the number of creatures per day that a seeker can affect. The animal does not receive a save, as this ability affects it in no way whatsoever. This is a supernatural ability.

Preternatural Hearing: At 4th level, a Seeker can "focus" his hearing. He cannot hear any better than before, but he can tune out obstructing noises, listening only to that which he wishes to hear. For example, in a tavern full of people talking, he is able to hear a conversation on the other side of the room as if the rest of the tavern were completely silent. However, if the conversation were held in a low whisper that would not normally be audible beyond about six feet, the Seeker will still not be able to hear it, unless he were within that distance. This is a supernatural ability.

Darkvision: At 7th level, the Seeker can see in the dark as though he were permanently under the affects of a darkvision spell. This is a supernatural ability.

Spell Use: Beginning at 7th level, Seekers gain the ability to cast low-level divine spells. A seeker may choose his spells from either the Ranger or the Druid lists, and can even mix and match his spells from the two lists if he desires. A seeker's spells are based on his Wisdom ability. A seeker with a Wisdom score of less than 12 cannot cast spells until 8th level. A seeker's caster level is shown in the table above. If the seeker has caster levels in other divine classes, he can add his seeker caster level to those levels.

Chameleon: At 10th level, the Seeker gains the power to blend into his surroundings, looking like he belongs. For example, in a forest he may look like a sapling or bush. In the camp of a tribe of orcs, he may look like an ordinary orc. This is more powerful than blend with foliage, which requires there to be leaves and branches around the character. This ability remains operative for as long as the Seeker concentrates, although this means that other actions have a penalty applied (-1 circumstance penalty to all rolls), due to the attention needed to maintain the ability. This is a supernatural ability.

Seeker

Bastion Press Open Gaming Content

The entire contents of *Guildcraft* is considered Open Content, except for the cover, artwork, and other graphic elements. The cover, artwork, and other graphic elements are Product Identity and owned solely by Bastion Press, Inc.